One day. One milli
London to LA, Africa
Asia to Amer

24 HOURS

IN

JOURNALISM

A reporter's odyssey into
love, war, fame, bombings, sex,
football and Hollywood.

JOHN DALE

John Dale Publishing Ltd

Published in the United Kingdom
by John Dale Publishing Ltd
Copyright © 2012 John Dale

Author's website
www.24hoursinjournalism2013.com

John Dale has asserted his
right under the Copyright, Designs and
Patents Act 1988 to be identified
as the author of this work.

ISBN-13: 978-147830-774-7

A CIP catalogue record
for this book is available
from the British Library.

Cover design
Stuart Bartlett

Pre-press production (UK)
www.ebookversions.com

PHOTO CREDITS

Cover photos (from top left to bottom right)

MAIN CAST

Anonymous, Ex-Murdoch reporter
Banks, David, Media commentator
Barsby, Jenny, BBC radio presenter
Baty, Louise, Freelance
Bhagwandas, Anita, Beauty Assistant, Stylist magazine
Blackledge, Sam, Reporter, Dorking Advertiser
Blundell, Kathryn, Editor-in-chief, Mother & Baby
Bolotin, Louise, Freelance, Manchester
Booth, Samantha, Freelance, Glasgow
Bowes, Peter, BBC News Correspondent, Los Angeles
Brown, Raymond, Crime Reporter, Cambridge News
Burkitt-Gray, Alan, Editor, Global Telecoms Business
Cain, Kathryn, Reporter, Bedfordshire on Sunday
Capello, Fabio*, Football manager
Carpenter, Adam, Freelance
Chunn, Louise, Editor-in-chief, Psychologies
Clancy, Abbey*, Footballer's wife and model
Clancy, Paddy, Freelance, Donegal
Cole, Peter, Professor Emeritus, Sheffield University
Condliffe, Jeremy, Editor-in-chief, Congleton Chronicle
Corry, Robin, Freelance
Courtenay-Smith, Natasha, Owner, Talk To The Press
Dacre, Paul*, Editor-in-chief, Daily Mail
Dean, Adam*, Photographer, China
Dattani, Meera, Travel writer
Duffy, Kevin, Freelance, Manchester
Dunne, Colin, Humourist
Durrani, Arif, News Editor, Brand Republic
Dye, Natalie, Freelance
Evans, Katie, Features writer, Talk To The Press
Evans, Katy, Editor-in-chief, Soul & Spirit
Figeon, Greg, Editor-in-chief, Yellow Advertiser and North
London & Herts series
Findlay, Heather, Feature writer, Medavia
Fleming, Rebecca, Editor-in-chief, Take a Break
Foster, Jill, Freelance
Fraser, Katie, Agony Aunt
Gallagher, Tony*, Editor-in-chief, Daily Telegraph
Gardner, Frank, BBC News Security Correspondent
Gray, Adam*, Photographer
Harris, Marcus, Editor, Mint magazine

Hearsey, Sophie, Editor-in-chief, that's life
Hobsbawm, Julia*, CEO, Editorial Intelligence
Holliday, Graham, Reuters correspondent, Rwanda
Hudson, Gill, Editor-in-chief, Reader's Digest UK
Hulme, Oliver, Chief Reporter, Wells Journal
John, Peter, Editor-in-chief, Worcester News
Leidig, Mike, Editor-in-chief, Central European News
Leveson, Sir Brian*, Chairman, Leveson Inquiry
Lustig, Robin, Presenter, The World Tonight
Macaskill, Jamie, Assistant Editor, Hull Daily Mail
Mackenzie, Lt-Col Gordon, Media head, HQ Task
Force Helmand
Mackenzie, Kelvin*, Columnist, Daily Mail
McGrath, Nick, Showbiz writer
Mohan, Dominic*, Editor-in-chief, The Sun
Moore, Malcolm, Daily Telegraph correspondent, Shanghai
Murdoch, Elisabeth*, mother of Rupert
Murdoch, James*, son of Rupert
Murdoch, Rupert*, Chairman and CEO, News Corporation
Newton, Kirstie, Editor-in-chief, Cornwall Today
Nicholson, Lindsay, Editorial Director, Good Housekeeping
O'Riordan, Nicola-Marie, Reporter, Avondhu Press
Oxford, Adam, Freelance
Peake, Jon, Editor-in-chief, TV Choice and Total TV Guide
Pike, Rebecca, Business presenter, BBC Radio 2
Preece, Stephanie, Head of content, Worcester News
Randolfo, Mario*, Investigative journalist, Brazil
Read, Ian, Editor-in-chief, Kent and Sussex Courier
Redknapp, Harry*, Football manager
Roberts, Helen, News agency editor, Delhi
Rodwell, Lee, Health editor
Russell, Helen, Online Editor, Marie Claire
Satchwell, Bob, Executive Director, Society of Editors
Sharp, Rhod, Presenter, BBC Radio 5 Live
Sidwell, Julia, Commissioning Editor, Take a Break
Solomons, Mark, Joint Owner, Specialist News Service
Sommerville, Quentin, BBC News Correspondent, Afghanistan
Spereall, David, Work placement reporter
Stewart, Steven*, Reporter, Daily Record
Storr, Farrah, Editor-in-chief, Women's Health
Sutton, Caroline, Media trainer
Thorne, John, Media trainer
Wallace, Richard*, Editor-in-chief, Daily Mirror
Watts, Susan, Science Editor, BBC Newsnight
Wheal, Chris, Freelance
Wild, Damian, Editor-in-chief, Estates Gazette

Wilde, Liz, Beauty editor
Wilson, Matt, Trainee Reporter, Stratford-upon-Avon Herald
Wilson, John, Deputy Editor, Worcester News
Wiltshire, Paul, Deputy editor, Bath Chronicle
Wintour, Anna*, Editor-in-chief, Vogue USA

Information regarding those marked with an asterisk* has been drawn from third-party sources, usually self-evident in the text, not from emails to the author.

CONTENTS

PREFACE

PREFACE
One Day, 8 February

Earlier this year, I set out to discover how the first draft of history is written. To do so, I decided to explore the hidden reality of ordinary mortals who are daily entrusted with such an extraordinary responsibility.

In short, were the hacks up to the job?

It was a question being raised by judges, politicians and an increasingly alarmed public and so, over one 24-hour period, I tracked the intersecting lives of hundreds of working journalists.

The result is a global journey into love, war, fame, bombings, sex, football, Hollywood and similar headline material – in other words, an average news day.

I encountered editors, reporters, war correspondents, feature writers, columnists, agony aunts, fashion gurus, showbiz writers, broadcasters, paparazzi, desperate trainees, unemployed hacks and billionaire moguls – in other words, an average cross-section of media folk.

Ranging from London to Los Angeles, from Kigali to Kabul, from Shanghai to Sydney, I was able to contemplate something which has long puzzled me: 'Why are some journalists so good – and some journalists so bad?'

And I identified a hidden global superpower – journalism itself – an entity to which most journalists offer allegiance above and beyond their nation states.

The seed for this book was sown while I was listening to evidence given at Lord Justice Leveson's judicial inquiry into press standards, in London. The loss of public trust in journalists was evident, not just to the judge but to the large online and television audience. So I circulated this appeal to colleagues around the world, with the support of Dominic Ponsford, editor of *Press Gazette* . . .

One day, one million stories
WEDNESDAY FEBRUARY 8: A DAY IN THE LIFE OF JOURNALISM
It's the big story that journalists ignore: their own.
Send a written snapshot of your day's work – in newspapers and magazines, TV and r adio – for a unique narrative of one 24-hour news cycle, from 6am Wednesday, February 8, 2012, to 6am the next day.

More than 70 journalists sent me detailed responses. Others replied more sparingly. Yet others I co-opted because they were either in the news or visible news-makers – their names are marked with an asterisk* in the preceding pages. And yet more were drawn in as supporting players from various sources, usually self-evident.

I then wove their stories together to form this 88,000-word narrative.

When people ask how journalists really work, they get different, confusing replies. Here then are answers direct from those who do the job day in, day out, in all its rich variety, from testing lipstick to putting themselves at the wrong end of a gun.

I want to thank everyone who volunteered and I hope they will not be too perturbed at seeing their contributions set in a dramatic context, supplemented by third-party information and, where appropriate, given a contentious edge. I am also grateful for assistance from the Society of Editors, the British Society of Magazine Editors and the National Association of Press Agencies.

I chose 8 February 2012 at random. This is a succession of snapshots – inadequate, I know – but I hope it reveals something about the secret lives, and power, of journalists.

JOHN DALE
London
August 2012

AUTHOR'S NOTE:

Project 2013 – you can join in next time

Monday, 11 March, 2013.

All I know for sure is that it is the date of Rupert Murdoch's 82nd birthday, and you are free to praise or pan him. Otherwise, anything could be happening: World War III, Obama joins the Moonies, maybe an extraterrestial invasion - shock is the USP of news.

As I finished this first book, I had other journalists saying they wished they'd taken part. Well, this will be their chance.

Because of the interest, I intend to produce a new version for 2013 – I stress it will be new, with many different characters and different individual stories (although current contributors will be welcome as well).

I hope it will be even more global, enlightening and compelling.

If you are a journalist, or affected by journalists, or involved in journalism in any way, then please email me a written snapshot of your day – 24 hours from 6am (GMT) Monday, 11 March to 6am (GMT) Tuesday, 12 March, 2013.

Add colour and dialogue, friendship and conflict. I am also interested in quiet, routine days. I want local journalists, as well as big shots.

Like this one, Project 2013 will be turned into a narrative ranging from Europe to India, from America to China, and all stops in-between.

Please adjust your times to GMT.
Email: 24hours2013@hotmail.co.uk
Website: 24hoursinjournalism2013.com
I look forward to hearing from you.

24 HOURS IN JOURNALISM

JOHN DALE

CHAPTER 1

6am
Pre-dawn

London: Her mind locked in a cycle of overactivity, Farrah Storr has woken up feeling more tired than when she went to bed. She looks out the window to see whether it is growing lighter. It isn't. Then she checks the time, again.

Six o'clock.

Sigh.

Only six o'clock. It seems ages since she kicked back the duvet, unable to sleep properly, her patience exhausted.

'But how can I sleep?' she keeps saying to herself.

The more she stares outside, the more elusive the dawn becomes.

Storr decides she needs to distract herself. She sits at her computer and lets her fingers rest upon the keys. Then she begins to write, something which comes easily to her.

'I'm tired . . . been up since 4.30am. I've been waiting for this day for what seems like an eternity.'

That is why she feels the urge to record it.

'Today *Women's Health* launches,' she continues. 'And the best bit . . . ?'

There is a pause before her fingers resume their choreography.

'I'm editing it.'

But to create, Farrah Storr may have to destroy.

She takes another glance out of the window. Here and there, bedroom lights are switching on behind drawn curtains as the capital city slowly stirs. But even with a full moon, the sky remains dark. The night has time to run. Be patient, be patient.

Bring on the day.

London: In contrast, Louise Chunn has slept normally and needs an alarm to jolt her awake. Her eyes open and, yes, somewhere in the back of her mind she may be aware of Farrah Storr's worldly ambitions.

But first things first.

The editor of *Psychologies* magazine gets out of bed, goes down to the sitting room and parks her bottom squarely on the floor. She looks at some pages she has torn out of a newspaper supplement. It's yoga mixed with Pilates. She follows the instructions, straining slightly, and persists for 20 minutes. She blames her bad back on sitting at a computer too long. Now she gets to her feet, rubs her lower spine, and wonders whether she's wasting her time. Mmm, it seems to be working.

She needs to be fit for battle. Like Storr, she's running a self-improvement magazine for women. Someone's parking their tanks on her glossy lawn. The phoney war is over. Now, in the world of paper tigers, the real thing is about to kick off.

Task Force Helmand HQ, Lashkar Gah: It is mid-morning on the outskirts of this regional capital of Afghanistan, four and a half hours ahead of London, and here war is being fought not with shiny paper and inventive coverlines but with bombs and bullets.

The blood spilled is real rather than printer's ink.

Suntanned faces tilt upwards as a Merlin helicopter rattles over the horizon, flying fast enough to avoid pot-shots and rocket-propelled grenades.

Then it pauses, as if applying invisible brakes, and slips out of the blue sky in a swift descent. It settles gracefully onto the helipad.

The passenger door opens and out jumps the figure of Lt-Col Gordon Mackenzie, ex-Reuters journalist, grateful to be back behind the fortress walls of the British military base.

Instinctively, he ducks his head beneath the rotating blades and, with shoulders hunched, hurries away from the flying machine.

Mackenzie has just delivered a high-value human cargo into the firing line. There are explosions going off out there, and snipers in the hillsides. Their guest is a prime target, a man risking his life for one objective.

The Story.

Fingers crossed for Sommerville.

Walthamstow, East London: Dawn is precisely 87 minutes away over the other side of London's Olympic Stadium when Nick McGrath rolls out of bed and glances briefly through the window. Here, in this eastern borough, the grey slate roofs are white with frost above streets that have been idling in nocturnal repose.

Now homes are coming alive one by one and down a quiet road, in a bedroom behind drawn curtains bearing a jungle theme, McGrath is more awake than most and under attack from a dinosaur.

He screams but mutely. It's too early to frighten the neighbours.

In another part of his mind McGrath reminds himself that he's due to conduct two showbiz interviews after breakfast.

The flesh-tearing T-Rex dives in for the kill, wielded by his two-year-old son. McGrath screams again.

Kingston, Surrey: On the opposite shoulder of the awakening giant that is London, as far west as the eye can see before semis give way to farmhouses, freelance Natalie Dye feels the great metropolis shrug. She emerges from dreams at the same time as Nick McGrath is fighting a plastic T-Rex and many others are stirring.

It doesn't matter if Dye knows McGrath or Farrah Storr, Louise Chunn or Lt-Col Mackenzie personally, because even at a distance they still have much in common. They are all badge-wearing members of the same working fraternity.

Journalists.

At this precise moment, that unity may not be entirely apparent in either thought or deed but all are aware of its presence.

Blonde hair on pillow, Dye hardly moves, except to register the clock. She glimpses the silhouette of her husband, Gino, as he gets up to go for an early-morning swim at the local pool.

Nar-e Saraj, Helmand Province: After being helicoptered in and dropped off by fellow Scot Mackenzie, the BBC's Afghanistan correspondent Quentin Sommerville is now on an active operation with the Afghan National Army.

'Anything happening?'

'Two IEDs have exploded this morning.'

'How many have you found?'

'Fourteen.'

That is 14 improvised explosive devices. It's a grim start, and a warning. The bombs and the blasts are a reminder that this asymmetrical war is not phoney.

As the convoy's most important passenger, Sommerville climbs into a British armoured vehicle with 2 Rifles, better protected than the Afghan ones. It is a dangerous assignment, although he is well used to that. Only volunteers get the Kabul bureau, a post which is prized, not feared.

Sommerville coveted this, to live and work with the breath of war on his face, only a tissue away from blasts and bullets, mayhem and mass murder. His life is one of bloody headlines. He is earning his journalistic campaign medals by seriously imperilling his life.

Wherever he is, that's the Big Story.

The convoy rolls forward. Sommerville knows it's not *if* another bomb will explode, it's *when* . . .

Tunbridge Wells, Kent: Oddly enough, despite being 3,500 miles away, it is the discordant noises of Afghanistan that are replaying in Sharon Marris's head, keeping her awake in the darkness of her bedroom on the edge of London's commuter belt.

Like Quentin Sommerville, she wants the Big Story.

She lies staring at a blank ceiling, having just flown back from Helmand, reporting for the *Kent and Sussex Courier*. You'd think she'd sleep more easily at home again, but you'd be wrong.

3

She's listening carefully and hearing only the sound of nothing. She can't get used to it. She hates it, the emptiness of silence. She wants the aural definition of noise, of people and shouting, of transports and helicopters.

She jots down her thoughts in a diary.

'Despite the dust, the blisters on my heels, the bruises on my hips from body armour that is not really shaped for the female figure, the dry hands, assorted scratches and general stresses and frustrations of working in a war zone, I still want to be there – doing that. But, as my boss reminds me, there's no need in Northcliffe for a war correspondent.'

Then she adds: 'So that's another reason I'm lying awake – trying to find a way to prove him wrong.'

London: Channel 4 News anchor Jon Snow opens his eyes and almost wishes he hadn't. He is usually fit and invincible, whether under shell fire in a war zone or reporting from the home front. Yet today that invincibility has cracked. He is achy and feeling weak. It must be that bug going round. Should he even get up?

Truro, Cornwall: *Cough-cough.* One cough triggers the other, creating a stereo effect for Kirstie Newton, editor of *Cornwall Today*. She opens her eyes to the sounds of her partner and their 18-month-old daughter hacking away in chorus, like a pair of Victorian consumptives. She tries to get back to sleep but is too distracted. She's thinking about a features idea. She'll put it up on Facebook.

She'll ask readers: *What Makes You Cornish?*

London: Helen Russell, Online Editor of *Marie Claire*, wakes up excited, with a mantra running through her head like a Frank Sinatra song . . .

New York, New York . . .

First thing, she reaches for her BlackBerry. She's got all her complex life locked up in that electronic matchbox. Well-manicured fingers tap keys and she starts looking at her diary. She sees meetings, meetings . . .

In her head, Russell is already choosing the wardrobe she needs to wear, to look like her readers would like to look themselves.

In their dreams.

Fashion can be a bitchy world but she defies the stereotype with the face of a young Julie Andrews, a personality to match, and a smile which is genuinely angelic, not fake. But that doesn't mean she should dress like Mary Poppins.

Now, what should she wear today?

When you're this kind of journalist, you have to look and live glossy.

Leeds: David Spereall is a journalism student who is completely mad about sport. At 19, he has taken a big step by getting a work placement on the sports desk of the *Yorkshire Evening Post*. He wakes up early, hardly able to believe how lucky he is.

He reckons it's the best job in the world and can't wait to start another day. He goes downstairs to make himself breakfast before his flatmates wake. He watches the TV news before taking advantage of the quiet to squeeze in two games of FIFA. The previous evening he'd seen one of his cricket articles uploaded onto cricketfancast.com.

It's all so exciting.

Like Farrah Storr 200 miles away in London, he is watching the clock, desperate to set off for work.

London: Other sports reporters – equally fanatical but a little older – are waking up with one-track minds.

Today, at Southwark Crown Court, the jury is expected to return their verdicts in the trial of National Treasure Harry Redknapp. He's favourite to become the next England football boss except for two obstacles in his path. He may be behind bars. And there's no vacancy.

So the People's 'Arry is probably awake too at this ungodly hour, wondering whether he is about to watch his last sunrise on the outside for a few years. Just an ordinary sunrise. The ordinary – the fresh air and starlight – has never seemed so precious.

The reporters know he's not the only one of his ilk feeling the pressure.

The current England football manager, Fabio Capello, is stressed out too.

Later today the reporters will be there when the Italian Capello arrives for a meeting with the Football Association at Wembley. Only he really knows what he's going to do. Not Redknapp, not the FA, not the writers and snappers. Only Capello.

According to this morning's headlines, it is National Treasure 'Arry versus National Scapegoat Fabio.

They are part of the country's unfolding narrative. *Narrative.*

That's the pseud's term for what working hacks call *stories* and *yarns*. What twists and turns lie in store for the rest of today?

While UK journalists rub sleep from their eyes and sputter into action, international correspondents check their Rolexes and office clocks and synchronise with London time. The UK's a big market and they need to keep in step.

Santa Clarita, California: As a shivering Britain rises from slumber, it's the end of the day for Peter Bowes, BBC freelance correspondent in the warmer clime of America's West Coast. Like Afghanistan's Quentin Sommerville, he has his own territory to cover. But there most similarities end.

While Sommerville is choking on Afghan's red dust and watching for roadside bombs and hidden snipers, Bowes is back on his 5-acre ranch 32 miles north of Hollywood. He has his own studio and runs and swims, and keeps goats and a llama.

He lives the Californian good life and sometimes he can hardly believe he's escaped the less glamorous environs of England's County Durham. Now he has just recorded a piece with *Good Morning Scotland* about American gay marriages and done a report about a school sex abuse scandal. He's also filed for 5 Live radio and the BBC World Service.

It's getting late and he's got another big day tomorrow, this time in Hollywood. Time to call it a night.

Hollywood, Los Angeles: A limousine sweeps along Wilshire Boulevard and swings between the palm trees which mark the driveway of an undistinguished chain hotel. It pulls up beneath the tropical fauna that drapes the entrance and a uniformed commissionaire steps forward and reaches for the handle of the rear door.

He pulls it open and a woman's legs emerge. As she eases herself out into the glaring porch lights, he recognises her face and says: 'Good evening, Madam.'

There is a flurry of deferential activity.

The woman smiles and walks through the doors into the lobby.

Outside the grounds, a man strung with cameras makes a call on his mobile.

'She's here.'

Rwanda, Central Africa: It's not just Hollywood that's able to enjoy days of sunshine and blue skies. Reuters correspondent Graham Holliday sits down on the patio of his home in the capital, Kigali, at a dining table carved out of eucalyptus wood.

This is a kind of paradise. He is surrounded by papaya and avocado trees and watches the sunbirds steal pollen from the flowers. Overhead, black kites circle and he can hear the quiet buzz of cars and moto-taxis heading up the main road towards the Milles Collines Hotel, otherwise known as Hotel Rwanda.

Kigali is going to work in its own relaxed way. Even when it's busy, the city moves with a lithe calmness, revelling in an all-year springtime which is the antithesis of the dash and hurry of the newsrooms from which he has escaped yet serves faithfully from afar.

Holliday fiddles with a battered old iPhone and scans emails, an RSS Reader and Twitter. Not much happening. Some days, to an outsider, it could be a scene in a Graham Greene novel.

It can only be a kind of paradise, an imperfect one, unable to erase its collective memory of genocidal hell.

Kingston, Surrey: As her husband leaves for his swim, the half-asleep Natalie Dye thinks back to the 1990s. Then she'd have been flying home on the red-eye plane scribbling a Hollywood profile five miles above the dark Atlantic Ocean. Now she's ghostwriting magazine columns, taking a rebellious pride in calling herself a slovenly suburban mum.

She rolls over and goes back to sleep, perfectly content to let Gino swim alone and the last remnants of night-time unfold without her attention.

Later, when she is awake, she will go on a journey into the space-time continuum, something she will not be entirely comfortable with.

Congleton, Cheshire: Although he drums in a punk band, Jeremy Condliffe is old-fashioned enough to still wear pyjamas in bed, and now he is sitting in them at his desk, having been up and at work for an hour already. He pads into the kitchen and puts the coffee on.

He is editor and managing director of the *Congleton Chronicle* series and Wednesday is Death Day; all their funeral reports (yes, they still print a full list of mourners) and death notices come in on a Tuesday, so his first job today is to sort them out for the sub-editors. There are long lists of names, just as his readers expect in a weekly newspaper.

That's why he got up at five o'clock.

One of his friend's fathers has died; a nice chap. Jeremy finds it depressing – life's achievements being summed up in three paragraphs and a standard *'He will be sadly missed'.*

Manchester: Kevin Duffy is looking lively considering it's so early. He gets ready quickly and hurries out of the door. He wants to beat the morning rush hour. At the wheel of his car, he threads his way towards the M6. He is heading for Preston, to teach journalism at the University of Central Lancaster. It's a career switch he never intended but he's throwing himself into it.

He joins the motorway and starts wondering why so many truck drivers drive like homicidal maniacs.

North London: Editors are paid well to worry, to wake up in the early hours with the screaming abdabs and now Rebecca Fleming opens her eyes and within seconds feels a sense of worry descend upon her.

She's thinking about a picture she's putting on the cover of *Take a Break* magazine. She's got a husband, three kids, and they get priority.

But in the back of her mind she can see a woman's face staring at her with cold, accusing eyes.

You've used my picture. Did I give you permission?

If ever a look spelt trouble, it's that one. Should she pixelate it – or take a risk? Deadline today. She will have to decide.

Right, kids, what're we having for breakfast?

Unemployed Ex-Murdoch Reporter: This is a journalist who once worked at Wapping - News International's London headquarters - when that was something to boast about. He flew around the globe, interviewed big names. Now he's out of work. He's not just lost his job, he's lost his sense of self. He calls himself 'an untouchable'.

Without identifying himself, he is at his keyboard and blogging to an unsympathetic world about his slide into poverty and misery.

'The central heating clicking on woke me and Chaplin my cat,' he says. 'A friend lent me money so I don't freeze as headlines scream "minus 15 and more snow on way". We yawned and stretched in unison, then crawled out of bed . . .'

Today he reckons it could be different. He's got an appointment, perhaps a step towards rehabilitation after his disastrous experiences as a foot soldier in the Murdoch empire.

Langwarrin, Melbourne: It's good that the sun is shining on Cruden Farm this day, the most important date in its annual calendar.

The estate looks beautiful, with its vineyards and gardens, lawns and horse paddocks, lakes and pools.

While London awakes to sub-zero temperatures, here on the other side of the world it is teatime in mid-summer and Dame Elisabeth Murdoch is enjoying her 103rd birthday. For someone her age, she is bursting with vitality and, dressed in flowered shirt and pink jacket, she is being taken to a concert arranged in her honour.

She is accompanied by two of her grandchildren, Elisabeth and Lachlan, both attentive to her needs.

'Sorry, Dad's not here, grandma.'

She's sorry too.

But everyone understands.

London: Even at this early hour there are many people waking whose destinies will be inextricably linked with Dame Elisabeth's son, Rupert, during the next 24 hours of this narrative.

As soon as they open their eyes, some think about the High Court. Others wake up and think about the Leveson Inquiry. Others emerge from sleep and think about the police investigations.

And yet others, investors and shareholders, will think about News Corporation's quarterly figures, right now being readied for release on Wall Street.

Even in these difficult times, Murdoch's presence seems to be everywhere, rivalling God's.

Vienna, Austria: Mike Leidig has been at his desk for one hour precisely. He is a British journalist who has been running Central European News since 1993. In front of him now, he has 18 news items sent from correspondents in other time zones. They need to be checked before he includes them in his regular newsfeed to the UK and elsewhere. He deletes five as uninteresting and sends the rest through to a sub-editor.

He's got another story on his mind, his undercover one.

Enfield, London: The bug that's afflicting Jon Snow in London and Kirstie Newton's family in Cornwall is probably the same one that has taken up residence inside Arif Durrani's home.

With two poorly kids, both under four, it's been a restless night for the group news editor of Haymarket's *Brand Republic*.

He gives up trying to sleep, goes into the kitchen and turns on his laptop. He's got a deadline. He wants to finish writing up a big interview, this one with Andrew Rashbass, *The Economist*'s global chief executive.

He needs to publish it later today, while it's still hot news. His fingers start tapping the keyboard, pausing while he thinks, then start tapping again.

London: Working to his personal schedule, Jon Peake, editor-in-chief of *TV Choice* and *Total TV Guide*, wakes, sees it is still dark outside and buries his head briefly back beneath the duvet. He needs his sleep. This will be his busiest day of the week.

Bath, Somerset: As news editor and deputy editor, Paul Wiltshire likes to lead from the front at the *Bath Chronicle*. He is the first one to arrive and takes advantage of an unnaturally quiet newsroom to deal with a stack of emails. When he's finished, he updates the news list, shaping the day ahead.

Then he watches the door, impatient for other faces to appear. He's like a terrier on a leash, hardly able to wait.

Bring it on.

London: *Bring on the day.* That's what Farrah Storr keeps thinking, still bursting with excitement over the launch of her magazine, *Women's Health*. She tries to distract herself again and pops a DVD into the TV. It is Nigel Slater's *Simple Suppers* and she does some hand weights while watching him make his 'teatime mackerel'.

'Forget exercising to music,' she thinks. 'Working out to your favourite foodie show is the way forward.'

Mmm, that'll make a good feature.

She glances out of the window, hoping to spot the elusive dawn. The dark sky continues to torment her.

Task Force Helmand HQ: Inside the British military fortress, Army press chief Mackenzie shakes off the dust after his helicopter ride. He unbuckles his body armour and drops it off, checks his rifle into the armoury and grabs a cup of tea.

He sips it as he talks to his press team.

'What's happening?'

He gets an update. He's shown an article just written by a *Washington Post* journalist. He scans it, looking for security breaches.

'Fine. Publish . . . '

Then he discusses various plans. He employs the language not of a soldier but of a PR professional.

'Media narrative . . . blah-blah . . . communications goals.'

When that's finished, Mackenzie goes to the gym and – in his own words – 'smashes 600 calories'.

He is committed to his work. But in this harsh semi-desert of Afghanistan, he sometimes misses the beach outside his house in the Scottish capital of Edinburgh, the lazy baths, the whisky, playing with his son and talking to his wife, Judith. He's 47 and thinks this will be the last Afghan tour he volunteers for.

Nar-e Saraj, Helmand Province: *Phwuumph.* A noise loud enough to be heard over the roar and rumble of a military motorcade sends a pressure wave in the direction of its most high-value passenger. Reaching vehicles, it presses against them like the hand of a delinquent giant.

The BBC's Quentin Sommerville swivels and stares through plastic eye-protectors and sees the crystalline blue sky being smeared with smoke.

Part of the road surface is erupting in a black cloud of rock and soil, rising in a column which then begins to collapse around itself, raining debris back to earth, sending fragments clattering down onto any nearby vehicle rooftops.

It's only 150 metres away.

He holds a microphone close to his lips, stabs the *record* button and starts speaking calmly ready for broadcast later . . .

'We've just heard an explosion, another improvised explosive device, a big one. We're told that the Afghan National Army so far have managed to find about 14 of these devices and they are doing that because they are pushing forward.'

Vehicle doors are thrown open, officers start shouting and troops move swiftly. This is the third blast today. The IEDs are embedded in the physical and psychological landscape. In one way it's routine but not the kind of routine you ever get used to.

Sommerville listens to the voices on the radio.

'Report injuries . . . both British and Afghani.'

He's a muscular man, bulked up even more by body armour. The tension is palpable as they wait. The reports come in.

No one is hurt. Another lucky escape.

Engines rev.

The convoy rolls on, every few metres kicking up a ton of dust as fine as talcum powder, flagging their position for snipers wishing to take optimistic pot shots from the low hills or distant dried-mud buildings.

If they knew about his presence, which thankfully they don't, Sommerville would be a prime target, a big prize.

Ahead, troops keep searching for the next IED, aware that their lives are being toyed with by luck and fate.

Again, it's not *if* the next bomb will go off, but *when*.

London: Media networking queen Julia Hobsbawm leaves home just as a more irregular army – that of newsagents in the service of the great British public – are making an unwelcome racket, slamming up shop front shutters and opening their doors. It's their contribution to the dawn chorus, a sleep-destroying reveille. They cut open bundles of daily newspapers and arrange them on their counters.

The displays look humble considering what they are.

The first draft of history.

Hobsbawm is driving to Heathrow Airport. Traffic has overloaded icy roads and she's wondering if she will miss her plane.

Delhi, India: It is late morning on a warm, balmy day and Helen Roberts is working hard at the features agency she has just set up. She is writing a piece for a corner of Rupert Murdoch's empire, a British magazine called *Fabulous.*

It is about a young Indian woman who, at 13, defied her parents by refusing to get married. She went on to save other girls from becoming child brides.

Roberts emails UNICEF India and asks: 'How many child brides are there every year here?'

She waits for a reply.

London: Time ticks on and now it is 6.45am and freelance Chris Wheal has been enjoying a rare lie-in. He's had eight hours sleep which, for him, is unheard of.

Finally, he stumbles out of bed, steps into the kitchen, makes tea and wakes the family.

While they surface, he sits at his computer and clasps the mouse. It's taken ten minutes from duvet to desk and already he's a journalist at work.

KwaZulu-Natal, South Africa: Usually Meera Dattani's breakfast view is an elevated one looking across North London rooftops. Now she sits at ground level over coffee outside the Umkhumbi Lodge and gazes at the sand bush, aglow in the bright low-angled sunshine.

It has been stupidly hot of late, although rain last night has made things fresher.

As a travel writer, she can't help think it's strange to be tapping out guides and money-saving features, her regular UK work, while parked next to a cage containing two huge boa constrictors. She tries to ignore their unnerving, serpentine stares. She does slightly miss waking up to the familiar voices of Radio 4's *Today* programme.

Shepherd's Bush, London: *'You're listening to Today on Radio 4 with Justin Webb and James Naughtie. The headlines this morning . . . The Chancellor has warned that the row about paying bonuses threatens to undermine jobs . . . but Labour have accused him of putting the economy into reverse . . . A report says older people needing care have been let down by services which pass them round like a parcel . . . Argentina is to make a formal complaint to the United Nations about what its president calls British militarization of the Falklands . . .'*

London: In this pre-dawn hour, the BBC's *Today* programme is uniting many journalists across the country, with the authoritative tones of Naughtie and Webb sweeping away the nation's night sweats and nasty dreams.

Their programme sets the news agenda.

Among the keenest listeners are the big beasts of old Fleet Street absorbing their first briefing as they armour themselves for their daily tournament.

Theirs is an amazing world, one where they hold lasting power which transient prime ministers can but envy.

11

But as they wipe the steam off their bathroom mirrors, they see faces staring back that are unusually tired and uncertain, and perhaps a little frightened.

To some of them, it is beginning to feel pre-revolutionary, with the mob enraged and threatening to turn their nice, cosy world upside down.

The stress is not confined to Murdoch, Redknapp, Capello and a few other headliners. It penetrates deep into the heart of the media industry, to an obscure elite whose exercise of power is made all the more effective because it is so well hidden.

This mighty band of newspaper Goliaths is being cut down to size by a man called Brian.

London: Sir Brian Henry Leveson, QC, better known as Lord Justice Leveson, is preparing himself for another day chairing his eponymous Leveson Judicial Inquiry into the regulation of the media.

It was set up by the British Prime Minister, David Cameron.

At first glance, Leveson seems as harmless as a puppy. But that is deceptive. If he is a puppy, it is of the pitbull variety, one which is rapidly acquiring a taste for chewing at the ankles of passing giants.

Cambridge: By his own admission, Bob Satchwell is a Leveson Inquiry junkie and, like most addictions, it is wrecking his life, turning him into a man running up a down escalator.

To find time for it, he has to make an early start and he is already checking his emails while listening to *Today*. He has different newspapers delivered every morning. In front of him now he's got the *Sun*, *Mail*, *Telegraph* and *i*.

He begins flicking through their pages.

Lincoln: The alarm is intentionally annoying on John Thorne's mobile so he cannot even think about ignoring it.

Not that it's necessary this morning. He's had a night of broken sleep in a hotel room next to the city's cathedral. He switches on the TV news and ponders briefly on his altered circumstances.

Until recently, the six-footer Thorne would have been on the other side of the screen, talking to camera, linking into the studio, giving his live reports as the BBC News Correspondent for the North of England.

Now he's switched teams. He's poacher turned gamekeeper, not without pangs of conscience. He washes his face, trying to rinse away the guilt.

London: Footballer's wife Abbey Clancy makes a living from looking good and today she is near the top of almost every newspaper picture list. Married to Stoke City's Peter Crouch, she is the face - and body - of a multi-million pound launch for *Lynx* cosmetics.

She and Crouchie also have a date with the High Court, next door to the Leveson Inquiry.

First she has to slip into something extremely clingy.

China: Having just landed aboard a flight from Kunming, Malcolm Moore comes loping across the concourse of Mangshi Airport with an air of practised calm.

He is trying to appear as inconspicuous as a European can in this distant part of the country. He passes police and uniformed officials who look but do not stop him.

This is a great relief to Moore, who doesn't want to lie.

On the walls, he sees adverts for jewellery carved from precious jade. That's part of his assignment: the fight for control of the Burmese jade mines. But he's not telling anyone.

At his side is photographer Adam Dean, keeping his cameras out of view.

They have travelled 1,500 miles from the coastal city of Shanghai. Maybe they look like tourists intending to visit the Wuyun Temple or the Sanxian natural cave. They sit down briefly and order two bowls of Chinese rice and porridge. They see the familiar KFC sign and grab quick coffees.

Then, wasting no time, Moore and Dean climb into a car and join the motorway, heading south-east, still trying not to attract attention as they drive across this corner of Yunnan.

Far from home, beyond effective protection, they have worked out a plan. It's risky. They could get arrested and thrown into jail. But that's part of the terms and conditions of their employment.

They are journalists.

Barra do Pirai, Brazil: Journalist Mario Randolfo is asleep at his home, the only place where he feels even moderately safe these days. But it is not a fortress and he remains vulnerable. He has been a brave, outspoken voice, just doing his job.

But now the gangsters have had enough.

Randolfo lies next to his girlfriend, Maria Guimarães, who is equally courageous. A contract has been taken out on his life and, in this impoverished state, there is always someone willing to fulfil it for a fistful of dollars and the benefits of personal notoriety.

Here, a dissident journalist's life is worth no more than a sackful of coffee beans.

Like those roadside bombs in faraway Afghanistan, it's not *if* but *when* . . .

Whether in Europe or America, Africa or Asia, the hidden superstate of journalism is at work as Wednesday 8 February gets underway.

CHAPTER 2
7am-8am
Bring It On

Cambridge: Two people have been found frozen to death in the open air on this sub-zero morning, in separate incidents. As crime reporter Raymond Brown takes in the news, he gets breakfast for his two boys while munching on toast.

They sound like his kind of stories; hard, serious, mysterious, maybe sinister.

The trouble is he's down in the newsroom diary to cover two important visitors, Prince Charles and Education Secretary Michael Gove.

Brown is more interested in covering dead locals than live VIPs for his newspaper, the *Cambridge News*.

He's going to have to do a lot of juggling.

Notting Hill, London: A twisting staircase runs steeply up t he back of Shannons Market Bar on Portobello Road. It's still dark when Natasha Courtenay-Smith arrives, threading her way between last night's rubbish bags being collected from outside the pubs and restaurants.

She wends her way up to the top floor, unlocks the door and steps into offices which were once Victorian servants' bedrooms. She adjusts the Venetian blinds, gazing down on the street like Philip Marlow in the *Big Sleep*. This is one of the city's most famous junctions. If you wait long enough, everyone will walk past once.

She sits at her desk and opens the *Sun* newspaper.

'*TRUSTING Janey Byrne thought she'd bought a trendy micro pig — then watched her balloon into this 17st monster.*'

That's Courtenay-Smith's story. It perks her up b etter than a cappuccino. Not a bad start to the day.

Stedham, Sussex: In a cottage overlooking the village green, veteran humourist Colin Dunne is waking up and running through a checklist to see if he's properly alive . . .

14

'Eyes open. Well, half open. What does the day hold? Golf, of course. And writing. Arranging black marks on white paper with a view to pleasing editors and/or earning cash? Well, maybe. Retired? Writers cannot retire unless fingers encased in set concrete.'

He gets up a nd has a bowl of porridge, briefly yearning for the five-Bensons-and-a-bacon-banjo-breakfast of his old *Daily Mirror* days. He tells himself he must keep his ancient heart ticking and brain simmering.

Why? He's no idea.

Nar-e Saraj, Helmand Province: Just south of Highway One, BBC man Quentin Sommerville is accompanying 900 A fghan soldiers and police searching for Taliban fighters. The Afghani troops outnumber their UK advisers nine to one.

It's less than an hour since the last IED exploded and everyone is watching for more. It makes them nervous.

Sommerville collars the man in charge, Brigadier-General Sheren Shah, and asks him: 'Will Afghani forces be able to do these operations on their own?'

Brimming with self-confidence – not universally shared – Shah stands in front of the camera and replies: 'Our foreign friends are in the back giving us support, but we know this place better. We know the language and only we can search the people and houses, not the foreigners.'

Sommerville is not so sure.

It is a two-day military operation and he has told his London newsroom, via the Kabul bureau, that he won't be doing any live TV or radio from out here. That would reveal his presence, draw attention and tempt fate.

Working for the world's best-known broadcaster carries danger as well as prestige.

His capture or killing would be a Taliban propaganda dream.

Sommerville is observing closely, nursing a heap of awkward questions. He's looking for a chance to start interviewing ordinary Afghan soldiers. Are they as confident as their commander?

Glasgow: Freelance Samantha Booth slips out of bed, goes into the kitchen and makes the first coffee of the day. She perches at her computer and opens her emails.

Gimme work, gimme work.

She's been sending out lots of ideas, reckoning at least one of her stories was a shoo-in. She scrolls down the screen.

Nothing. Sod all. Zilch.

Booth is starting to feel sidelined. Freelancing is proving to be a tough new world. She puts on the TV and stares at the news, hardly taking it in. Why don't editors reply?

London: He's just got back from the Indian Ocean and no one knows better than Frank Gardner how terrorists like to target BBC reporters. Now he is woken by a phone alarm that is not his own.

He stirs and, for a moment, he wonders where it is coming from. Then he realises he is at home and it is from another bedroom in the house. The ringtone belongs to his daughter and Gardner says to himself: 'That's extremely irritating. I'm going to ask her to change it. It's the least she can do for her old man.'

The BBC security correspondent has been making a film about modern piracy, flying in a helicopter to scan the sea off the African coast. He's found that fascinating.

Today, he gets to sit in a darkened room and do the edit which, for someone who likes action, is much less so.

London: Still waiting for dawn, Farrah Storr, Britain's newest editor, makes tea and drops a slice of wholemeal bread into the toaster. She takes an avocado out of the fridge, mixes it with marmite and spreads it on the toast. It's her favourite, an old Australian recipe, and reminds her of when she used to live in Sydney. She hopes it will keep her full until lunch.

There's a table booked for her at the Soho Hotel, as cool as you can get. With the launch of *Women's Health,* this is the biggest day of her career.

London: Having finished her yoga and Pilates, *Psychologies'* Louise Chunn sits down for breakfast with her husband and 11-year-old daughter. They skim the *Guardian* and *The Times*, in their printed editions, and then she showers, dresses and applies makeup. It's an 'outfacing' day, one where she will be representing *Psychologies* to others, so she is careful about looking the part.

People have their expectations of top editors.

London: As she gets ready, Helen Russell's mind keeps leaping forward to New York Fashion Week. She will be attending on behalf of *Marie Claire.* It's a big trip, a lot of work and a great experience.

But first she has things to organise here, not least what she's going to wear. She looks in her wardrobe and sees her clothes need pressing.

For fashion journalists, the personal melds with the professional. They are judged not just on their journalistic talent but on how they dress and look, every hour of every day. It's harsh but true.

Now she gets ready and selects the outfits she will wear in Manhattan next week. She slips them into a bag.

Bristol: Caroline Sutton wakes up shivering in a freezing hotel room. For some reason, the heating's off. She switches it on and starts getting in the right frame of mind. She's travelled from Brighton to give some media training. Her audience will be a very bright group of journalists. It's a c hallenge. She's looking forward to it.

Watford, Hertfordshire: Susan Watts, science editor of BBC's *Newsnight*, has woken up feeling pleased. She's still thinking about last night's studio special on PIP breast implants. It was TV journalism at its best, informative and revelatory, packed tightly into the first eight minutes of the show.

A woman had allowed them to film her operation as a surgeon removed and replaced her flawed implants.

That prompted a studio discussion and an unlikely alliance between Naomi Wolf, the cerebrally enhanced feminist, and Katie Price, the mammary enhanced self-publicist, aka Jordan. Together they accused the British government minister Anne Milton not just of getting her facts wrong but of lying.

Lying! You couldn't say that in the House of Commons. Watts wonders what today's reactions will be.

Now she helps marshal the children out to school with their dad. First things first.

KwaZulu-Natal, South Africa: Sitting on her hosts' patio, Meera Dattani has finished breakfast and is staring at her computer screen. On behalf of the Umkhumbi Lodge, she goes onto Twitter and Facebook, greeting new followers, re-tweeting interesting nuggets and adding more tips to an ever-expanding 'social media strategy' document.

She may be in the South African bush but she is as electronically hooked up as anyone back home in London, or in New York or Beijing.

A few paces away is a snake house and an enclosure with two iguanas. As someone who arrived from Britain scared of m ost bugs, large spiders and definitely snakes, this is proving to be a life-changing experience. Instead of Radio 4's *Today*, it's birdsong, wild guinea fowl and, in the evenings, the sound of cicadas.

She finishes her coffee and applies herself to her work.

London: As the alarm goes off, the radio comes on. Robin Lustig, presenter of the BBC's *World Tonight,* lets his semi-conscious mind meld with the voices on his early-morning sister programme, *Today.*

Ah, he recognises the mellifluous tones of Naughtie and Webb, reassuring in delivery if not always in content.

He listens to the headlines, noting what has changed in the eight hours since he went off air. *Chancellor George Osborne on business bonuses; NHS reforms being sent back to the House of Lords; Argentina protesting about Britain's Falkland Islands policy.*

Lustig wonders what will survive for his broadcast 16 hours ahead. NHS, Falklands, probably Syria? It's anyone's guess.

London: Having ensured all his family is up and about, freelance Chris Wheal is writing his first post for *AOL Money*. He is tapping away when he realises the bathroom has become free. He jumps up, has a quick shower and gets dressed. When he returns to his desk and resumes work, his wife rewards him with a bowl of cereal and a fresh smoothie. No wonder he calls her The Good Lady Wife.

Outside, it is still dark but the sky is starting to lighten.

Hollywood, Los Angeles: *'Hi, man, d'ya wanna know where she's staying?'*

17

'Yeah.'
'On Wilshire Boulevard. This is the hotel . . . '
'Thanks.'

The paparazzi are buzzing as information sparks round their private circuit. Info. Names. Where and when. *Tell me, tell me, I wanna know. Money, money, money.*

Info is their currency, a commodity to be bought and sold. It comes from delivery girls, pizza boys, call girls, rent boys, florists, waiters, bodyguards, drug dealers, pilots, priests, masseurs, cops and drivers – anyone. You can't blame the hotel. They try to respect privacy. This is a city like a sieve.

There are three days to go to the Grammy Awards at the Staples Centre.

LA lives and breathes celebrity. And now, as if it's not got enough famous faces, even more stars are flying in from the music industry's far-flung outposts – New York, Nashville, London and all points in between.

It's a toxic overdose of fame yet LA has big enough nostrils to snort every line of it, and the paparazzi are tooling up with the cynicism of a southside street gang.

'Confirm it again . . . '
'Whitney's on Wilshire Boulevard.'
'Got it.'
'You know where to send the money?'
'Sure.'

Rwanda, Central Africa: This is a slow start for Reuters man Graham Holliday in Kigali. He makes his way to the Place de la Constitution and steps inside the Blues Cafe. He's meeting a PhD student from the School of Oriental and African Studies, in London. He's here researching local industry: coffee, tea, mining, tourism and horticulture.

For a journalist, the tables are turned and now it is Holliday who answers the questions. It doesn't seem much but this is how good reporters work. Talking to anyone and everyone. Keeping informed. Building contacts. Sifting facts. Looking for angles. Letting things bubble on the back burner. Good stories often emerge from left of field, when you least expect it, as an experienced hand like Holliday knows.

Blackheath, London: The alarm wakes Alan Burkitt-Gray, editor of *Global Telecoms Business*. He tunes into *Today*, listening on an earphone so as not to disturb anyone, and continues to lie in bed while resisting the temptation to doze off again. After 15 minutes, he gets up, makes tea and steps into the shower. This is press day. He's got deadlines.

Better get moving.

Tunbridge Wells, Kent: Deadlines – a whole sequence of them – are waiting like dominoes, to be knocked down one by one. As editor of the *Kent and Sussex Courier*, Ian Read is first to enter the dark, deserted newsroom.

He rattles about in the kitchen, filling a bowl with Cheerios and milk, and making a mug of coffee. He flicks through some national newspapers while eating, then pushes his dish aside and gets down to work.

There is a lot to do.

He starts by tinkering with two page leads and sending them through ready for the subs. He looks up at the door half-expectantly, knowing his colleagues will be huffing and puffing through it at any moment.

He just loves it.

Dorking, Surrey: In the darkness, twin headlight beams swing off the road as Sam Blackledge turns carefully into a car park glazed with ice and snow. When he steps out, his shoes start slipping and it's a treacherous skid of a walk to the office door.

As chief reporter of the *Dorking Advertiser*, he reckons extreme weather has a strange effect on journalists. Blackledge likes it because readers send in pictures. You don't need much training to write *Brrr, Dorking Shivers.*

But he also hates it because it is impossible to avoid the clichés and puns, like the one reeling through his head right now: *Snow Joke.*

He pushes at the door and finds it still locked. There is no sign of anyone else. The paper recently moved from a tiny, crumbling office to this larger open-plan one, with Fort Knox-style security. He waits. The time passes slowly in the cold and it's 20 minutes before he sees a colleague slip-sliding across the ice towards him.

'I can't get in,' Blackledge says.

'I've got a key.'

The door unlocked, they enter the newsroom. Others start arriving.

Someone says: 'Who's getting the tea in then?'

Barnet, London: Having just become a mum, magazine deputy editor Sara Ward is pitting journalistic theory against reality.

She is woken by the cries of her three-week-old son, James. Her husband, Stuart, gets out of bed and changes him while she goes into the kitchen and makes porridge and tea. It's been a wakeful night but no more than she expected. She's spent ten years writing true-life stories about mums for the best-selling weekly, *Take a Break.*

Now she's a mother herself, she is discovering whether the clichés are true.

Yes, she decides as she takes Stuart his tea, they really are: life becomes an endless round of feeds and nappy changes and – yes, again – you're carried along on a wave of emotion and love.

She knows it's not unique to her.

When she gets the chance, she'll write it up as a feature. She and Stuart drink their tea, sighing between sips. Today is going to be different. They don't say it but they feel sad.

Enfield, London: Just down the road from Barnet, at Arif Durrani's home, it has been sickly mayhem during the night, with two poorly children. He says to himself: 'They're great, of course, but not today . . . '

He's got a lot of work on his plate and now he beats a retreat out of the front door.

As he strides out for the train, he's already got final copy structure whirling around in his head. He reaches the still-dark Gordon Hill station and grabs a cappuccino. He sips it and thinks it's the worst coffee of the day and yet still the most needed. This is rush hour and other commuters are filling the platform.

Towards the east, the black clouds' underbellies are beginning to soften.

Walthamstow, East London: Having fended off his son's dinosaur attacks, Nick McGrath has climbed the stairs to his attic office. From there he can see the Olympic Stadium, an arc of light against the fading night sky.

McGrath has two interviewees lined up for this morning: Gregg Wallace, presenter of *Masterchef*, and somebody called Lydia Bright.

Lydia who?

Reluctantly, McGrath decides that he'll have to make the ultimate sacrifice. Yes, he'll watch *The Only Way Is Essex*. Deep inside, he emits a muted groan.

From the window, he sees the dawn starting to break.

07:28; Sunrise. The rising sun dispels the dark and casts a low watery light over the chilled rooftops of Britain. It is still cold.

Melbourne, Australia: In warm sunshine Dame Elisabeth Murdoch is being pushed along the pavement in a wheelchair towards the Melbourne Recital Centre. People are filing into their seats for a concert being held in her honour on her 103rd birthday.

Her son Rupert, himself 80, is not the only notable absentee. Her grandson James is also not present.

Syria: Having just disembarked at the airport, Bill Neely, the international editor of ITV News, has got through passport control and is making the drive into the capital city of this war-torn state. He has already detected a degree of governmental paranoia. He Tweets: '

Welcome to Damascus, where we are about to be watched . . . '

Lincoln: A winter sun strikes the cathedral spire first, then penetrates the windows of the hotel occupied by ex-BBC correspondent John Thorne, poacher turned guilt-ridden gamekeeper.

Behind the glass panes, Thorne reports for breakfast and sees his colleague, Richard Wells, already seated at a table. He takes the chair opposite and they survey the menu.

Both Thorne and Wells spent many years as the BBC's Northern reporters and now they are putting their past experience to commercial use. Over cereal and fruit, they scan the newspapers, looking for stories to add topicality to their day's work.

Ah, the *Daily Mail* is expressing 'outrage'. As per usual. That will do nicely. They mark the page.

They are running a high-grade media training course.

Everyone hates the press in these Leveson days and Thorne wonders: 'Will our "clients" hate us too?'

London: *Marie Claire*'s Helen Russell leaves her flat, carrying favourite dresses and other clothes in a bag. She calls at the dry cleaner's nearby and drops them off. She wants them back pressed and folded, all ready for packing for her trip to New York Fashion Week.

Dropping off her own stuff? Shouldn't she have an assistant catering to her every whim? Yes, if you are Anna Wintour and edit American *Vogue*. No, if you are Russell and edit the digital and online material at *Marie Claire* UK.

There is a difference.

Russell powerwalks to the tube, slim forearms high and pumping, getting into the mid-town Manhattan mode and mood.

Preston, Lancashire: The 50-mile race up the M6 against speeding juggernauts has brought out Kevin Duffy's paranoia. With relief, he turns off the motorway and reaches the university. He finds a £4 a day parking spot and realises he is ridiculously early and wonders whether to snooze in the car for an hour, to make up for his early start

No, it's too cold. He trudges over to the on-campus Starbucks and joins the queue. He orders a caramel shortcake and skinny cappuccino with double shot. He finds a seat and, as the first sip hits the spot, imagines this is how desperate smokers must feel these days.

He would have asked for a triple shot but fears it might arouse suspicion. He reads one of the Starbuck's newspapers, already looking a bit used.

Lancaster: Just up the coast of the Irish Sea, ex-editor Peter Cole is setting off from home, pondering on the best laid schemes of mice and men etcetera. He thought he'd got the day all sorted. Now his plans are falling apart.

As Professor Emeritus of journalism at Sheffield University, he'd arranged a lecture for his students this lunchtime from Sue Ryan, head of the *Daily Mail*'s training scheme, who had promised to come up from London.

But last night Ryan texted Cole. She said she couldn't make it. She apologised and explained that she was ill. Could she send a replacement?

He accepted, of course.

But now, as he drives across northern England, the distinguished Cole worries. Will the substitute be any good?

Unemployed Ex-Murdoch Reporter: 'It's nice to have a warm flat,' he blogs, 'because we (him and cat, Chaplin) have both been sleeping on the settee by the halogen heater, a gift from a friend, in recent weeks. I've been living on beans on toast and Chaplin, a food snob, has been forced to eat store-brand cat food. If this cat knew how much I've relied on him for company because I'm too poor to go out, I think he'd laugh or leave.'

He blogs to keep in practice, to maintain a sense of self-worth. But a blogger is not journalist. He's desperate to get back to being a journalist.

Bristol: Heather Findlay, senior features writer at Medavia news agency, calls at the newspaper shop on her way to the office and collects the *Sun, Daily Mail* and *Daily Mirror*. As the shopkeeper takes her money, he says: 'Hey, I wanna sell my story, Heather. D'you wanna buy it?'

Is he joking? Everyone claims to have a story. Findlay is unsure.

Syria: The *Guardian*'s Middle East correspondent Martin Chulov tweets to his 14,000 followers: *'Attack on Homs district of Bab al-Amr more intensive than ever this AM. Residents know no one's coming to help & they can't escape'.*

London: Farrah Storr, Britain's newest magazine editor, leaves home walking on air. She wants to skip, dance, perhaps break into song. Then, the first disappointment . . .

As she arrives at the underground station, she sees there is only one *Metro* newspaper remaining. Someone goes for it. So does Storr, and she is more determined. She wrestles it out of the hands of the other woman who submits, wondering why a free newspaper should be so prized. Storr turns away, flicks through to page 15 and there it is: an advertisement for *Women's Health*.

Fantastic!

The train pulls in and she steps aboard.

London: With his family getting ready around him, Chris Wheal finishes his AOL story and it's not yet eight o'clock. Then he sits at his computer planning a motorbike trip to East Anglia for this Sunday. He'll be camping. He needs a decent ride-out anyway as he is off to Spain next week with Honda to test and review their new 'adventure' bike.

Great job. He's looking forward to that.

London: It's not much use being known as the 'networking queen' when you are stuck in traffic going nowhere. The irrepressible Julia Hobsbawm, founder of *Editorial Intelligence,* needs to get to Sweden. She tweets anxiously: *'On way to airport. Gridlock.'*

Will she miss her flight?

Cambridge: As he prepares for another crowded day, Society of Editors' director Bob Satchwell flicks through newspapers, then scans websites – *Media Guardian, Hold The Front Page* and *Press Gazette*.

The previous evening he'd got back late from London after appearing at a seminar to launch a collection of essays, *'The Phone Hacking Scandal – Journalism on Trial'*.

He's thinking about it right now. Some contributions were erudite, brilliant even. Others were not and left him appalled. He sums them up to himself in three words.

Inaccurate, ignorant, drivel.

Nar-e Saraj, Helmand Province: As the column of military vehicles halts, the BBC's Sommerville clambers down from the Husky transport and accepts an invitation to go on foot patrol with Brigadier-General Shah. One of Shah's company commanders walks alongside him and says: 'I prefer to travel on foot rather than in armoured vehicles.'

'Why?'

The officer laughs. 'We Afghans,' he says, 'have good eyes. We can spot the bombs before we stand on them.'

He's entitled to his opinion. But three bombs have gone off already. Sommerville climbs back aboard the Husky. He'll take his chances behind its heavy-gauge armour plating.

London: Before starting work, the BBC's Frank Gardner arrives for a gym session with his trainer. It's a weekly appointment. He needs to maintain his strength and fitness more than most, ever since being gunned down by al-Qaeda sympathisers in Saudi Arabia and having to use a wheelchair. In the attack, his cameraman was shot dead.

Now he does a series of pull-ups on a bar, dips on a bench, and balances on a rubber ball. He struggles with the latter.

Gardner jokes: 'I've got all the poise and elegance of a recovering drunk.'

London: TV Anchorman Jon Snow is sure it is 'flu. A keen urban cyclist who looks younger than his 64 years, he's normally as fit as a fiddle. Will he be well enough to present this evening's Channel Four News?

Tunbridge Wells, Kent: Having burped over his bowl of Cheerios, Ian Read is still on his own at the *Courier*. The phone rings and he answers it. It's a headteacher.

She says: 'Have you been trying to get hold of me?'

'Yes, I want you to put your side.'

Two of her school's employees have been jailed for sex offences, in unrelated cases.

She says: 'I'll send over a quote.'

He replies: 'Okay, and then we'll do a feature on your school's progress.'

'Thanks.'

Next Read compiles front-page teasers. He's not just running one newspaper. The *Courier* has *six* editions. It's a complex job.

Essex: While organising her three children for school, agony aunt Katie Fraser switches on her computer. She runs dozens of Facebook groups dealing with everything, from drugs and desertion to panic and premature babies.

She checks her messages.

The first one says: *'I've had enough of feeling like this now. Docs keep giving me pills wot [sic] don't work. Can u find me a Buddy?'*

Unlike most problem page editors, Fraser doesn't confine herself to letters that make good stories. She acts as if she is running her own little social services department, helping anyone, any time. It's her kind nature.

Fraser's got the dog to walk as well as get her kids ready.

'Come on, everyone,' she keeps saying. 'Get a move on. It's Wednesday and do you know what that means?'

'Yes,' they chorus, and nod.

Enfield, London: The 7:48 overground train pulls into Gordon Hill station and Arif Durrani steps on board and finds a seat. Two years ago he would have opened a newspaper. Now, like half his fellow passengers, he peers at his phone screen instead, seeing breaking news as it happens.

He gets the latest for the media industry.

First, LOVEFILM's CEO Simon Calver is leaving to head Mothercare. Then, via email, he receives Virgin Media's full-year results.

As the train flits in and out of tunnels and cuttings, his phone reception comes and goes. He writes two briefs about Virgin's topline figures, waits until the signal is strong enough, then sends them.

Seconds later, he checks Twitter and they're already up there.

Islington, London: At the Angel crossroads, it is traffic gridlock and Anita Bhagwandas is panicking. As beauty assistant at *Stylist* magazine, she's got an appointment to keep. She left early without even breakfast to give herself extra time. But it's worse than she expected and now she's not just frustrated but hungry.

She starts tapping on her mobile, releasing a flurry of traffic-rage Tweets.

London: *Daily Mirror* editor Richard Wallace is getting himself ready for the journey to his office at Canary Wharf, keenly aware that his newspaper is about to take a big gamble today.

It is relaunching its website.

The old one looked clunky, like something out of the Flintstones. If online is the future, then the *Mirror* has slipped badly behind. Something has to be done.

But Wallace is no fool. He knows that these high-tech projects invite disaster. Anything can go wrong.

He's keeping his fingers crossed.

China: As they drive along the Yunnan motorway, *Daily Telegraph* correspondent Malcolm Moore and his photographer Adam Dean are feeling parched. It's proving to be an arduous journey and by the roadside they see a lady who has set up stall. They pull over and buy some fresh oranges from her, then peel and eat them as they drive off.

It's not too hot because they are at altitude, in the mountains. Even here, right at the furthest edge of China, they note that the motorways are immaculate.

London: As he prepares for another marathon day – 16 hours or so – *Daily Mail* editor Paul Dacre is trying to control his irritation. He's got enough on his plate – not only running the newspaper but chairing a board meeting of the parent company, Associated Newspapers.

Now, dammit, he's being recalled to give further evidence to the Leveson Inquiry.

He is going to be cross-examined over the actor Hugh Grant – *again*.

In a 40-year career, Dacre has always ducked the spotlight while happy for his newspaper to shine it on others. He has avoided exposing himself to the harsh grillings his reporters dish out daily, to live argument and debate, always saying in effect: 'My newspapers do the talking for me.'

He also says he's 'shy'.

Dacre's influence on the nation's politics and culture are matched only by his personal obscurity.

Suddenly, alarmingly, that's all changing.

This time the spotlight is being turned on him, full voltage. He is caught in its televisual beam and cannot switch it o ff. Good god, at t his rate he'll become *famous*.

No wonder he dislikes the whole Leveson shananigans.

Now Dacre gets ready for work, one part of him locked in the default mood which readers expect of a *Daily Mail* editor-in-chief.

Truculent outrage.

London: Some say Dacre verges on genius in the way that he has edited the *Mail* for the last 20 years, building its sales and influence and turning it into the newspaper *du jour*. It's some achievement to make the *Mail* not just popular but a fashionable must-read.

Others agree but worry that he's become a c ult figure to his own unquestioning staff. Yet others simply fear him, not just for his journalism but for his commercial vision and acumen, and his temperament.

Amongst the latter are his rivals at Express Newspapers where no one takes more pleasure in the *Mail's* public discomfort.

While Dacre commands a large budget, his counterpart Hugh Whittow has to edit the *Daily Express* on a relative shoestring.

Whittow stares out of the window and finds inspiration as free as the air. Forget everything else. This is what ordinary people are talking about. It's right in front of his nose. Whittow's got his next front page sorted already.

Brrr, it looks like snow.

CHAPTER 3

8am-9am
Breakfast Bugle

London: When she gets off the tube at London Bridge station, Farrah Storr buys flowers. They are for her team, as a thank-you for all their hard work.

She cannot resist going into the WH Smith shop. Sure enough, there is *Women's Health* on the shelves. She strolls towards it, then past it and back again, and when she halts to admire it further she hopes people don't think she's a mad woman. She snaps a picture on her mobile, pleased with the way an ultra-fit Kate Beckinsale projects from the cover and catches the eye.

This is the first time she's been able to compare it alongside all its rivals such as *Psychologies,* to see if it stands out.

It does.

West End, London: *Psychologies'* editor Louise Chunn emerges from the underground and drops her daughter at school. She looks at her watch, sees she's running late and flags down a black cab. The driver uses the bus lane to penetrate the rush-hour traffic and delivers her quickly to 195 Piccadilly, home of the British Academy of Film and Television Arts.

She climbs out, pays the fare and follows a sign announcing: *The Jasmine Awards: Celebrating Excellence in Fragrance Journalism.*

Last year, *Psychologies* was a winner. Chunn's hoping to repeat that success.

Bermondsey, London: Mark Solomons, joint owner of S pecialist News Services, arrives at an empty, cold and half-painted office on the unfashionable south side of the Thames. The painter has switched the boiler off, there's wet paint on the doorframe (and on Solomon's hand now) and the radio's been left on. Worse, in his view, it's been left on Heart FM.

He sits down and opens snail mail and receives his first, and possibly last, pleasant surprise of the day. They've been paid £30 by the *Guardian* for a tip to the diary column. It's not much but this is the penny-pinching *Guardian,* for God's sake! He jokes to his partner: 'Thirty quid. That must be half their daily editorial budget.'

Scissors and pens in hand, they start gutting the morning newspapers. Solomons opens the *Sun* and sees a page lead story he was chasing and couldn't stand up. He's been scooped.

'Sod that,' he says.

The day has hardly started and he is pissed off already.

Leeds: Student David Spereall only has one pair of black shoes and needs to keep them shiny and clean to impress his temporary bosses. That's why, in his work placement at the *Evening Post*, he has been taking the long route to Headingley station rather than the muddy shortcut. He wants to look smart, to play the part of the would-be sports reporter.

Now, with the morning frost hardening the ground, he looks out of the window and decides to risk it. Wearing a thick grey coat with skiing gloves, and shirt and tie underneath, he steps out the door and starts to run the route, with the reckless enthusiasm of a sports-mad young man. It's nearly a mile. Half way, he looks at his shoes.

Oh, crikey, that was a mistake.

Too late now.

Nar-e Saraj, Helmand Province: On ops with the Afghan army, it's already turning into a frustrating day for the BBC's Sommerville. He keeps asking to interview ordinary soldiers. The commanders keep refusing.

But why?

An officer replies: 'They may say something bad.'

Sommerville's unhappy.

He explains that he needs more material for TV and radio. The whole point of this assignment was for him to assess their capabilities.

So he defies the officers, goes ahead and speaks to the troops anyway.

But the men are as cautious as their commanders and their replies are predictable and disappointing.

Sommerville says: 'It's just the usual complaints about pay and holiday, universal soldierly grumbles.'

Now his armoured vehicle turns round and heads back towards the local base at Spin Mujib.

Blackheath, London: Briskly eating his morning muesli, Alan Burkitt-Gray props the *Guardian* up in front of him to read. Then, online, he checks the trains are running on time. They are, thank goodness. He doesn't want any hold-ups at *Global Telecoms Business*, not today.

Manchester: Freelance Louise Bolotin has overslept. She gets up and in swift succession makes coffee, feeds her intern (aka the cat), reads emails and flicks through her RSS feed. She does this while tuned into BBC Radio Manchester, where she used to work.

There is no such thing as a typical day for her which is why she calls herself a Jill-of-all-trades. She specialises in news editing and subbing and also in financial editing for non-journalism clients. She works for blue-chip investment banks, accountancy firms and specialist publishers. On the writing front she mainly covers society issues, technology, finance and food.

So what will today bring?

Essex: Agony aunt Katie Fraser gets her three kids up and moving. She prepares breakfast, drops them at the bus stop and takes the spaniel for a brisk romp. Then she gives a goodbye kiss to her lawyer husband Jamie and goes to the railway station. Normally she works from home but this is the one day of the week when she breaks her routine.

She likes to get away from the house and sit in an office full of people, just for a change.

The train pulls in and she hops aboard. As it heads towards London, she considers the desperate email begging for a friend and thinks: 'Now who fits the bill?'

Delhi, India: Helen Roberts finishes writing her piece on child brides for *Fabulous* magazine and realises the morning has whizzed by and it is now lunchtime. She and her colleague, Tanzeel Ur Rehman, pop round the corner to their favourite restaurant for a cheap and tasty tandoori chicken and biriani. But it's hard to switch off. She's checking her BlackBerry and much of their conversation is an extension of work, a discussion of stories and ideas.

They gulp their food, risking indigestion. Britain is waking up and they must hurry back.

Barnet, London: As she looks after her three-week-old son, *Take a Break* deputy editor Sara Ward knows that this is the end of her husband Stuart's paternity leave. It's a big wrench to see him pull on his coat. It's not as if he's off to Afghanistan or anything, but they both feel sad. One last cuddle all round, then he opens the door and leaves, and the door closes.

He's going to his job as a magazine designer.

Ward finds herself testing yet another seemingly self-evident truth so beloved of women's magazines – this one that new mothers feel isolated and lonely at home with just a baby for company.

It was one of the reasons *Take a Break* set up a social network called Chums for Mums: 20,000 readers signed up.

She feeds James and then, when he starts to sleep, she has a doze too.

Rwanda, Central Africa: At the Blues Cafe, Reuters correspondent Graham Holliday finishes his chat with the visiting student researcher and starts to plan his day. He writes in a moleskin notebook, the sort that might have been first choice of Boot of the *Beast,* in Evelyn Waugh's *Scoop.*

Holliday arrived here from Rugby, England, via postings in South Korea, Vietnam and France. He's got a French wife, Sophie, and earlier this morning he did the school run with his son.

He usually covers breaking news, business, inflation, GDP rates, anything impacting on the local and regional economy. He also does environmental and photo stories.

He loves the weather. Kigali is sunny with blue skies and gets to around 28°C, but not humid. Having lived all over the world, he likes to think it has the best year-round climate, a sort of springtime of the eternal scribe.

Euston Station, London: The Manchester train pulls out and among its passengers is *Estates Gazette* editor Damian Wild. He's got an exciting day ahead of him and stokes up on a good breakfast.

He's going to need it.

Twitter: From Selkie, aka Thais Porthilo-Shrimpton, co-ordinator of *Hacked Off,* a campaign to raise press standards – *'God, I ha te mornings. YAWN. Actually been busy some time nudging support for @nataliepeck who will be covering the latest phone hacking case from 10.30 at High Court.'*

Selkie also has a big day ahead, covering the Leveson Inquiry. But her early morning lassitude may be the symptom of something more serious. Is she coming down with 'flu?

Twitter: From WatchMurdoch – *'Pressure on News Corp mounts as FBI steps up bribery probe'.*

Syria: Bill Neely, international editor of ITV News, has arrived in the city of Damascus and his first report is transmitted to London and is immediately broadcast on the channel: *'At the Four Seasons Hotel, the echoes were deafening . . . Welcome to Damascus . . . city of echoes.'*

Piccadilly, London: More journalists are arriving at the BAFTA building where they join *Psychologies'* Louise Chunn. Among them is Lindsay Nicholson, editorial director of *Good Housekeeping,* who has taken 90 minutes to get here from Hertfordshire where she's had five inches of snow. Now she hops up and down on one leg in the doorway, trying to change out of snowboots into heels. She's not the only one doing so and swaps smiles. She gets into the right footwear and only then feels right. She steps through the door and glides on pedicured feet towards the room hosting the Fragrance Awards.

London: First Greg Figeon drops his eldest son at school, then he heads into the heavy traffic to Enfield where he is editor of the *North London & Herts* series. He is also editor of the *Yellow Advertiser* series, based at Basildon, Essex. Lots of titles, lots of distance, lots of blood, toil and sweat. This is press day and he's got 15 hours of non-stop work ahead of him.

London: Even after his late evening anchoring the BBC's *World Tonight*, Robin Lustig is already listening keenly to one of his morning equivalents, Jim

Naughtie on *Today,* elegantly skewering Stephen Hester, chairman of the Royal Bank of Scotland, over his proposed £1m bonus.

It's the big centrepiece interview and Lustig is following Twitter at the same time. It's getting a lot of reaction.

BBC: *'You're listening to Today on Radio 4 w ith Justin Webb and James Naughtie . . . '* Webb reads out listeners' email comments on the news . . . *'Stephen Hester gets £1m for saving our economy – and Fabio Capello gets £6m for managing a very average football team..!'*

Dorking, Surrey: The *Advertiser* news editor phones in sick - it's that 'flu bug again - and now chief reporter Sam Blackledge has to step up to run the newsdesk. He switches chairs with mixed feelings. The newsdesk is the hub and it gets fraught even on the best of days, and this is not the best of days.

A reporter files copy for a page 2 lead on council tax. Blackledge starts changing it – a lot – and sees the angry look on his colleague's face. But it's got to be done. This is no place for egos.

Glasgow: Disappointed at having none of her story ideas accepted, freelance Samantha Booth is in danger of sinking into torpor. She stares at the TV screen, distracted by an old re-run of *Frasier*. It's not funny enough to cheer her up or dull enough to stop her watching.

She knows, as every lone freelance knows, that working from home requires self-discipline. It's different from her days on the *Daily Record* and *Sunday Mail*. She gets up and makes a second coffee, an alternative displacement activity to staring at the TV.

Bristol: In her under-heated hotel room, journalism trainer Caroline Sutton hears a knock on the door. She opens it and breakfast is wheeled in. She loves room service although the food, like her surroundings, is chilly. She tucks in, stoking herself up for a long, demanding day.

Tunbridge Wells, Kent: Following a fitful night, reporter Sharon Marris gets out of bed. She knows she needs to restore her routine at the *Courier* after her two weeks in Afghanistan. It's difficult. The sounds of Helmand, the call of the Big Story, have been replaying in her head and keeping her awake.

She loved the constant thwump-thwump of helicopter blades. She went up in Merlins ten times flying to villages and front-line operations. On her final trip, a Chinook took her from Lashkar Gah to Camp Bastion. She got used to the noise going on all through the night – darkness made flying safer – and now dear old Kent seems so quiet, almost silent, devoid of even birdsong because of the frost.

Marris is worried.

She's not at *Apocalypse Now* stage lying in a feverish delirium below swirling ceiling fans. But she's having to switch back to local stories, writing about car parking and council tax instead of 14-year-olds being arrested for planting murderous bombs.

She tells herself to get a grip.

Piccadilly, London: At the *Fragrance Awards,* Louise Chunn and Lindsay Nicholson sip coffees and gossip with other magazine journalists. These events are excuses for catch-ups. There are hugs and air-kisses and business talk interlaced with minor office gossip. Who's moving, who's going up, who's going down, who's got married and/or divorced, who's having a baby and/or an affair?

'Anyone seen *Women's Health*?'

'No chance yet.'

They all realise it could affect Chunn and others.

Although they are linked through the American corporation Hearst, both Chunn and Nicholson are not corporate clones. Nicholson declines to remove her coat, saying the room is too cold. Perhaps she should have kept her snowboots on after all.

Not everyone's arrived yet.

On the other side of the West End, *Stylist*'sAnita Bhagwandas is still stuck in traffic. She is getting more panicky, more tweet-happy, more hungry, more desperate for a coffee. Will it all be over? Without her!

London: Arif Durrani is on a jam-packed train and already getting stuck into his job. He calls the office and plugs in with Dan 'the Rock' Farey-Jones on the newsdesk. Dan's already organised full coverage of the Virgin results and LOVEFILM news.

Durrani is group news editor for *Brand Republic*, a news service for the marketing, media and advertising industry.

They run through the day's agenda.

Durrani is supposed to be going to Oxford later. But it's a two-hour round trip and he's beginning to wonder . . .

Preston, Lancashire: After his Starbucks coffee, tutor Kevin Duffy receives an email from a student saying: 'I won't be able to make it today.'

He adds: 'Major road traffic accident has just closed commute route from home to city train station.'

Duffy replies in bluff newsdesk style: 'Get pix and words.'

After a delay, the bemused student replies: 'Will try.'

Duffy is amused.

He starts tweaking and polishing some of his lecture material. He has a lot of experience – 20 years as a staff journalist, four years as a newspaper editor (with Newspaper Society awards) and four years as a TV journalist with live presenting.

But lecturing is different. He is relatively new. He loves journalism and hopes that shines through.

31

Bristol: At the Medavia news agency, Heather Findlay opens the *Sun* and sees it is carrying a feature about a glamorous psychic. It's her story. Result! She has porridge and tea at her desk.

Everywhere journalists are wielding scissors and chopping up the morning newspapers – whether in newsrooms and news agencies, magazines and freelance offices – and trying to come up with their own ideas and angles.

Brussels, Belgium: Veteran EU correspondent Chris White steps off the cold pavement and into the warmth of La Clé de Vert cafe by the railway station. Pinot the barman, who knows him well, asks: 'Do you want a brandy, Christopher?'

White replies: 'No thank-you, Pinot. Are you descended from a St Bernard rescue dog?'

Pinot says he is not.

White takes a coffee and a seat and logs on to La Clé internet. It is his favourite place to start the day.

He sees the release of an al-Qaeda suspect called Abu Qatada is making UK headlines, and that Fleet Street is blaming Brussels as per usual. White thinks: *Oh no, not that nonsense again . . .*

Congleton, Cheshire: He may be at home in his pyjamas but *Chronicle* editor Jeremy Condliffe has been hard at it for three hours already. He's completed his Death Watch – sorting the death notices – and now he turns his attention to his current pet project.

He wants to produce an edition of the paper containing all the news from a single year – 1912 – and so he starts scanning in news stories from big, heavy-bound volumes that are the *Chronicle*'s priceless archive.

He's listening to Radio Five. He loves the breakfast show and the phone-ins but it drives his wife mad.

He tweets that the *Guardian* may claim to have invented 'Notes and queries' but the *Chronicle* had one in 1898.

Anything of interest goes on one of their Twitter feeds. They have four, one for each edition, plus a 'what's on'. Condliffe tries to annoy the reporters by being overly frivolous ('If you could live in a house shaped like an animal, which animal would it be?' got a very good response.)

China: It is mid-afternoon and the *Telegraph's* Malcolm Moore and Adam Dean stop for a late lunch in Yijiang. They have to dodge into a courtyard hotel to keep out of view. Chinese police have been on the lookout for journalists like them.

Three dishes, soup and rice come to £2.40. Moore says: 'Should manage to get that through expenses.'

They resume their journey.

Tunbridge Wells, Kent: Editor Ian Read welcomes his colleagues as they start to traipse through the door, taking off their coats and logging on. The newsroom of the *Courier* warms up with human and electronic heat.

Meanwhile, senior reporter Sharon Marris is at the wheel of the office car. As she drives, she can't help thinking about Helmand. It was two weeks on the go, interviews and story-gathering from first thing in the morning until well after dark, an assignment full of incomparable thrills for someone from a lo cal weekly.

Now she's heading towards the small town of Edenbridge.

It's for the draw of a loyalty card winner. The competition is run by shops which are trying to reinvigorate the high street. She knows it's important locally. She's coming down to earth with a thud.

Esher, Surrey: Freelance Robin Corry watches ITV's *Daybreak* while perusing the *Sun, Mail* and *The Times*. He doesn't bother with fancy new cereals but sticks to Kellogg's cornflakes. He first got a taste for them, oh, almost 70 years ago. He pours himself a second coffee.

Nar-e Saraj, Helmand Province: It's lunchtime and the cool, fresh air has sharpened appetites, not least that of the BBC's Sommerville. There hasn't been a roadside explosion for an hour and his military convoy halts like a modern version of a Wild West wagon train.

While some troops set up security, Sommerville prepares to eat. He's been up nine hours now, since 4am, and he's secretly glad to see he's being served British rations, not Afghani ones. He gets cold tuna pasta.

The Taliban let him eat in peace.

Dorking, Surrey: Sam Blackledge feels like he's been thrown in at the deep end at the *Advertiser*. They're falling even further behind and now, as stand-in news editor, he is proofreading pages as fast as he can.

The proofing subs – who make a final check of pages before they go to press – are struggling. So everyone has to speed up, which means mistakes may slip through.

The local radio station phones and asks him: 'What's in this week?'

Blackledge gets five minutes to prepare and then he's live on air, talking down the phoneline to listeners.

He gives his headline stories – bin collections and snow – and says: 'It's pandemonium.'

Has he gone too far? In the back of his mind he keeps thinking he might have a *Network*-esque meltdown, a sort of Tourette's rant. It doesn't happen. The interview ends and he returns to his other tasks, now mounting minute-by-minute.

Someone tells him to write the placard bills to put outside newsagents' shops. He hunches over his pad, thinking. How do you distil the lead stories down to four words each – without giving away the endings? He makes a few scribbles. Thinking harder. It's not as easy as it looks.

Task Force Helmand HQ: Press chief Mackenzie grabs a sandwich and sits down at his screen. In a blink, video call technology eats up the 3,500 miles to London and he's talking directly to his colleagues at the Ministry of Defence in Whitehall.

Who's visiting next?

They have a list – Kim Sengupta, of the *Independent*; Deborah Haynes, of *The Times*; Sam Kiley, of *Sky News*.

They are high-value players. Not quite up there with the BBC, but still first-rank. They'll want to get out there, on operations, with the soldiers, because that's there job. Real danger makes good copy.

Just don't die for a headline.

Essex: On the train, agony aunt Katie Fraser is busy running her one-woman unofficial social services and taps out an email to a reader/volunteer she has selected: '*Dear Laura, I've had a message from a woman who is struggling with depression and would like support from someone who understands. Do you think you might be willing to help out?*'

She presses *send* and waits for the answer as her carriage sways into the eastern outskirts of London.

Cambridge: Society of Editors' director Bob Satchwell is driving his wife to the train station and calls his office to check if there is anything urgent he needs to deal with. *Yes, loads.*

London: Gill Hudson, editor-in-chief of *Reader's Digest*, is at her desk and eating porridge and congratulating herself on making a nutritionally good start to the day. She scrolls through her emails, deleting time-wasting PRs, then jots down notes from yesterday's meeting with her CEO.

It was about marketing and reader research. As an editor, she welcomes all the data she can get. It's a tough world out there.

She knew it would be a challenge when she took on the 90-year-old title, and so it is proving. But Hudson has a terrific record and is a fighter.

The office lights go out. She waves her hands around until they spark up again. Five minutes later, her email freezes. She logs in again. *Twice.* Switches off, switches on. Waves hands around. Email returns. She's got enough to think about, without coping with a doomsday scenario every five minutes.

London: Freelance Jill Foster has been preparing for a breakfast meeting with PR. At the last moment, the woman calls, adopting an apologetic tone.

'Sorry,' she says, 'I've got a conference call. It is with a client. I have to cancel.'

Foster feels put out.

Wells, Somerset: This is usually the quietest day of the week for Oliver Hulme, chief reporter at the *Wells Journal*, in England's smallest city. The paper went to bed at nine o'clock last night and now he's got time to catch his breath.

He checks his emails but there's nothing exciting. He does some tidying.

Tomorrow, when it hits the streets, the *Journal* will be carrying an upbeat piece about preparations for the Queen's Jubilee, as well as exclusive pictures of the wedding of a local actor Kris Marshall.

He's proud of it. He thinks readers will like it.

Camden Town, London: Freelance Adam Carpenter disembarks from the Northern Line tube and rides the escalator up to street level. He isn't a fan of gadgets but he loves his BlackBerry because he can work on the move. This morning he has already been tapping out a spoof agony aunt column he's been commissioned to write.

The words flowed easily, which he takes as a good sign.

It offers advice supposedly from the royal couple, Wills and Kate.

Carpenter depicts Wills as a bit snobby, Kate as down-to-earth. And in the background, the Queen keeps interfering . . .

On Camden High Street, he sends it as an email.

Oh dear.

As soon as it's gone, he has second thoughts. It's so easy to love your own material. He's kicking himself. He should have waited.

London: In his box-room office, freelance Chris Wheal is checking out campsites. As a motorbike reviewer – one of his many roles – he is planning a tour of East Anglia. He needs a decent ride-out anyway to prepare him for his test ride with Honda in Spain next week.

London: The *Mirror's* new website is up a nd running and editor Richard Wallace starts to see the first reactions.Ex-*News of the World* features editor Jules Stenson tweets that he's 'not sure'. But this is more than counter-balanced by praise from Britain's top media blogger, Roy Greenslade, himself a former *Mirror* editor. On *MediaGuardian,* he says it is 'a vast improvement'.

With *Mail Online* about to become the world's no. 1 newspaper site, Wallace knows the *Mirror* has a lot of catching up to do.

It had better work.

London: At home on his iPhone, the BBC's Robin Lustig scrolls through Twitter. It's all about Rick Santorum winning three US Republican primary contests. Lustig is fascinated, but is anyone else?

Again on his iPhone, he skims through the *New York Times*. He sees a story about the US Embassy in Baghdad halving its 16,000 workforce. Interesting, so he Tweets it.

Now he picks up the *Mail, Guardian* and *Financial Times* –delivered the old-fashioned way via the letterbox – and starts to leaf through their pages. An ex-*Observer* reporter, he reckons he's just an old inkie at heart.

Bath, Somerset: Keen to get things revving at the *Chronicle*, deputy editor Paul Wiltshire has already knocked out a couple of articles himself, including one about a new restaurant and another about a row over travellers' sites.

The newsroom has filled up with staff and he talks to the news editor.

'What's the splash?'

'Bath City football stadium to get a new name.'

'Great! What else?'

'An armed robbery. We're on to it.'

'And what else?'

'Tesco versus Sainsbury over the new store site.'

As they talk, someone offers to get the teas in and sets off to fetch several rounds of bacon sandwiches to share out.

Southbank, London: *Marie Claire*'s Helen Russell arrives at th e Blue Fin building which, unsurprisingly, is covered with blue aluminium fins, all 2,000 of them. She goes up to her office, talks to the news editor and looks over the news list. She checks the stats for the website – what stories did well and what didn't from the day before – and starts to tweak content accordingly. She does a second sweep of her email.

Stratford-upon-Avon, Warwickshire: It's press day at the *Stratford Herald* and trainee reporter Matt Wilson is busy looking for last-minute stories. He has been working here for five months. He phones a former Mayor about a £10,000 design competition for Stratford's Town Square, gets an answering machine and asks him to call back.

He goes on the website, Twitter and Facebook to flag up tonight's council planning meeting. On the agenda is a proposed cinema. It's very controversial and he will be covering it.

It looks like a 16-hour day ahead. He's very keen.

Bring it on.

Brussels: Veteran correspondent Chris White opens an email from someone on the *EU Reporter* saying: 'Disgraceful that Abu Qatada can't be deported to Jordan'.

White sighs.

He suspects that a cool and careful look at the facts might throw-up some serious questions about Fleet Street's role in stirring this up. He decides to make inquiries.

He calls the press office of the European Court of Human Rights in Strasbourg. No reply. A message in French and then English tells him to call back later.

He's irritated. He's got work to do.

For God's sake, how many people work there?

Tunbridge Wells, Kent: In the *Courier* newsroom, editor Ian Read is briefing reporters individually.

First, it's his Weald reporter on the head teacher conversation he had earlier – concerning the sex cases – as it will shape the front page of her edition.

Next, it's the Tunbridge Wells chief reporter on the sale of part of the historic Pantiles walkway.

He says: 'That's the page 6–7 spread. Let's get reactions and quotes.'

As the clock reaches 8.50am, he finally remembers to have a Vitamin C tablet, hoping it might fend off the 'flu bug going round.

Leeds: Student David Spereall arrives at the *Evening Post* in the black shoes he'd hoped would impress. They do make an impression, but the wrong sort: mud imprints. So he starts cleaning them. He shouldn't have run. He takes his work placement very seriously.

This is the sports editor's day off and today he is being supervised by the chief football editor. He sits at his desk and checks the latest stories on the internet before knocking off a couple of press releases.

He sees it's a big news day. There's the Harry Redknapp trial verdict expected. And then there's Fabio Capello's meeting with the Football Association. Spereall is full of enthusiasm.

Oh boy, I'd love to be covering one of those.

Hollywood, Los Angeles: The Big Star has arrived and disappeared into her fourth floor suite and the paparazzi are drawn to her hotel on Wilshire Boulevard like dogface moths.

These men - they are mainly men - are journalism's version of stalkers. They include high-earners and low-earners, the skilled and the unskilled, but they all share an appetite for the hot picture.

They are patient, remorseless, merciless and now they loiter kerbside with the scent of fresh meat flaring their nostrils.

It is not only war and money that write the most dominant narrative of our times. It's a deviant form of showbiz, one which thrives on a self-destructive, symbiotic relationship with the media.

If the star needs peace and quiet, she's come to the wrong place. If she wants to self-destruct, then she's welcome to do it here in this city like a sieve, to have her disintegration recorded, dollar by dollar, in real-time, sob by sob.

The paparazzi are on their marks. She's one of those 24-hour people. She could pop up any time in the kind of drunken, dishevelled state that makes their day.

Ker-ching, ker-ching.
It's Whitney Time.

Barra do Pirai, Brazil: It is dark, the middle of the night, and hired men arrive outside the home of journalist Mario Randolfo.

The men are being paid to do a job and they are determined to do it properly. Only six months earlier, others failed at this task. They will not make the same mistake.

The building offers little protection and they get inside and wave guns at a frightened Randolfo and his girlfriend, Maria Guimarães.

Randolfo and Guimarães can guess at what is to follow. These intruders are determined to justify their modest fee, by carrying out their instructions to the letter.

The couple are ushered out of the door and taken away in the darkness.

CHAPTER 4
9am-10am
Kicking Off

The Strand, London: Photographers and TV crews are competing for prime positions outside the Royal Courts of Justice, erecting tripods and pointing lenses at the Victorian Gothic entrance. It is where people will start arriving shortly, on foot or by cab, to take part in one of two media hearings, separate yet linked.

One stream – such as comedian Steve Coogan and ex-footballer Paul Gascoigne –– will be heading for the High Court, which is hearing multi-million pound phone hacking settlements against Rupert Murdoch's defunct *News of the World*.

The other stream will go to Court 73, where Lord Justice Leveson is chairing the judicial inquiry into press standards.

Some days there have been so many photographers that the police have herded them into a block three deep, where they look as if they are in a cage. With their tired, pasty faces, the snappers resemble enemies of the state arraigned for trial in a Stalinist dock.

Maybe cops do have a sense of humour.

Southbank, London: On the other side of the River Thames, more photographers and TV crews are jostling for territorial rights on the steps of Southwark Crown Court for the final day of t he Harry Redknapp trial. The crews all know one another, seeing the same faces on job after job. They share coffees, cigarettes, office gossip and bad jokes.

South London: At King's College Hospital, *that's life!* magazine editor Sophie Hearsey is 32 weeks pregnant and waiting for a scan. She sits with her husband, Stuart. This will be their first baby and they are as thrilled as any couple.

If she seems preoccupied, it is because in her head she is juggling some words and ideas.

'I'm trying to sort out a coverline,' she tells Stuart.

'What's the story?'

'This woman, she's told she's having a Down's baby and she insists on going ahead with it. It's her decision. Then her boyfriend offers her money to have a termination.'

Stuart nods. He is aware, as is she, that they are in a maternity unit and why, but he leaves it unsaid.

Sophie glances round at her fellow mums-to-be as she – with Stuart's help – starts to scribble down some words. Then she reads it back to him . . .

One life inside me; then in the real world, one life under threat from a cold-hearted creep. She chose the baby over the bloke – and he is the most beautiful little boy now.

Stuart nods again.

'That'll do,' she says just as a dismbodied voice announces over a loudspeaker: 'Sophie Hearsey to the scan room please.'

They go in together.

Worcester: Stephanie Preece, head of content at the *Worcester News*, emails staff: 'Great start to the morning with our health reporter James Connell getting praised on live national television. Well deserved JC!' Connell broke a story about 'a boy trapped in a girl's body' and now it's been picked up and published everywhere.

Notting Hill, London: At Talk To The Press, features writer Katie Evans is competing against two other agencies to sign up a story. It's about the first man in the UK to donate sperm to a lesbian couple – and get both of them pregnant.

Agency boss Natasha Courtenay-Smith sifts through the overnight messages to their website.

She says: 'A teenage boy has emailed UFO pictures. They look like car headlights to me. A woman wants to talk about her time in an Abu Dhabi jail. Someone says they have a sex tape of a Hollywood celebrity – what's the price?'

It's an average collection.

Then a magazine asks her to help find someone who fits a specific editorial idea. Courtenay-Smith circulates the request through her own network of freelances, Case Study Link.

The question asks: *'Do you know a daughter who loves a vajazzle while her mum goes au naturel?'*

Piccadilly, London: A flustered Anita Bhagwandas finally reaches her destination, the BAFTA building, and bursts breathlessly through the doors. Remaining the right side of elegant, she rushes into the room hosting the Fragrance Awards.

Relief! It's not all over, and she gets a coffee.

She starts to talk to others about her bad start and when she has a second coffee, it triggers a tremor. She's had too much excitement already.

The presentations begin and Bhagwandas makes notes furiously.

And the top award goes to . . .

Everybody waits during an X-Factor-style pause.

Vicci Bentley . . . !

It's for Bentley's article *Eau to be in England*, published in the *How To Spend It* supplement of the *Financial Times*.

Louise Chunn and Lindsay Nicholson leave empty handed and, with Bhagwandas, head towards their offices.

West End, London: Farrah Storr does not attend the Fragrance Awards. If she had, she would have been able to talk to Louise Chunn and gauge her opinion on her new magazine. Instead, she arrives at her desk to find cardboard boxes waiting for her.

She greets the sight with undisguised delight. As she pulls them open, it feels like Santa has finally answered her wishlist. They are full of *Women's Health,* enough for her to revel in.

Her team are looking at comments on Facebook.

'Love, love, love it,' reads one.

Another says: 'Rushed out this morning to get one of only two copies my newsagents had. Feeling lucky!'

Storr's mobile is going crazy with Twitter comments. Her favourite is from a man who suggests she give away free subscriptions to all the wives and girlfriends of men who subscribe to their sister magazine, *Men's Health.*

But she knows they mustn't get carried away.

She sits down for a quick debrief with the team. They swap pictures of store displays they saw on the way into work.

Then she looks at the time, grabs her coat and says: 'I've got to go.'

She rushes out.

Delhi: Helen Roberts looks at her watch and calculates the time difference between India and London. She hopes she is timing the message perfectly. She double-checks the email, then presses *send . . .*

It vanishes from her screen and sets off on its 5,500-mile journey.

London: A few seconds later, a quarter of the way around the globe, Helen Roberts's email pops up s imultaneously on a dozen computer screens in newsrooms which are just beginning to come alive.

They are filling with people sipping Starbucks coffees, fiddling with sticky pastries, unwrapping bacon rolls and chatting about last night's TV . . .

'Did you see the breast implants piece on Newsnight?'

'I caught it.'

'Jordan ganged up with Naomi Wolf. She came over well.'

'What have we got?'

'One from Delhi, looks okay.'

'Yes?'

'Conjoined twins. Two girls abandoned by their parents. They've been cared for by the hospital for eight years. They're going to operate to separate them.'

'Could make.'

'I'll ask for more.'
Tap-tap, tap-tap.

Delhi: A message pops up on Roberts's screen . . . 'Hi Helen, we like the conjoined twins story. Can you send more pix please . . . ?'

She replies, attaching extra photos.

It looks promising.

Axminster, Dorset: Photographer Adam Gray, on his first assignment of the day, looks for a cloud of smoke as he arrives on the fringe of this small town. Ah, there it is, that's the place. It's a better locator than a GPS system and he drives towards it.

He draws up alongside the smouldering remains of a barn.

It is part of a cookery school on Hugh Fearnley-Whittingstall's River Cottage farm, well known from television.

Gray moves into action, pointing his camera and starting to shoot. It's a bright day and the light is good. He steps round the edge of the building, covering as many angles as he can, showing how it disintegrated last night in a blaze so intense it turned expensive ovens into shapes from a Salvador Dali painting.

He asks someone on the scene: 'Is Hugh about?'

'No, he's away.'

On his mobile, Gray tells his office: 'They're good images.'

'Okay,' say his bosses at South West News Service, in Bristol, and within a minute or so they are alerting the London picture desks.

The London picture editors ask: 'Is Hugh in the pictures?'

'No, he's away.'

'Can we snap him later?'

'He doesn't even know yet. He's filming in Antarctica and he's out of radio range. They spent a million quid doing up this 400-year-old barn. No one's told him its wrecked.'

Congleton: Still at home in his pyjamas, Jeremy Condliffe checks with the Chronicle's general manager/sub, Vanessa.

He asks: 'Do you need more letters for the letters page?'

'No,' she says. 'The paper is pretty full.'

He says: 'Hold a space for Mr Grumpy.'

'Okay.'

Their star columnist Mr Grumpy is turning 50. Condliffe Photoshops a bulldog's head onto Mr Grumpy's body.

A lot of people say to Condliffe: 'Is Mr Grumpy you, Jeremy?'

He always replies: 'No, it's not.'

He takes a break and does some yoga. Last year he had lower back problems and the physio advised him against sitting down for hours on end.

As he says: 'I'm in the wrong job!'

Watford, Hertfordshire: On the commuter train carrying her through the London suburbs, *Newsnight's* Susan Watts hardly has time to register the fields and houses flitting past her carriage windows. She is working.

She is gathering her thoughts for a meeting this morning. It is with her editor and it is important. They want to discuss stories for this year, especially 'Big Thoughts'

The programme takes science seriously, digging beneath the superficial headlines and asking how advances will really affect society. To Watts, it's a privilege to report on such matters, and also a responsibility.

At this moment she is thinking about biotech issues which, in their complexity, are a challenge to anyone's journalistic skill. It's easy to trivialise but that is not her way. How can such large issues be encapsulated in a few minutes of serious TV? How best can she explain their wider significance.

She jots down a few notes for later.

West End: Kathryn Blundell, editor of *Mother & Baby* magazine, starts the morning with a visit to John Lewis's flagship store in London's Oxford Street. It's a press day, when consumer journalists are invited to see the latest products. Blundell examines items which might appeal to young mums. She asks: 'What's selling? How is John Lewis responding?' Then she sets off for her office.

North London: At home, health editor Lee Rodwell sits at her desk scribbling a list of questions. She is about to phone Katie Piper, a model who was blinded in an acid attack. Her sight has been restored, thanks to organ transplants.

Now Rodwell wants to ask Piper to head up a *Take a Break* campaign for more readers to register as NHS donors.

Will she do it?

Kigali: Reuters correspondent Graham Holliday makes the ten-minute walk from the Blues Cafe to the National Bank of Rwanda. He ascends to the third floor and witnesses the signing of an MoU – a memorandum of understanding – with the Rwanda Capital Market Authority. It's not much in the way of 'real news' but he gets to meet Robert Mathu, the executive director.

An official says: 'Mr Holliday, we wish to invite you to the Monetary Policy Committee press conference. It is at the Serena Hotel tomorrow.'

Holliday's news antennae twitch.

He thinks: *'That could mean a change in interest rates – a real story.'*

'I'll be there,' he says.

Brighton, East Sussex: Technology freelance Adam Oxford arrives at the office he rents above an estate agent, plugs in gadgets that need powering up, and checks on his RSS feeds and news sites. He does a quick reblog of the latest story about Google's Android OS.

An email pops up. It's from South Africa.

'Adam, just a gentle reminder about your column,' it says. 'Here's a few suggestions, if it helps . . . '

43

Suggestions? They must be desperate. He'd better get on with it.

Glasgow: The newsroom at the *Daily Record* is getting busy. Reporter Steven Stewart is summoned over to the newsdesk. He takes a note as he is given a briefing. He returns to his desk, picks up the phone and taps out a number . . .

London: *Guardian* deputy editor Kath Viner is on the underground heading towards her office at Kings Cross. She uses the journey to do some discreet market research, hoping she doesn't seem oddly nosey. She looks at her fellow passengers and checks what they are reading.

When she disembarks she Tweets: 'On my tube carriage this morning: *9 Metros, 2 G uardians, 2 St ylists, 1 Mi rror, 1 S un, 1 Kindle, 1 Lolita, 1 Commodities for Dummies.*'

Metro and *Stylist* are both given away free at stations. The rest are paid for. It is ominous.

Task Force Helmand HQ: The phone rings on the desk of Army press chief Mackenzie who has just got back from a long-overdue haircut with the camp barber, Aziz.

He raises the receiver to a well-shorn ear and hears a voice say down the line: 'Hi, this is Steven Stewart at the *Daily Record* in Glasgow.'

'Hi, Steven.'

Stewart: 'I'm writing a piece about the Black Watch, Third Battalion, and what they've been doing out there.'

'Oh yes . . . '

'I understand they've been taking part in a major operation against bomb makers. Can you tell me a bit more about it?'

'Certainly,' says Mackenzie, and he starts to fill in the details for the reporter who is scribbling them down furiously 3,500 miles away.

Stewart: 'That's great. Thanks. Do you have pictures?'

Mackenzie: 'I'll email some over.'

'Fantastic. Are you missing Edinburgh?'

'Of course.'

County Donegal, Ireland: Today's plan for veteran freelance Paddy Clancy is to start on a news feature about a lo cal girl who survived the sinking of the Titanic, saving 25 lives with her tiny pen-knife.

Her name was Margaret Devaney and she has relatives still living nearby.

The Titanic centenary gives him a peg. The media has gone Titanic-mad.

Colchester, Essex: Katy Evans, editor at *Soul & Spirit* magazine, sits at her desk and starts her day with a spiritual health check.

She looks at her 'Success Now' calendar. She likes the way that every day carries a different inspirational message. Now she reads today's . . .

'Self-knowledge is the jewel in the crown of success . . . '

She will bear it in mind.

She has 27 overnight emails, many from PRs, which she deletes. She emails the promotions department to liaise about a *Mind Body Spirit* show. Then everyone on her desk picks an 'angel card', giving each another daily message.

Katy looks at hers. She's drawn the Crown Chakra and it tells her: *'Pay attention to your ideas, as they are a message of true Divine guidance sent in answer to your prayers.'*

Good. She welcomes Divine guidance.

She gets on with her work, keeping the two messages in mind.

Glasgow: Right now, Samantha Booth is in need of some spiritual uplift. Trying not to get discouraged, she gives herself a shake and stops watching morning television. She checks emails again. Oh, there's one from Talk to the Press in Notting Hill.

Do you know a daughter who loves a vajazzle while her mum goes au naturel?
Booth laughs. Nothing she can help with there.

Otherwise the email is quiet – still no commissions.

She writes a to-do list.

Then emails come in from her two private PR clients, work she enjoys even if she feels she's selling her soul. It is not so much PR as a 24-hour advice service.

She goes to make coffee number three but, fearing an overdose, switches to green tea.

Stedham, Sussex: Booth is not alone in feeling frustration as a freelance. At his cottage overlooking the village green, veteran columnist Colin Dunne traipses down the garden path to a shed containing a desk and a computer.

He looks at his emails, searching for gushing praise.

He has a number of projects on the go – a spoof golf column, and a book outline called *'How I Made Sex the Popular Pastime It Is Today, with the Help of Maureen Ashton.'*

There is nothing.

He returns to the house and tells his wife (who is not Maureen Ashton): 'Email contains only 32 offers of Viagra. Out of the last 50 years, I must have spent 45 years waiting for editors' responses. Editors and publishers are appalling people, heartless.'

He gives a sigh.

She tries to look sympathetic but hears it every day, sometimes several times, and anyway it's time he forgot about that flippin' Maureen Ashton and moved on.

Camden Town, London: Adam Carpenter is shifting at *that's life!* magazine, editing copy by staffers and freelances, choosing pictures and headlines, helping to make stories work on the page.

He is looking at a true-life story about a woman whose terminal illness will leave her children orphaned. Carpenter decides to turn it round. He rewrites it from the angle of all the kids working together to look after their dying mum.

He says: 'Suddenly a potentially tragic story becomes life-affirming.'

He adds: 'These true-life magazines are dismissed as trashy and gossipy but as human beings we thrive on gossip – yes, even readers of *The Times* and *Country Life*. More than that, though, these stories offer hope.'

Enfield, London: Editor Greg Figeon arrives at the offices of the *North London & Herts'* newspaper series. Chief sub James Lowe gets there just after him, blaming the trains, and makes the first cuppa, as they brace themselves for a long day.

Cornwall: Kirstie Newton, editor of *Cornwall Today*, arrives at her desk with not much to do. The glossy county magazine goes to print tomorrow. Deadline week can be very hectic, but this week they are well on schedule.

The team's hard work has paid off.

She sits down and goes wild with a mug of Earl Grey and half a Twix.

Bristol: Trainer Caroline Sutton leaves her hotel, walking alongside Tom Bureau, CEO of her client, Immediate Media. She is running seminars for the *Get Creative . . . Stay Creative* day for 200 s taff of t he newly-formed company – now owner of a raft of magazines from *Radio Times* to *BBC History*.

Sutton sets up a room for her workshop. She wants to make an impact and it's title is self-explanatory.

Make Every Edition An Event.

Mitchelstown, County Cork: It's not just press day for reporter Nicola-Marie O'Riordan, but her birthday. She's 29. As she starts on the *Avondhu* newspaper, she first opens her cards. But she doesn't dwell on them. She gets on with work, putting stars next to the important stories on her list, procrastinating for a few moments but then getting stuck in. She knows she's got a lot to do.

First, she phones a charity shop.

She says: 'I'm calling about the slimathon you're hosting. Can you tell me more about it?'

'Certainly . . . '

Bermondsey, London: Agency boss Mark Solomons goes through magazines and supplements looking for ideas. He has a talent for re-angling stories for different markets. He groans as Heart FM plays Adele after a 'no repeat guarantee' promise.

He says: 'That must be the 159th day running.'

'What about this one?' he says to his colleague and business partner. 'Male excursions banned by Kuoni.'

'Sounds alright.'

'Oh, hold on, it's not what it looks – "Male" isn't a man.'

'It's getting better . . . '

'No, Male is the capital of the Maldives. Didn't realise. Ah well, another one bites the dust.'

Solomons starts writing stories for tomorrow's papers and holds back the better ones to offer exclusively to the Sundays, which pay much better.

City of London: Slightly late, Alan Burkitt-Gray hurries out of his Blackheath house and catches the train. When it reaches Blackfriars, he joins the throng along Queen Victoria Street and arrives at his office. He has been editor of *Global Telecoms Business* since 2000.

He plugs in his laptop.

As it boots up, he goes into the kitchen and uses his own cafetière to make a cup of coffee. It's his own coffee. He won't touch the free stuff, in a giant, always open, catering container.

Bath, Somerset: As staff finish their bacon sandwiches, the *Chronicle*'s deputy Paul Wiltshire starts penning a leader column. He likes it. It combines dog poo, the youth parliament and the council budget-setting meeting, which is a pretty nifty mix.

He chats with the chief sub about the running order of stories and starts sending through copy for live pages.

West End, London: *Reader's Digest* editor Gill Hudson is discussing two commercial matters: readers' offers and new ad business. Then she realises there is another deadline pressing - the annual awards of the Periodical Publishers Association.

Hudson is a serial awards winner. It's not vanity, it's business. Awards impress readers and advertisers.

But time is short.

And now she looks at her screen and sees her computer password has expired. She pulls a face.

Oh drat!

Nar-e Saraj, Helmand Province: After lunch, the military convoy is on the move again, carrying the BBC's Sommerville. Like everyone, he peers not just at the horizon but at the road. That's the danger point. Has some farmer been planting bombs not crops?

It makes for an uneasy journey. But there is little sign of the Taliban. The vehicles come under occasional small arms fire but it's winter and most of them are laying low.

They reach a base and Sommerville visits the operations room. It's clear to him that, despite the claims, the Brits are still providing a lot of necessary support to the Afghan National Army.

Vienna, Austria: Agency boss Mike Leidig is looking at his watch and growing impatient. He's waiting for a lawyer. He's arranged to meet him but the man is late. Where the hell is he?

For two years Leidig has been investigating the Natasha Kampusch kidnap case – much of it undercover – for a British daily. But he's reaching a dead end.

Thirty minutes pass before the man turns up.
Leidig explains his problems. Can he help?
The lawyer shakes his head.
'Nein, nein . . . '
Disappointed, Leidig returns to his offices in the 14th district.

London: Having listened to *Today,* Robin Lustig goes upstairs and gets on his computer. He is checking for stories: BBC News Online, BBC news diary, RSS feed (oh dear, more than 1,000 unread articles – has Twitter taken him over instead?). He reads emails, sends emails, and tries to go through the papers a bit more thoroughly.

Lincoln: Poachers-turned-gamekeepers John Thorne and Richard Wells meet their 'clients' – the senior council officers who deal with Lincolnshire's young criminals and tearaways.

They eye the ex-BBC reporters suspiciously. Thorne tries to impress with a summary of his career – Belfast, Argentina, Africa and Iran. They look unmoved.

One man says: 'I h ad a bad experience with the media. I do n't trust journalists.'

Thorne and Wells nod, encouraging him to continue.

'It was local radio and the presenter told me he'd start with a gentle opening question. In fact he began straightaway with the most awkward question.'

Thorne gives a knowing frown.

'That's why we're here,' he explains, 'to teach you how to keep out of difficulty.'

They still look unconvinced.

London: Freelance Louise Baty is 37 weeks pregnant and determined to keep busy until her very last moment. Her husband, Chris, says she'd file a story from the delivery suite if she could.

She has coffee, toast and a look at the daily papers online. She keeps the TV on in the background because working from home can get lonely. As a result, she thinks she's become unintentionally addicted to *Homes Under the Hammer.*

Now she starts to write up a feature for a national paper on women who spend fortunes on their children's designer wardrobes. The interviews and photo shoots have been done. She lodges her keyboard in front of her rounded tummy and starts to type steadily.

Camden Town, London: Editor Rebecca Fleming feels twitchy as she looks at the new *Take a Break* cover she's working on. To pixelate or not to pixelate? It shows a woman's photo they lifted directly off her Facebook profile.

Are they invading her privacy? If so, can they justify it?

Now they send the woman another message. No reply. This one's going to the deadline.

The features team are arriving armed with Pret coffees, croissants, sticky buns, bananas and instant porridge.

Commissioning editor Julia Sidwell sifts through emails sent by agencies and freelances offering true-life stories.

She sees the one from Helen Roberts in Delhi about conjoined twins. But it's not for them. *Take a Break* wants British stories.

The phone is ringing off the hook, again with agencies.

Sidwell sits just two paces from editor Fleming in an open-plan office. In just a few moments they can spend thousands of pounds – or nothing. Sometimes it feels like Monopoly money.

Alongside them Siofra Brennan and Laura Brown are clipping the papers and writing up a story list. They give a running commentary.

Brown says: 'Why's Karl Lagerfeld calling Adele fat? If h e wants to see something funny, he should look in the mirror.'

Writer Stephanie May chases the end of a Crown Court trial. She calls a police officer and he promises to phone back.

Fleming is holding the latest cover in front of her, studying it critically and asking other opinions, not just about the pixelation.

She says: 'Are the cover lines strong enough?'

Everyone stops and looks. Some like it, some don't. Just like readers then.

Bristol: They start the day with a brainstorm at the Medavia agency, sitting down together to think of new angles. They come up with some good story ideas – people getting depressed if they look in the mirror too long; underage girls having contraceptive implants without parental consent; a girl of 11 hiding her pregnancy.

That's fine – but the next question is: how do they turn these into sellable stories? It requires ingenuity.

They get to work on solutions.

Bedford: Reporter Kathryn Cain makes routine morning calls to the police and fire service. Nothing today for the *Bedfordshire on Sunday*.

She phones a school to find out why they were the only one in the borough to close because of snow – especially when a special needs school next door did not.

An angry reader calls and says: 'Why didn't you cover my friend's child being in a dancing semi-final?'

Cain doesn't wish to be rude and so allows her to let off steam.

She writes up her notes on a man accusing a doctor of being unprofessional during his benefits assessment examination. It may make something.

It's a quiet start.

Wells, Somerset: Someone has fly-tipped five bags of suspicious material just off the high street and now the *Journal's* chief reporter Oliver Hulme goes to investigate. He calls out a photographer, interviews people, knocks on doors and has a coffee. It is clinical waste. It shouldn't be there. He returns to the office, goes on Twitter, has another coffee.

Camden Town, London: Jon Peake, editor-in-chief of *TV Choice* – Britain's biggest selling magazine – rides up from the underground and strides to his office. He drinks tea and eats a banana while savouring a nice, clear desk, saying to himself: 'It won't be like this for long. Not today.'

Sigh.

This is the day the magazine goes to press, along with his sister title *Total TV Guide.* It's the craziest day of the week.

Cambridge: Crime reporter Raymond Brown arrives at a church, the one where the body was found, and inspects the doorway, the scene of the death. The poor man froze there while seeking shelter from the snow piling up around him. Brown goes into some nearby shops and talks to people, then to parents at the church nursery. He's trying to build up a picture.

Tunbridge Wells: 'Damn, you've scuppered my cartoon,' says *Courier* editor Ian Read as a reporter briefs him about last night's council U-turn.

A U-turn may be fine for the community but not for Read' front page. He rings the design editor to cancel the artwork.

Read spends a few minutes discussing legal problems with another reporter. Next, he gets an update from the Sussex chief reporter.

He's busy.

Then he gets an email from a man asking: 'Please don't run that story about us yet because we're not ready for the publicity.'

Read is irritated. The story's on page eight. But it's not a big enough deal to fight over.

He replies: 'Okay, I won't run it.'

Walthamstow, East London: The internet connection is terrible for showbiz writer Nick McGrath. He's ground to a halt before he's even started and now he is bashing his desk in frustration.

KwaZulu-Natal, South Africa: Ten thousand miles from Walthamstow - and her north London home - Meera Dattani's internet is just fine. She finishes writing a piece on France's Atlantic Coast, then turns to an article on Berlin. She feels conflicted, seeing that she's sitting on the patio of Umkhumbi Lodge. But the UK work keeps coming, and she lives and dies by the freelance motto: *Never say no.*

Because if you do, they never call you again.

Southbank, London: Online editor Helen Russell holds a 'stand up meeting' – meaning nobody has the comfort of sitting down – with her tech team. That way it's over quickly.

She returns to her desk and ploughs through other tasks – writing up a training plan for a new starter; reporting on the *Marie Claire Blog & Twitter Awards*; planning team jobs, workloads and duties for when she's attending next week's big event, New York Fashion Week.

Cambridge: Bob Satchwell has a tea and a sandwich at his desk, knowing it gives his administrator Angela Varley an excuse to nip out for a cigarette. As director of the Society of Editors, he is planning the launch of the Regional Press Awards.

He dips into some of the entries and is impressed by their quality.

He says to himself: 'I wish politicians and the public could see the brilliant best of British journalism. I have already offered Lord Justice Leveson the opportunity.

'It would be my luxury on Desert Island Discs . . . '

JFK Airport, New York: Paparazzi photographers are stretching their necks like meerkats, standing on tiptoe to scan over the heads of arriving passengers. They are looking for celebrities coming for New York Fashion Week.

Suddenly they surge forward in pack formation and the cameras whirr.

Hidden in the midst of them, Victoria Beckham remains unfazed. She's famous for being famous and she'd be worried if it didn't happen. She gives her trademark pout.

Then her small daughter, Harper, decides to join in. She is sick on her mother, an act of maternal defilement swiftly recorded in a dozen images.

Mum pouts for real this time.

Anybody want to buy vomit pictures? Something different? With Posh Spice? You bet!

Melbourne, Australia: In the aptly-named Elisabeth Murdoch Hall, Lord Mayor Robert Doyle shares a slice of birthday cake and addresses the distinguished audience.

Glancing at the guest-of-honour, he says: 'Dame Elisabeth is one of the most loved citizens of our city . . . never underestimate the warmth, regard and genuine affection in which she is held across the whole nation.'

Anyone seen Rupe?

Hull, Yorkshire: It's a relatively late start for Jamie Macaskill, assistant editor of the *Hull Daily Mail*. He begins with a quick catch-up with the newsdesk.

Earlier in the week, their splash about an 11-year-old boy drinking alcohol in the street with his mother was so strong it also made the *Sun* front page.

He'd love a story like that every day.

Edenbridge, Kent: Sharon Marris has arrived at the shopping centre and now, notebook and pen in hand, she watches the shoppers' draw taking place. The winning ticket is pulled out and everyone gathers round to read the name. They stare at some confused scribble.

'It's illegible.'

'Can't read it.'

'What's it say?'

No one can decipher it. So that's her story. She can see the headline now . . .

'Are YOU the Mystery Winner?'

It's drama but no one's dead; it's not Helmand.

Southwark Crown Court, London: Someone says: 'Look out, here he comes . . .'

The photographers crane their necks and recognise Harry Redknapp's distinctive footballers' gait. As shutters click, his hangdog look turns into a smile even if these may be his last few moments of freedom.

He disappears inside the building.

Reporters trail behind him, then veer away and enter the courtroom through another door. They slide into the press bench. They're early and they want to make sure they get a good seat.

London: Fabio Capello is almost certainly amongst the millions tuning in to the fate of Redknapp, on TV and online. The only things the two men have in common are their age – sixty-five – and football. Otherwise they are chalk and cheese.

Yet, while Redknapp has been on trial, Capello has been having his own troubles. Today he is preparing for a showdown with the Football Association.

London: The BBC World Affairs Unit is probably the most powerful editorial force on earth, a geo-political body with the weight of a nation state. Now it holds its morning conference call, connecting its web of editors, bureau chiefs and on-the-spot reporters spread across the planet.

There are too many to participate in every session – 44 foreign news bureaux as well as correspondents in almost all of the world's 240 countries.

But they pay careful attention as this sets the agenda.

One participant is security correspondent Frank Gardner, cooled down after his gym session.

Top today is Syria, with its insurrections and massacres. They have all been listening to BBC correspondent Paul Wood's courageous reports from inside the besieged city of Homs.

Then there is Afghanistan.

'How's Quentin?'

But they want to keep his assignment low-key until he's back in the relative safety of Kabul. They need to minimise the risks.

Tasks are assigned, strategies devised, and the conference finishes.

Decisions made by the Unit will be noted by policymakers from Washington to Beijing, from Moscow to Delhi.

If the BBC is like an independent nation state, then it is a modest one compared to journalism itself.

Journalism, with its borderless pursuit of ideas and information, is more like an ill-defined superstate, a subversive wrapping overlaying most of the planet, sceptical and disagreeable, inconveniently speaking truth unto power.

Most journalists, even the parochial, intuitively feel membership of this omnipresent fraternity, their loyalty to its ideals trumping allegiances to nation states. To them the job title 'journalist' is both a badge of honour and an entry card to a vast international network committed to high principles rather than low pragmatism; the annoying, preachy sibling of politics.

They wear their badge with pride, the sign of the cussed and the troublemaker.

This journalistic superstate exists in culture as much as in constitutions, and has flourished hugely with the growth of the internet. Its strength is in its size, spread and diversity, uncontrolled and now uncontrollable.

West London: Freelance beauty writer Liz Wilde gets a message about her regular magazine column, saying: 'Sorry, Liz, one of your Q & A letters has just dropped out. It leaves a hole. Can you replace soonest please?'

She replies: 'No problem. When?'

'This morning, no later.'

She starts getting on with it. The only problem is those pesky PRs.

Wembley, London: Photographers assemble at the Asda superstore for the launch of Lynx's first product for women. The snappers have been lured into this unlovely suburb by the prospect of picturing Abbey Clancy, former Lynx girl and now wife of footballer Peter Crouch.

They can snap her against the Wembley arch. Will she live up to the hype?

The Strand, London. Other photographers are recording the arrival of witnesses for both the Leveson Inquiry and the High Court phone hacking hearings.

Inside the labyrinthine building, in his chambers, Lord Justice Leveson prepares to enter Court 73 and start today's hearing. He rises from his chair and steps into a corridor which is partly sealed for security reasons. He approaches a doorway . . .

It's all kicking off.

CHAPTER 5

10am-11am
News at Ten
By now the news industry is rolling . . .

China: Dusk is falling as the *Telegraph's* Malcolm Moore and Adam Dean drive down from the mountains. The micro-climate changes and the air grows warm and tropical. Cicadas are strumming in the trees and the road, now running along the Burmese border, deteriorates.

This is the riskiest part.

Way ahead in the distance, they see the lights of a border checkpoint, manned by armed guards from both sides. They approach and then, just a few hundred metres before they reach it, they swing down a dirt track, scattering a litter of black-haired piglets. Ahead is a small bridge. They roll straight across it.

As the wheels reach the other side, they arrive in Burma, the unofficial way.

They drive on.

The first person they see is a young man, barely out of his teens, dressed smartly. He is carrying a rifle, a modified AK-47. They stop and explain what they are looking for.

He says: 'I am a Kachin soldier.'

They are lucky. He points them further down the road and they drive on.

Wembley: At the Asda superstore, photographers are waiting for Abbey Clancy. When she appears, they are not disappointed. She makes a dramatic entrance in an electric-blue dress, which clings to her curves like a second skin.

Even world-weary snappers show some life. The cameras point.

'Look this way, Abbey.'

'Over here, love.'

She pouts, struts and wriggles in the over-the-top style demanded by the Lynx brand, putting on a show that's worth the hype and following the marketing department's script.

'Ever since my stint as a Lynx girl,' she says, 'I have been calling for them to make a female version. I can't wait to see the mayhem that will happen now both sexes have the Lynx effect.'

'Thanks, Abbey, love. That's all.'
The photographers pack up and head back to their offices.

Cambridge: Society of Editors' director Bob Satchwell sits at his screen and watches the door open at the back of Court 73 and sees Lord Justice Leveson enter and take his seat. The inquiry into press standards begins and the first witness steps into the witness box and swears in.

Cambridge: Two miles from Satchwell's office, Raymond Brown sits down in the newsroom of the *Cambridge News*. He sends the news editor a list of stories he is working on. Today, it is relatively short as he has to cover a visit from Prince Charles and his wife, Camilla.

He sees that a photo of singer Peter Andre has arrived for a fan with Down's Syndrome. Brown got Andre's people to send it with a message for her funeral. They did – with a second-class stamp and it is too late. The funeral is over.

He speaks to a friendly detective for an update on the murder of a pensioner.

Wapping: The *Sun* picture desk sees the agency pix from JFK Airport, New York. Baby Beckham is being sick on her mum. Vomit worth its weight in gold. *Buy!*

The adjacent newsdesk is offered a story about an unusual pair of twins – Sierra is 5ft 1in, and Sienna 4ft. It comes from an agency, Barcroft Media, and the picture shows the girls standing side by side with the working headline: *AMAZING PLUCK OF DWARF GIRL, 13 . . . Little sister is my twin.* *Buy!*

Worcester: Editor Peter John starts his editorial conference at the *Worcester News* promptly. Head of content Steph Preece runs through her story list: a murder, a travellers' site inquiry, and the Asda store development.

She says: 'It's shaping up to be another good news day.'

John agrees. He says: 'It's a good mix of stories to be getting on with. Let's see how they develop.'

Preece returns to the newsroom and notes the chatter about stories and last night's TV has been replaced by the tapping of keyboards. It's music to her ears.

One reporter, Tony Bishop, is down at Worcester Crown Court. A local man, Roger Troughton, 74, is accused of beating his cousin to death with a spade.

Now the judge sends the jury out to consider their verdict.

Bishop calls his newsdesk, files the latest development, then hangs around the court and waits . . .

Congleton: Still in his pyjamas, editor Jeremy Condliffe receives the copy from his regular columnist, Mr Grumpy. He reads it and declares: 'Oh dear, this man has no idea of libel, plagiarism – or good taste!'

Condliffe is closely following the Leveson Inquiry. He says: 'We've never tapped a phone, obviously. The only bugs we get are the insects people bring in jars for us to identify. Usually wood-boring wasps for some reason.'

He has breakfast, showers, dresses, tidies the house to avoid his wife's ire and sets off for the office.

London: While Condliffe has been up and about for five hours, Marcus Harris, editor of *Mint* magazine, is only just coming awake. He's got a good excuse: Wednesday is his lie-in day.

He runs a club on Tuesday night – publishing is merely a sideline labour of love.

He turns the TV on and reaches for his laptop which means – by his own definition – that he's now at work. He sees 68 new emails staring back at him, as if to say: *'There you are. We've been waiting...'*

Kingston: Natalie Dye is on the phone interviewing a 'psychic' for his magazine column. She's ghostwriting it, no pun intended. She loves talking to him. He is witty, down-to-earth and tells it like it is; what she calls 'her kind of person'.

He claims to be an expert on reincarnation, a subject which fascinates her. She reads a reader's letter to him.

Dye: 'OK, this is from Sarah, 46. She wants to know, "If you meditate, go back to a past life, and see yourself making better choices, does it change history?"'

Psychic: 'We're talking about the space-time continuum here . . . '

Dye (heart sinking, wishing she had chosen the letter from Tim, 24, who simply wanted to know whether or not he was a steward on the Titanic): 'OK, hang on a sec. Take me through it slowly. Let's try an example. Say I'm terrified of fire. I meditate, go back to a past life and discover I was trapped in a burning building in Victorian times. So I visualise myself escaping. Now, according to you, I'm not so afraid of fire anymore. But have I changed history?'

Psychic: 'You've changed your 'soul history', and this will be recorded in the akashic records, where our soul histories are kept.'

Dye (slowly): 'OK . . . '

She pauses to think this through. She's just about hanging in there with it, but suddenly imagining the vast universal consequences of changing the past.

Dye: 'But how does this work? Are they changing history for everyone?'

Psychic: 'Only their soul's personal history. It doesn't affect other people.'

Dye: 'So, for example, if they change their life paths it doesn't mean certain people wouldn't be born? Or that ancient artefacts vanish from museums?'

Psychic: 'No. They wouldn't be changed.'

Dye: 'And if others meditate and go back to the exact same place and time, do they see the original events?'

Psychic: 'Yes. They will see the original actions. The person is just changing their personal history.'

Dye (eager to give readers something concrete to do): 'OK. So how could readers have a bash at this?'

The interview continues . . .

Edenbridge, Kent: The illegible winner of the shopping draw has still not been identified despite lots of people trying to decipher the scrawled name and address. Sharon Marris sets off back to the *Courier's* main office, thinking about the two edition pages she still has to sort out when she gets there. She's got some catching up to do after her Afghanistan trip.

Glasgow: The phone rings for Samantha Booth and it is an 88-year-old man who used to interrogate Nazi war criminals. She was interviewing him for a story.

Now he says: 'Would you like to come for lunch?'

She replies: Oh, I'd be delighted.'

He says: 'I'll be round at 12.30.'

She gets her head down to finish a spread on a wannabe war artist.

Stedham, Sussex: Veteran columnist Colin Dunne is at his desk in the garden shed noting down some thoughts for the next episode of his humorous magazine series, 'Diary of a Bus-pass Golfer'.

Most golf writers aim at players who wish to excel. Not Dunne. His column aims at those who have to stop every 200 yards for a pee. He points out that half of Britain's four million golfers are too old and knackered to play anyway.

Great, that's his readership.

Notting Hill: At Talk To The Press, agency boss Natasha Courtenay-Smith gets a call from a man whose daughter was murdered by an immigrant supposedly deported. Now the authorities have accepted the blame and apologised.

As a result, the father wants to talk.

Murder. Bereaved father. Immigrant. Failing authorities. It's got a lot of trigger points. Courtenay-Smith contacts a Sunday newspaper and sets up an interview with him.

All her team are chasing stories and photographs.

Courtenay-Smith is not just a journalist, she is an entrepreneur, importing bags and dolls for sale in the Portobello Market in the street below her window, thronging with tourists.

BBC Radio 4: ' . . . *Woman's Hour has been following three female entrepreneurs over the last 12 m onths as they've been trying to survive the impact of the recession. We teamed each of them with a mentor – to give support and guidance as they tried to grow their business. They join us in the studio to tell us how they've got on: to pass on the most useful pieces of advice, crucial lessons learnt, the value of having a mentor – and the benefits of being one . . .* '

West End: *Reader's Digest* editor Gill Hudson is steadily getting through her to-do list. Next item is the Queen's Jubilee and the London Olympics.

She asks her team: 'What can we offer that's distinctive to RD?'

She wants great ideas!

While they are thinking about it, she makes changes to two layouts, offers input to the ad team, and agrees to some student work placements.

Then she starts writing submissions for the PPA awards. But it's a fiddle. She needs photos of the right format and size, ABC certificates, commercial stats, four lots of three issues and entry forms. It is admin hell.

She has eye strain. She munches crisps.

Southwark: The Redknapp jury is now out and no one knows how long they will take before they reach their verdict. It could be hours, it could be days. Journalists mill around and some step outside for a smoke.

They wonder how Redknapp's coping. He is used to stress watching from the managers' bench while his team, Tottenham Hotspur, win or lose. In an aside to reporters, he said at the start of the trial: 'There's absolutely nothing to worry about . . . '

But no one can be sure. No football match was ever as tense as this.

Glasgow: At the *Daily Record,* Steven Stewart receives material from Army press chief Mackenzie at Task Force Helmand HQ. Once he's got words and pictures, he starts to knock it into shape.

Tap-tap, tap-tap.

'Black Watch troops helped capture a Taliban bomb factory holding almost a ton of explosives. The haul included 27 improvised explosive devices – the roadside bombs that are the biggest killer of British soldiers.

One Afghan policeman was killed . . .

. . . six bags of explosives, 64 pressure plates and 14 controllers for remote detonations . . . the whole lot was blown up in a spectacular desert explosion.'

His news feature will make a double-page spread on Saturday.

Dorking: A lot of tweeting is going on in the *Advertiser* newsroom as journalists follow various running stories – especially Redknapp and Leveson.

Looking round, Sam Blackledge says: 'Twitter has absolutely revolutionised the way we work, but it has also changed the atmosphere of news rooms. Reporters are constantly tweeting with in-jokes and trying to use social networking to get one over on each other.'

Tunbridge Wells: A flash of inspiration strikes *Courier* editor Ian Read as he is being briefed by the Tonbridge chief reporter about last night's council decision to increase council tax.

Read decides to link it to £1m in uncollected council tax and and give it a clever headline.

The Million Pound Drop.

Great stuff, even if he says so himself.

To keep out of trouble, he'll give the council plenty of space to put their side.

But they're slipping behind schedule.

He starts nagging reporters. With multiple editions, he needs to approve six front pages – and so far he's only sent through one. Five more to go.

He tells them: 'The earlier the better . . . good intentions and all that.'

He wants a coffee but they've run out of milk. He dashes out to Iceland and when he returns he hands out Kit Kats and Animal biscuits. It's bribery, which doesn't work, but it cheers people up.

Bermondsey: Acknowledging no national frontiers, agency boss Mark Solomons does up a story from the Massachusetts Institute of Technology in America. It says, basically, that Facebook is good for you.

He says to his colleague: 'I bet it doesn't do as well as our 'Facebook is bad for you' story last year.'

Leveson Inquiry: Will Moy, founder of the campaigning body *Full Fact*, tells Lord Justice Leveson about the problem of 'wilful inaccuracy' – stories which are deliberately distorted in order to make a more eye-catching headline.

He gives an example: a headline said house prices were going up whereas the story showed they were actually going down. But 'going up' was thought to be a better seller.

Walthamstow: Showbiz writer Nick McGrath is sitting in front of the TV, notepad in hand, forcing himself to watch *The Only Way Is Essex*. It is essential if painful. He needs to prepare for his interview with Lydia Bright for the *Sunday Mirror* magazine, *Celebs On Sunday*.

He is not impressed and thinks: 'Staggering level of intellect on the screen.'

He is also jotting down questions for *Masterchef* host Gregg Wallace, for a *Sunday Telegraph* section, *Fame & Fortune*. He has spoken to Gregg before and thinks he's like a puppy in a butcher's shop.

It is drizzling outside the window of his loft office. He can see the lights of the new Olympic stadium being tested.

He drafts a letter of complaint about his dodgy broadband connection.

Then he makes his first call.

Wallace answers and the interview begins.

'How did your childhood influence your attitude to money?'

Wallace: 'Well, I had a poor upbringing . . . no bathroom and an outside toilet . . .'

Bristol: At Medavia news agency, in her search for stories, Heather Findlay starts going through her long list of people to call. She rings six, gets six no answers, and wonders if it's going to be one of those days. She makes a round of tea, carrying a tray of mugs up four flights of stairs, feels better, and hits the phone again.

Finally she gets through to a woman being stalked.

'So what's he keep doing?'

'Stealing my knickers and wearing them.'

'When did you first notice something strange?'

'When I saw a hand coming through the bathroom window.'

'What did you do?'

'I shouted and it scared him away.'

'Had you noticed anything before that?'

'Yes, I remembered my knickers had been going missing. But my parents owned a guest house and I blamed it on housekeeping.'

After that, Findlay tries some of the other numbers again and gets through to another woman.

She says: 'I'm addicted to entering competitions.'

'Oh really . . . '

Knightsbridge: Having dashed out of her West End office, Farrah Storr is in the lift at the ultra-posh Harvey Nichols store. She's running late. She gets out at the fifth floor, looks round the airy cafe and sees someone waiting at a neatly-set table.

'Hello, Wanda.'

Wanda Longo is a make-up artist and head of press for the beauty brand, Cover FX. She's flown in from Canada especially for this meeting with the *Women's Health* editor, on her debut day.

Storr sits down, takes in the views, talks and sips her first coffee.

West End: 'Flu, gastric and otherwise, is racing through the *Psychologies* team, which is small anyway. Editor Louse Chunn has a quick catch-up with her deputy Clare Longrigg, then retreats into her office to finish writing the cover story. It is about actress Anna Chancellor. It's urgent and she is working quickly.

The magazine specialises in Q and A interviews – what they call 'on the couch' – and they try to ensure they are more perceptive and psychological than the average profile.

Chancellor has uttered a few choice quotes: *'If you think men are all arseholes, they're not going to fancy you, are they?'* . . . *'I was really unsuccessful for years.'*

North London: Freelance health editor Lee Rodwell is putting together her three-page *HeartBeat* copy for *Take a Break*. Now she checks it word by word for errors, literals, length and sense.

She finds relevant pix and/or info for the picture desk and has more coffee. She checks her in-boxes and sees a freelance is offering her a story. It's not suitable but Rodwell commissions her anyway, asking her to interview a reader about having a baby with a cleft lip and palate.

The freelance accepts the assignment.

Wells: Having investigated clinical waste dumping off the high street, Oliver Hulme starts work on the *Journal's* regular *Yesteryear* feature. It's 900 words from 100-year-old issues, a cheap but popular space filler.

Hulme discusses next week's centre spread with the editor, news editor and sub. They decide on a picture-led feature on a classic car show taking place this weekend.

Then he gets a court report about two tramps fighting in the bus station.

He goes out and has a coffee with a contact who says he's got a scandal about nepotism and cyberstalking. Hulme listens. He's keen. But how's he going to stand it up? And it's a national story. He wants local.

Camden Town: It is time for a production meeting at *TV Choice* and *Total TV Guide*. Editor Jon Peake holds three of these a week, so they can keep track. They work on four issues of both magazines at once. Now they go through each one to check progress: interviews, features, pictures, layouts.

The singer Olly Murs is due to call today to talk about his part in *Let's Dance For Comic Relief*.

Peake is not holding his breath. Celebs are notoriously unreliable . . .

There's a flurry of excitement when a large box arrives. Staff watch as it is opened. It's full of everything a five-year-old would need at a birthday party: jelly, juice, chocolate spread sandwiches and enough Twiglets to build a tree house.

Who's it from?

At that moment identical parcels are being delivered to magazines and newspapers all over the country.

Breaking news . . . breaking news . . .

High Court: Rupert Murdoch's News International agrees to make payouts worth millions of pounds in 60 phone hacking lawsuits.

Comedian Steve Coogan gets £40,000; former footballer Paul Gascoigne gets £68,000; Simon Hughes, deputy leader of the Liberal Democrats, gets £45,000; and maverick politician George Galloway gets £25,000.

After each settlement, Michael Silverleaf, QC, says Murdoch's company accepts responsibility and regrets the damage caused by the now-defunct *News of the World*.

The judge is told that up to 56 lawsuits remain unsettled.

Afterwards Coogan tells reporters: 'This has never been about money. Like other people who have sued, I was determined to do my part to show the depths to which the press can sink in pursuit of private information.'

Enfield: Editor Greg Figeon holds a meeting with news editor Kim Inam to plan *Barnet Press* editions. They have some great local stories including a father and son who spent four hours digging drivers out of the snow on London's North Circular; shopkeepers protesting over increased parking charges and a church choir procession being mistaken for a Klu Klux Klan march.

Figeon makes cuppas all round.

Donegal: Freelance Paddy Clancy has driven over to visit a brother and sister who are the only living relatives in these parts of the Titanic pen-knife girl, Margaret Devaney.

He sits in the kitchen, notebook open, sharing a plate of scones as they start revealing the family's own story of what Margaret did as the ship sank. She climbed from steerage, past locked gates to second-class and made it to the lifeboat. There she used her pen-knife to cut a rope to save 25 lives.

It's a good interview. Clancy thanks them.

West End: Kathryn Blundell leaves the John Lewis store and returns to her *Mother & Baby* office. She sits at her desk and starts reading proofs. It's slow progress because she is answering queries from staff and constantly making decisions, big and small.

She talks to the art editor and they sketch some layouts.

London: In his box-room office, Chris Wheal is working alongside his new trainee, Rhian. She looks over his shoulder as he writes posts for *AOL Money*. He does one about car accessories being dangerous as well as expensive and she suggests a couple of good amendments. Then they search PA's photo library for a suitable picture. They choose one, crop and resize it, and write a headline.

Twitter: From MediaGuardian – *'Northcliffe revenues fall by 9 per cent.'*

Heathrow Airport: Networking queen Julia Hobsbawm has just arrived, having finally got through the traffic. She tweets: *'There is a word for a woman like me who drives and parks at the airport she is not scheduled to land at on her return.'*

She doesn't say what it is.

Camden Town: Agony aunt Katie Fraser opens more snail-mail post. Lots of letters are from lonely – mainly older – readers asking to be put on her penpal list. Younger ones usually get in touch via email or Facebook.

She slips them into an envelope which she sends to her assistant Kerry who, working from home, will reply to every one.

She calls Kerry to asks: 'How's our Adopt a Granny scheme going?'

Kerry replies: 'Very well.'

They both like helping people.

Rwanda: Reuters' Graham Holliday is still having a quiet news day in Kigali. He collects his son from school and they head home for a family lunch of bread, cheese, ham, saucisson and salad.

Shepherd's Bush: At the BBC Television Centre, science editor Susan Watts arrives at the *Newsnight* office. She discusses last night's implants special and colleagues express their surprise that the health minister was not tougher.

They hold an editorial meeting and run through the agenda for tonight's show: health bill, Greece, bond market, hacking, Syria.

Helmand: The BBC's Quentin Sommerville discovers that his cameraman Dean Squire was travelling in a convoy which was hit by one of the IED explosions. The vehicle behind took the blast. It was a lucky escape. Again, no casualties.

Southbank: Online editor Helen Russell welcomes a n ew intern to *Marie Claire*. Straightaway, the newcomer starts being trained: cutting pictures and uploading stories and galleries.

Vienna: Agency boss Mike Leidig meets some Austrian students in journalism, trying to persuade them to give some time to a charity project he is running, *Journalism Without Borders.*

He tells them: 'It centres on an investigation into human trafficking. The final report will be handed out for free . . . '

He adds: ' . . . so we can't afford to spend a lot of money on it.'

When they hear that, they lose interest. He is disappointed.

After they have gone he says: 'At the end of the day these students want to work for a named publication – the idea of working for an agency that they haven't heard of doesn't seem to push the right buttons here. Interestingly, UK student journalists are more than ready and willing to help. Austrians don't seem to think the same way.'

Wapping: At the *Sun*, political editor Tom Newton Dunn is filing an exclusive: *'Falklands hero Simon Weston is bidding to become one of Britain's first civilian cop bosses. The terribly burned ex-Welsh Guardsman will take on former Labour Cabinet Minister Alun Michael to be Police and Cr ime Commissioner for South Wales.'*

Brussels: Veteran correspondent Chris White boards the metro to the EU headquarters, using the journey time to arrange meetings.

Disembarking at Schuman, he goes to the Grapevine bar and talks to a parliamentary official. He says he'll have a coffee. The official suggests a beer or a glass of wine. He sticks with the coffee.

White gets a d etailed run down on some questionable business activities involving a senior European Commission figure. But as he takes notes he wonders if he is being used to spread political mischief.

He jokes that the EU seems to run on booze and business, and finally accepts a small beer.

West End: After the Fragrance Awards, Anita Bhagwandas gets back to *Stylist* magazine in time for the daily production meeting. Then she opens the mountain of post and starts sorting through beauty products sent by PRs.

She tries a new perfume from Viktor & Rolf.

Lincoln: Trying to win their trust, ex-BBC reporter John Thorne tells his class of service managers: 'I'm a pussycat – not a John Humphreys or a Jeremy Paxman.'

They are split into groups for radio interview practice.

Thorne explains: 'Remember, ninety per cent of interviews are collaborative public information exercises.'

They nod unconvincingly.

But then he throws in a couple of 'googly' questions – something surprisingly hostile – and warns them: 'There – never completely trust a journo.'

He's just confirmed their worst suspicions.

Shepherd's Bush: BBC security correspondent Frank Gardner descends to the edit suite to put together the film on counter-piracy. It is timed to coincide with Prime Minister David Cameron's conference on Somalia.

He is shut into a windowless room with coffee and banks of screens and is relieved to see they have the assistance of Neil, one of the best editors, a man with both patience and artistic talent.

The raw film begins to run.

Most of the time, it shows Gardner as just another talking head, speaking into the camera, but one shot pulls back when he boards an aircraft and reveals him in his wheelchair. Gardner is not just a reporter, he is an inevitable part of the story, a living witness against terrorism.

They write an introduction . . .

'Piracy off the Somali coast is estimated to be costing the shipping industry nearly $7bn (£4.4bn) . . . Frank Gardner has become the first British journalist to be allowed aboard an Australian maritime patrol aircraft, as it flew a counter-piracy mission over the Somali Basin.'

Tunbridge Wells: Reporter Sharon Marris gets back to the main office, thinking about the two edition pages she still has to sort out for editor Read.

She was also down in the diary to cover inquests at the police station but another reporter, who was sitting idle, has been sent.

Instead, she starts chasing a front-page story about a police station having its two sergeants switched to another town. She already has responses from angry councillors – but is struggling to get the police to say anything. They won't even confirm it.

Task Force Helmand HQ: Press chief Mackenzie records a weekly broadcast for BFBS – the British Forces Broadcasting Service. In this job, he has to be a jack-of-all-trades.

He is different from most Army press officers, having been a journalist first. He worked on trade magazines and at Reuters, all the time serving with the Territorial Army. When the TA formed a Media Operations Group, he volunteered.

He tells colleagues: 'At first, it seemed like a busman's holiday, but gradually I realised that I was in a position to influence the way the Army looked at media, at a time when it was beginning to develop a more open approach.

'Eventually I decided to become self-employed as a journalist and PR adviser, spending about a third of my year doing stuff all over the world with the Army, including going on operations.'

He was in Iraq and this is his third time in Afghanistan.

He says: 'Sometimes taking a journalist out can mean going on patrol and taking the same risks as everyone else. We wear body armour, but no one is completely bulletproof.

'On this tour, Thomas Harding, Defence Correspondent of the Daily Telegraph, was on a patrol that came under fire; an armoured vehicle transporting the BBC's Caroline Wyatt narrowly missed hitting a roadside bomb; and Oliver Harvey from the Sun was close to a suicide attack in Lashkar Gah.'

Mackenzie adds: 'Of course, it gave them all great stories.'

It reminds him, if he needs reminding, of the danger Quentin Sommerville is in. His cameraman has just had a narrow escape. The Taliban don't nail up posters but every war correspondent automatically has a price on his or her head. Mackenzie – and Sommerville too – are only too aware of it.

Delhi: Sitting in front of her screen, Helen Roberts goes onto *Mail Online* and sees her conjoined twins story is already up, with big pictures. They've wasted no time. It's also proving popular with magazines in Dubai and Australia.

In the previous few days, Mail Online has been confirmed as the world's most popular online newspaper and is expected to break into profit shortly. It has displaced the New York Times as leader.

The Daily Mail says it has 're-invented popular journalism for the digital era . . . The site has become renowned for its unique mix of breaking news, fascinating feature projects and unbeatable pictures and brilliant coverage of the entertainment world.'

Today's new issue of Private Eye magazine tries to puncture the paper's self-praise.

It says: 'So why was the screengrab used to illustrate this puff cropped to leave out all the stories highlighted down the right hand of the site which provide most of its hits? Surely not because this is where it pushes the celebrity-driven tripe and photos of scantily clad reality TV stars which editor Paul Dacre claims to abhor?'

It is a fair question.

On the one hand, Dacre has made the Mail newspaper a force for family values.

On the other, Mail Online is a flesh-fest, with all the semi-staged crises of manufactured celebs.

Mail Online has 70 staff, including offices in New York and Los Angeles, and one of the secrets of its success is being 'a guilty pleasure'.

It's a new business model, one which may one day displace its parent print newspaper. At 63, Dacre retains an old-fashioned love for the printed page, something he inherited from his father, Peter, a showbiz writer on the Sunday Express. He hopes it won't happen in his time.

Preston: Having finished his first seminar, Kevin Duffy hands out assignments to his students for next week. He deals with questions, giving one of them an idea for a feature for the campus newspaper. Then he hurries off to his Year 1 group in a distant building.

Stratford-upon-Avon: Trainee reporter Matt Wilson has just picked up a good local story: 300-year-old lead piping has been stolen from the house of Shakespeare's daughter. He tells the editor who says he wants it for tomorrow's front page. Wilson starts making calls – police, owners, experts – while finding time for his first coffee.

Barnet: Deputy editor Sara Ward is keen to keep in the loop despite being on maternity leave from *Take a Break*. She is watching the Leveson Inquiry on her laptop. Her mum arrives to help out with the new baby.

Camden Town: Lots of things, big and small, are happening in parallel at *Take a Break*, in different corners of the busy editorial floor. A PR calls about food products. Then Becky Mumby-Croft reads out a Reader's Brainwave: 'If you're at a finger buffet and don't want to get hands mucky, use your key.'

They laugh. It's too silly to make the magazine.

Feature writer Laura Brown sends through her newspaper memo.

They watch and marvel at a video of Byron, the most helpful Labrador in the world. He makes the bed, fetches the milk and gets money out of the cash machine for his disabled owner. They want this story. It has great pics. But a quick Google shows it's already been in a rival magazine.

And so the *Take a Break* caravan moves on.

Southwark: The jury are still out at the Harry Redknapp trial. Everyone is waiting anxiously for their verdicts.

CHAPTER 6

11am-12 noon
Eleventh Hour

Right now, in most national newspapers, the executives are filing into the editor's office and sitting down for the first editorial conference of the day.

The department heads take it in turn to present their schedules to the editor.

The most important is the news editor. It is the news list which largely dictates what follows from pictures, features, showbiz and, to a lesser extent, sport.

The editor listens to ideas and stories and starts to think about the shape and emphasis of tomorrow's newspaper, asking questions and leading discussions.

'What's happening in Syria?'

'We're getting words and pictures from inside Homs.'

'Any verdict on Harry Redknapp yet?'

'No, we're at court and we expect one soon.'

'What about Fabio?'

'He's visiting the Football Association. We don't know what will happen.'

In some offices, these conferences are civilised. In others, they are less so, degenerating into humiliation and bullying for failing executives. Occasionally, tears have been shed.

It is too early to set tomorrow's paper in concrete. In the newsroom, there are spare reporters waiting like Battle of Britain Spitfire pilots for the order to 'scramble'.

The teams have to remain flexible, expect the unexpected, respond as new stories emerge from nowhere, synchronise and coordinate. News has a dynamic life of its own which journalists respect, like sailors respect the sea. No one controls it. You can easily drown. All you can do is react quickly, and hope to swim.

As traditional editorial conferences go, the exception is the Daily Telegraph. There, the editor Tony Gallagher doesn't hold them routinely any longer. Departments send their news lists to him, and one another, on iPads.

It's a deliberate physical break from a daily schedule which was designed for another age, another technology. It's not just a gesture. It is faster and more flexible and recognises that digital is not an add-on extra but has turned into the core of the business model. These days, 65 per cent of Telegraph stories are written for online – only 35 per cent for the paper.

Face-to-face has not been abolished. The wiry Gallagher likes to move about the Telegraph floor constantly talking, monitoring, supervising, helping. Computers have yet to replicate those other elements of a good editor – leadership and experience, inspiration and humanity, intuition and instinct. They are still there but the delivery mechanisms are changing, even at a human scale.

The editors also check front-page promotions. These are big sales drivers, which are often much more effective at boosting sales than exclusive stories and headlines – to the dismay of journalists.

Today's are . . .

Sun – *SAVE ON YOUR SHOPPING WHEN YOU S PEND £40 AT MORRISONS.*

Daily Mirror – *Free books. Ladybird. Token collect. Postage payable*

Daily Star – *WIN £1,000 B&Q gift card. TWO UP FOR GRABS.*

Equally important is the cover price and how it is projected on page one:

The Sun – 'Still only 30p'

Daily Mirror – 45p

Daily Star – 30p.

Wapping: At the Sun, editor Dominic Mohan has made it clear he wants the paper to get even more involved in the case of Abu Qatada, described as Osama bin Laden's right-hand man. He cannot be deported because of Human Rights law. Mohan decides to launch a petition.

'KICK OUT QATADA'.

It has an alliterative rhythm, a succession of hard consonants, which helps.

West End: After the Fragrance Awards, Lindsay Nicholson arrives back at her Soho office and gets a shock. Usually it's neat and stylish in a mirror image of the brand. As *Good Housekeeping* editorial director, she can't inhabit a slum.

She'd feared the worst when she saw all the fuss and worried faces.

'It's a water pipe, Lindsay,' someone explains. 'It's cracked. There's been a flood. It's ruined the furniture.'

The sofa has been removed and her office looks denuded.

Someone says: 'It's being sorted out, Lindsay. Facilities are onto it.'

This is a distraction she does not need.

Nicholson improvises. She gets her department heads together, sitting them in a circle of dining chairs, looks round and says: 'It's like an AA meeting!'

The tension is broken.

She reviews layouts, checks headlines and reworks the flatplan.

Helmand: Lunch ends and the military convoy carrying Quentin Sommerville is on the move again. He peers through the reinforced windscreen, searching the horizon and still seeing very little sign of the Taliban. There is occasional small arms fire. They are at altitude and the Taliban don't like the cold.

The vehicles halt, he climbs out and is shown into the operations room. He is seeing for himself and making his own judgement: that the Brits are still providing a lot of support.

Manchester: The train from Euston has arrived, delivering *Estates Gazette* editor Damian Wild for the start of a frenetic day. He is now having a coffee with a property developer who has big plans. The man tells him he hopes to overhaul a northern town in desperate need of modernising.

This is Wild's sort of thing.

Bermondsey: With his agency partner, Mark Solomons has come up with a couple of ideas for Sunday exclusives and they start offering them around. One is a consumer rip-off tale.

Solomons says: 'Let's put that to the *Sunday Mirror* first. They pay the most.'

They do and the paper comes back quickly and says: 'We like it. We'll buy it.'

A good start.

Then they offer a health story to the *Mail on Sunday*, another good payer. They take that too.

These are sales which make all the difference.

Solomons explains: 'One Sunday exclusive is worth around seven page leads in somewhere like the *Daily Express* and ten in the *Daily Record* as – like all papers – they now pay less than they did when we started our agency in 1993.'

Time for a cuppa. The office has finally warmed up. Normal tea has run out and all that's left is what he calls 'poncy stuff'. So he makes a cup of decaf Yorkshire and another of Assam with vanilla. *Yuk.*

He checks his Facebook page. In the last few weeks they've picked up a couple of stories and the odd job via Facebook contacts. But today it's mostly funny pictures of cats and Harry Redknapp jokes.

He checks the Redknapp trial.

The jury's still out. No verdict yet. Solomon's a Spurs fan. He loves 'Arry, an iconic Londoner right down to getting himself in hot water.

Worcester: At the *News,* Rob Hale has volunteered to make a round of tea. He thinks it's a humble but necessary task in keeping the team together.

Bath: At the *Chronicle*, deputy editor Paul Wiltshire is cracking on. He stops only to wish his wife a happy birthday, then gets back to the job.

. . . *Breaking local news . . . local council tax is going* DOWN . . .

It's a good story. After the bacon sandwich earlier, he reckons he can carry on without lunch, no bother.

Burma: In their hired car, Malcolm Moore and Adam Dean have followed the pointed finger of the young KIA soldier and are bouncing over a rough road leading them away from the Chinese border.

Ahead, they see shelters. They stop and realise they have reached the secret Dabang training camp.

They show their credentials. The camp officers question them. As the first British newspaper journalists to reach this base, they are welcomed. The KIA want the wider world to hear of the Kachin people's plight.

Moore asks: 'How many new recruits are there?'

An officer replies: 'A total of 237 have just arrived for basic training.'

To Moore's eye, some look suspiciously young, barely into their teens. They sport the red, crossed machetes that are the KIA symbol. He asks about their ages and the translator shrugs.

He replies: 'There's not much we can do to stop them turning up here.'

These are the youngsters who, dressed in sarongs and army fatigues, are bravely taking on Burmese Army mortars while armed only with AK-47 rifles and homemade explosives. Their courage comes partly from rice-distilled moonshine and, inevitably, they are outgunned by more professional troops.

With the high casualty rate, the KIA has intensified its training regime and soldiers now emerge after two months, rather than three.

Moore asks: 'What does Dabang mean?'

Translator: 'Dabang means camp. This is Camp Camp. It is to emphasise its purpose.'

Moore interviews some new recruits and is led to the camp commander.

Twitter: Job offer – 'Vacancy for a sub-editor on the Democratic Voice of Burma, based Chiang Mai, Thailand.'

Knightsbridge: Farrah Storr leaves the Harvey Nichols cafe, hurries down five floors and dashes back to the *Women's Health* office in Soho. She sits down with the team and at last they have time to run through the first issue of the magazine together.

Storr asks them: 'So what do you think?'

Everyone is bubbling with praise. It's taken them months to produce so holding it in glossy printed form is an incredible thrill. They turn the pages, saying what they love and what they can do better next time.

They try to view it as a reader, not a journalist, and want to be their harshest critics, but it's not easy. They laugh at some of the pages and wonder why they seemed to take forever.

West End: At *Psychologies,* editor Louise Chunn is discussing tomorrow's readers' event, *Make It Happen.* Readers will meet experts and take part in workshops.

It's all about . . . *'helping you achieve any goal, from quitting pesky habits to starting a dream business'.*

Chunn and her staff need to get the magazine into more people's hands. It is a crowded market, even more so now *Women's Health* has joined. Chunn believes that once people try *Psychologies*, many will become regulars. Should they give away the issue at the readers' event? Should they have posters? What about subscription offers?

It all costs money.

She is thinking hard.

Unemployed Ex-Murdoch Reporter: *At this exact moment, he is starting some part-time, temporary work giving writing tutorials to journalism students.*

Trying to sound upbeat, he tells them about his career at Murdoch's News International in Wapping, naming some of the stories he worked on. He doesn't tell them he's now living in poverty and wondering when it will end, if ever. He says one thing and thinks another.

'I fight the urge to tell them not to be journalists,' he blogs later. 'We need journalists and it is a great job. This isn't how I expected my life to turn out when I deferred gratification, studying for a journalism degree and tolerating the screams of my first editor.

'It's far removed from how I lived when working at Wapping: I never worried about the fare to work or whether I could have lunch; I didn't fret that my clothes might smell of damp because the radiator went off while drying and, even arriving with a hangover, I had more energy than I do these days.' In front of the eager students, he keeps up a positive manner while nursing dark thoughts.

'Many who now enjoy hating News International journalists would, no doubt, wish this life upon them. It's not what I expected to return to from Australia, thinking the UK was a better place to be due to fewer cockroaches, a civilised lack of sun and a journalism industry the envy of the world . . . '

Saying none of this, he gets on with tutoring the students, offering encouragement where he can, preserving their dreams.

Dorking: At the *Advertiser,* Sam Blackledge sends through the final front page. It is a strong story about a battle between a youth group and a supermarket developer, and the presentation looks great.

He discusses it with the group editor.

'A supermarket developer?' she says, raising an eyebrow. 'Sam, you'd better be ready for the backlash.'

Notting Hill: Agency writer Katie Evans is checking out a 'medical miracle'. Is it all it seems? She is talking to a neurologist and says: 'We've got this story. It's about a motorcyclist who was in a terrible accident, got very bad brain damage and then made a remarkable recovery. Is it a medical miracle – or just a bit better than normal?'

The neurologist replies: 'It sounds more like a very good recovery than a medical miracle.'

'Thanks,' she says. 'We don't want to over-egg it.'

The story is downgraded

At another desk, the phone rings and a male caller tells her colleague Georgette Culley: 'I've been at the centre of a public school abuse scandal and want to waive my anonymity. I'm willing to do an interview.'

'Will you definitely be named and pictured?'

'Yes.'

'Then we're interested.'

Meanwhile, agency boss Natasha is booking a train ticket to Preston to give a talk to journalism students at UCLan, the University of Central Lancashire.

Preston: At UCLan, Kevin Duffy misjudges the long walk between buildings and arrives five minutes late for his next class. His students are waiting and he apologises.

Trying to draw a lesson from it, he tells them: 'If I was actually reporting, then I'd have missed the press conference or the arrival or the deadline – perhaps the whole story.'

His students smile politely.

Delhi: Now Helen Roberts pitches the conjoined twins story to someone involved in making TV documentaries. She sends an email.

He responds swiftly, loves the idea and says he's forwarding it to a London production house. She knows TV is a lot slower than print. It'll be a few weeks before she hears but she's optimistic. Roberts believes the money could help the girls have a quicker operation and live a better quality of life.

London: Freelance Jill Foster meets a woman she interviewed for the Daily Mail six months ago. They took to each other and have kept in touch. The woman would like more publicity for her various causes – as Foster would like more stories. They bounce ideas off each other.

Foster describes how she helped cancer sufferer and charity fundraising athlete Jane Tomlinson and husband Mike write their bestselling books *The Luxury of Time* and *You Can't Take It With You*. Jane passed away in 2007 halfway through writing the third book, *How Good Is That?* – but Jill and Mike finished where she left off and it is now out in print.

She's looking not just for features but another big project like that.

Manchester: Another train from London pulls into Piccadilly Station and disgorges a horde of passengers. Amongst them is Rebecca Pike, e-business presenter on the *Simon Mayo Show* on BBC Radio 2.

She boards the tram which sweeps her across the city centre to Salford, and there she starts to prepare for an outside broadcast on Mayo's *Drivetime* show.

Cambridge: Crime reporter Raymond Brown gets a call about the man found frozen to death in the church doorway. It is from the church's vicar, sounding distressed. They both recognise the harsh symbolism, that of the poor seeking – but not finding – Christian shelter.

The story is like a parable, as are many human interest stories in newspapers.

Brown writes it up, already pushed for time.

Then he speeds off to Madingley Hall, a country house and conference centre, which is hosting a meeting of headteachers.

A helicopter appears in the sky and a few minutes later they recognise the visitor stepping through the entrance

Brown tweets: 'Prince Charles arrives . . . '

Holding his mini tape recorder, Brown latches onto him with the rest of the press pack.

Tunbridge Wells: It's turned into a race against time at the *Courier* with the sub-editors very understaffed this week. Editor Read mucks in, agreeing to sub five pages of community news. He finds it surprisingly liberating.

It gives him an idea – for one week, a reporter will go to every event listed in a chosen village. It will be a great chance to shout about how vibrant their communities are and to get out and meet local people.

Will it go down well with the reporters, making them do a lot of evening jobs? Probably not.

Read thinks: *'Tough.'*

Brussels: Correspondent Chris White arrives late for the European Commission's regular midday press briefing – they are an hour ahead of the UK – and slips in quietly at the back to join the 40 other journalists present. A lot of it is about the Greek debt crisis. He makes some notes.

Then he nods to the Press Association's Geoff Meade, another long-serving reporter.

Meade says sotto voice: 'Fancy a coffee?'

White whispers back: 'Good idea.'

They get up and leave.

Tunbridge Wells: Sharon Marris writes up her edition's lead story: *The Great Loyalty Card Mystery.*

Can anyone help decipher the illegible signature on the winning ticket? By the time she's finished, it's turned into a real drama, like *CSI Edenbridge.*

The news editor wants a few smaller items to fill the page and she starts looking for those.

Two of her Afghanistan photos haven't yet been Opsec-d – cleared by military security. On her first day out there, they held back her report because she mentioned troop numbers. They even objected to a particular type of computer being shown.

Now she emails the photos to Helmand.

Task Force Helmand HQ: Press chief Mackenzie's team receive the email from Sharon Marris.

She says: 'Please see photos. Are these okay for us to use?'

The media unit looks at them and ten minutes later they email back: 'Pix okayed for publication, Sharon. Go ahead.'

Kingston: Freelance Natalie Dye is still interviewing the famous 'psychic' for his magazine column. It's dragging on about the space-time continuum.

Dye asks for practical lessons.

Psychic: 'You can meditate and see your past life as a timeline – with red flashing lights at each point where you made decisions with important consequences. Then you see how life might have panned out if you'd made different choices.'

Dye: 'So they can go back, see where it went wrong and take a more positive path in their minds? This changes their lives today for the better, does it?'

Psychic: 'Exactly. They're reprogramming a happier memory, which will have a p ositive effect on their soul. Not all their other paths will be better though. They need to look and choose.'

Dye thinks: *'Hmmm. Might have a go m yself later. I always thought I might have been an axe murderer. I will visualise myself putting down the axe and taking up knitting.'*

She glances back over her reams of notes and reckons it's sufficient.

She does not wish to hear the words 'space-time continuum' again. It reminds her of A-level physics lectures during which, having already got a place on a journalism course – largely by going to the pub beforehand and offering the interviewer a cigarette as she strolled in half-cut – she sat at the back putting on Biba make-up.

She is a published author – of *Cosmopolitan's Sex Confessions* – which doesn't have much to do with the space-time continuum.

'Thanks,' she says drawing the interview to a close. 'That was interesting.'

She finishes the call and starts on the column straightaway. She stares at the screen murmuring to herself: 'Space-time continuum – how the hell do I explain that to ordinary readers?'

Bristol: Trainer Caroline Sutton strongly approves of the people she's meeting from Immediate Media. She thinks they're a refreshingly mixed group of journalists, editors, art directors and others from publications as diverse as *Wildlife* to *The World of Cross Stitching*.

She begins her training session.

Leeds: At the *Evening Post*, work placement student David Spereall is busy tweeting, discussing the value of Ian Bell to the England cricket side and gauging reaction to his online article.

He checks *Sky News* again for the latest from the Redknapp trial. Nothing. The jury is still out.

City: Alan Burkitt-Gray posts four news stories and pictures to his website, *Global Telecoms Business*. He goes through 70 emails and starts editing incoming features.

Busy, busy.

He ghost-wrote one feature for an industry expert at 850 words. The expert revised it up to 1,450 words, far too long for a page. So now Burkitt-Gray cuts it back to 850 again. He emails it to him, as it will need to have his byline – but he's in California and, presumably, fast asleep. He won't hear back for a few hours.

Lincoln: The training session is well under way and now John Thorne hopes he's overcoming the suspicions of those sitting in front of him. Their stares are slightly less hostile and he explores their fears.

Why are people so afraid of the media?

One woman, Jill, says: 'I worry about my speech patterns, my ums and errs, my waffling answers, the glaring black hole of silence as I d r y up i n mid-answer.'

Thorne reassures her.

He says: 'Don't worry, it is part of the natural, everyday speech pattern now quite acceptable to listeners. In the old days, interviews used to be de-ummed but we don't do that now. Anyway, preparation and practice will cure it.'

He begins to show them how and they start to sit up and pay closer attention.

Wapping: At the *Sun*, chief showbiz writer Richard White has got a story which presses three of the right buttons – Simon Cowell, *Britain's Got Talent*, and the other BGT judges.

He taps out his intro: *'Simon Cowell has put the other Britain's Got Talent judges in the shade -with special lights under his desk that give him a healthy glow . . . '*

Editor Dominic Mohan reads it. It's not earth-shattering but he likes it. It's just right for a page 3 lead.

Bedford: The reception desk rings up to the newsroom and speaks to news editor Keeley at the *Bedfordshire on Sunday*.

'Are you expecting a package?'

'Not really.'

'One's just arrived.'

Displaying her over-developed wit, Keeley replies: 'Right, I think it's a bomb. I'm coming down to collect it.'

She brings it up to the newsroom and everyone watches as she opens it. It contains a cake, party snacks and balloons – just like the one which arrived at *TV Choice* earlier.

Keeley looks at the card and says: 'It's from Virgin Media. They want us to celebrate their fifth birthday.'

Reporter Kathryn Cain says: 'Great. Do they know we haven't actually done any stories on them? Ever.'

Someone asks: 'Should we send it back?'

Everyone choruses: 'No way. It would be rude.'

West End: *Reader's Digest* editor Gill Hudson is talking to the ad team about an important presentation they're making to a big advertising agency. She asks what their main selling point is. They say: *'Er, you . . . '*

She is their ace card, a winner of many awards and current Editors' Editor as voted by her peers in the British Society of Magazine Editors.

She's at the top of the pyramid.

Afterwards, she looks at the first finished spread for April. She signs it with one reservation, saying: 'Can we please change one of the "funny" stories . . . because, frankly, it isn't.'

Shepherd's Bush: At *Newsnight,* Susan Watts goes in for the meeting she has been preparing for. It is with the programme editor and two deputies.

They discuss science stories for 2012. They talk for an hour and it is productive, with 'big thoughts' on issues which they can realistically tackle.

She is pleased.

She is fortunate to work on a show which believes it has a duty to spread public understanding.

This is not the case throughout much of the media – especially the tabloids – where science is either dismissed, mocked, misrepresented or senselessly sensationalised.

Camden Town: A freelance calls and tells *Take a Break* commissioning editor Julia Sidwell: 'I've signed up a brilliant love-rat story.'

Sidwell listens to the details and says: 'Great. I like it.'

Ten minutes later, a different agency phones and says: 'We're letting you know we have a love-rat story which we'll be offering you.'

Again Sidwell listens. She replies: 'Er, it sounds good.'

When she's replaced the receiver, she turns to editor Fleming and says: 'That's two agencies both claiming to have the same story under contract.'

Fleming says: 'We can expect trouble. They'll be fighting like cat and dog.'

Until fairly recently, at least one love-rat story would be guaranteed in every issue of *Take a Break.* They were the readers' favourites and it was a free-for-all between the magazines and tabloids to get the best, paying freelances up to £7,000 an article.

The most common source was the embittered wife, angry at her husband for running off with her best friend.

But then the law on privacy changed and the market collapsed.

Now prurience has to be justified by genuine public interest – involving a crime, for instance. But even this will not always suffice.

Fleming looks up to see the post boy walking towards the features team carrying a gift-wrapped basket of goodies.

Writer Anna Murphy says: 'Ooh, these need to be sampled and reviewed.'

The package is unwrapped. It's Virgin Media again, asking them to celebrate their fifth birthday party.

Murphy shares the goodies out and says: 'It's a tough job but someone's got to do it.'

Cornwall: *'What Makes You Cornish?'* – that's the question which editor Kirstie Newton is asking on behalf of *Cornwall Today*. She has posted it on Facebook and Twitter and is reading the replies . . .

From Australia, one woman writes: 'It's in the blood. I'm Cornish through and through; 500 years' worth of ancestry.'

Others disagree.

A man says: 'It is living here, the long-term commitment to Cornwall, not the accident of your birth.'

Another comments: 'Being Cornish means loving Cornwall, respecting Cornwall's people, history and language, and belonging and contributing to it.'

Newton reckons it will make a good column.

Congleton: Editor Jeremy Condliffe is looking at the *Chronicle's* front page lead – the splash – about a man who committed indecent acts with children. The paper got into trouble recently when the word 'penis' was placed too near a young girl's image.

The sub-editors are worried again.

The newspaper's policy is to define the different levels of indecent images from 1 to 5 – saying a 'serious Level 4 image' or 'Level 5, which can include penetrative sexual acts between children and animals'. These are the legal definitions.

Condliffe formally approves the necessary changes.

BREAKING NEWS . . . BREAKING NEWS . . .

Southwark Crown Court: Suddenly the milling around stops. There's an announcement from the Redknapp court officials.

The jury's coming back.

The words have hardly been uttered before reporters are texting their newsdesks.

There is the clatter of shoes on tiled floors and the busy corridors empty as everyone hurries back into the courtroom. Most of the journalists slide into the press bench, with an unofficial overflow perched in the public gallery.

Phones are primed ready to text – tweeting was banned by the judge earlier in the trial – and pens poise over open notepads.

They look up and see the top of Harry Redknapp's head when he emerges into the dock with his co-accused Milan Mandaric. Flanked by uniformed guards, the two men glance round at their relatives and friends. The strain is showing.

Next, the members of the jury file in through a side door and re-occupy their places, keeping their faces impassive.

Finally the judge, robed and bewigged, takes his seat.

With all the pieces in place, the tension is unbearable. The judge nods and the trial moves into its brief final act.

The clerk asks the jury foreman to stand and then reads out the first charge and says: 'Do you find the accused Mr Redknapp guilty or not guilty?'

The foreman takes a deep breath and gives the verdict . . .

As the words cross his lips, a dozen thumbs depress tiny mobile keyboards and a wave of texts rise unseen from the press bench, a ghostly evolution of Mr Reuter's pigeons during the siege of Paris in 1870. They penetrate the court walls and in a matter of seconds fly 360 degrees across London, Britain and then around the world.

Kensington: At the *Daily Mail,* someone shouts across the newsroom: 'It's here – the Redknapp verdict.'

At that moment, those words are being echoed in hundreds of other newsrooms . . .

Camden Town: Agony aunt Katie Fraser spots one last envelope at the bottom of her pile of letters. The writing looks familiar, but not in a good way. Her heart sinks. She tears it open and scans it swiftly . . .

Dear Katie

Am I normal? I have a problem I hope you can help me with . . .

It's him again. He gives a list of measurements in which he details the length of his male member. She sighs as she gets to the final sentence, which is always the same.

Please reply to ease my mind.

She bins it, having replied many times and now dreading to think what he does with the responses.

Petersfield: Veteran freelance columnist Colin Dunne blogs: *'Crisp day, blue sky, no rain. Instead of writing – thinking. Best place to think? Petersfield golf course, for research purposes. Elegant golf, intense pleasure, hence ideas cascading through ancient brain. It worked for Wodehouse. I'll play a few holes, write a few chapters. Easy, also peasy. Awf we jolly well go . . . '*

BREAKING NEWS . . . BREAKING NEWS . . .

Southwark Crown Court: In the public gallery Jamie Redknapp's eyes redden as he sees his father turn and hug his co-accused Mandaric and mouth a 'thank you' to his defence team.

Outside in the fresh air, TV sports correspondent James Pearce hears the verdict instantaneously, composes himself, looks straight into the camera and prepares to speak . . .

Shepherd's Bush: On BBC News 24, the presenter says: 'We are going over live now to James Pearce at Southwark Crown Court . . . we hear the jury have just returned their verdict in the Harry Redknapp trial. What's happened, James?'

Southwark Crown Court: Just outside, James Pearce says that, yes he has the verdict.

GUILTY!

Yes, he says, Harry Redknapp has been found guilty of one count of tax evasion.

CLANG!

There is a pause as he listens to his earpiece against the noise of traffic and other broadcasters and journalists.

His assured manner starts to crumble.

Pearce says: 'I am sorry, I was going to say . . . I am sorry, I am going to correct this because we have confusion here and that makes much more sense . .

.

'They have been cleared of all charges. We have got some wrong information that has come through here.'

He continues: 'A clarification, they have been found NOT guilty of all charges. I was getting very confused when I was speaking then. It was unlikely that they could be found not guilty of the first charge and guilty of the second charge."

He adds: 'That is now confirmed, they have been found NOT guilty of all charges.'

The verdict is being announced over the airwaves from every source: TV, radio and web.

Worcester: At the *Worcester News,* they see it as a snap on the wires and shout it round the newsroom: Redknapp not guilty. Someone makes a joke, perhaps one of thousands being blurted at that point.

London: Fabio Capello almost certainly sees it. His fellow manager, Harry, is not guilty. Now he can watch pictures of Redknapp being cheered out of court, people mobbing him and slapping his back. If only he, Fabio, were half as popular . . .

Leeds: Sports-mad work placement student David Spereall sees it on *Sky News.* He watches as Redknapp says in a faltering voice to a wall of microphones and cameras: 'It really has been a nightmare. It's been five years. It's been horrendous. The jury were unanimous . . .'

London: Robin Lustig sees it on the BBC News Channel. *Redknapp not guilty.* It's big news but *sport.* His programme, *The World Tonight,* doesn't do sport. And yet . . .

Bermondsey: Mark Solomons sees it on the net. *'Arry not guilty.* As a Spurs fan, he cheers.

Bath: The *Chronicle's* Paul Wiltshire sees it on the BBC and sends a tweet calling it a shambles – wrong announcement, rogue apostrophes, even misspelling of Redknapp.

Daily Express: Editor Hugh Whittow can almost see the court building from his office on the other side of the Thames. Redknapp's acquittal may be a great story but is it good enough for the front-page splash?

He gazes down at the streets and sees tiny figures bolstering themselves against the cold.

The wily Whittow is ruminating.

He's already got another splash in mind and when he stands at the window, it's right in front of his nose. It's still the nation's favourite conversational opener.

It's not Harry Redknapp, not for *Express* readers.

Walthamstow: Showbiz writer Nick McGrath is still on the phone putting questions to *Masterchef's* Gregg Wallace.

McGrath: 'What's been your single most profitable day of work?'

Wallace: 'Four hours for Sainsbury's. I'm not going to tell you how much.'

McGrath: 'What's the most you've spent on a single restaurant meal?'

Wallace: 'A table for four or five of us, about £1,300. We drank vintage champagne. It wasn't worth spending that much.'

McGrath: 'Do you spend a lot of money on food?'

Wallace: 'This will amaze you but I spend far too much money on takeaways.'

Foodie Wallace says he's a secret kebab addict. The interview ends.

As a reward, McGrath makes himself coffee number three.

Hammersmith: A new reporter has started at *Brand Republic* this week and it's down to Arif Durrani to ease him into the workflow. Today, he arranges internal training on their CMS (content management system) including how to file images and video.

Durrani says: 'Bedding in new staff takes time and patience, and both can be in short supply on the news team, and we vow to be considerate.'

He finally finishes the Rashbass feature ready for *Media Week*'s afternoon bulletin.

West London: After a morning chasing unresponsive PRs, beauty editor Liz Wilde finally gets an email with the details she's been requesting.

She receives it *twice*. She wonders what they're paid for.

Wilde says: 'You send an email to a PR, it comes back 'out of office'. You send another to the suggested colleague. It comes back too. You phone the PR number, get put through to an answer machine, phone again, get put through to another answer machine. You phone a third time, ask to be put through to someone who is actually there and you're told the exchange is in Birmingham so they have no idea who's in the London office . . . Hopeless! And I'm trying to give *them* publicity.'

Stratford-upon-Avon: Matt Wilson has just finished writing the story about the ancient piping stolen from Shakespeare's daughter's house. He finishes it and sends it through to the editor. As a trainee, he sits anxiously awaiting the boss's verdict.

London: Chris Wheal talks his trainee, Rhian, through the essential but boring bits of his freelance work: accounts, calculating earnings, negotiating and, most important, getting paid. He also explains more about having your own websites, and SEO (search engine optimization)
.

Twitter: From NewsLord – *'Have sent workie to cover Twitter joke trial. Give me some direct quotes sonny, or I'll insert a copy of McNae's (a journalists' law book) in you . . . .And file by three @ajhmurrat or don't bother coming back tomorrow. I don't care how many pubs (publications) you've got.'*

Bristol: At Medavia, Heather Findlay takes an early lunch at her desk with a book, Helen De Witt's *The Last Samurai*. She always tries to have a proper break but it's not easy. Now she ends up r eplying to emails and texts, and answering questions from her editor.

CHAPTER 7
12 midday-1pm
High Noon

Tunbridge Wells: After a brisk 20-minute walk, news presenter Jenny Barsby clocks on for her shift at BBC Radio Kent. A midday start suits her fine. She's used the morning to go to the gym and have a swim, and feels fresh and relaxed as she sits down in the studio and starts to prepare her news scripts.

Brussels: Chris White is sitting at a table in 'Meade Corner' – officially named after his current lunchtime companion, Press Association's Geoff Meade, who has been its most frequent occupant for over 30 years.

The two veteran correspondents are trying in vain to access the internet and White says: 'We'd be better off at La Clé cafe.'

Then he phones the Court of Human Rights, gets no reply and declares: 'My God, this is like the old days in Fleet Street.'

When they discuss the Abu Qatada controversy, White says: 'I smell something wrong with the coverage.'

They are joined by Bruno Waterfield, of the Daily Telegraph, and White asks him cryptically: 'Would you be willing to rock the boat politically?

'What is it?'

'A British problem.'

'When you are ready, try us.'

Waterfield places two glasses of white wine in front of them.

White: 'I'm not drinking.'

Meade: 'A small glass of white wine doesn't count.'

White: 'Oh, that's all right then.'

They drink up, then accept a second glass each.

West End: After the burst pipe, working in conditions which would shock her tidy-minded readers, Lindsay Nicholson approves the dummy of her new standalone print title, *Good Housekeeping's Chocolate Collection*. It contains nearly 200 chocolate recipes and she has memories of tasting every single one.

Oh well, she says, it had better be salad for lunch then!

Glasgow: Freelance Samantha Booth looks at the time and realises she hasn't even dressed despite being up for four hours. And shortly she'll have a visitor. She moves swiftly. Shower, hair, make-up and then she hears someone at the door. She answers it and greets her octogenarian interviewee who once interrogated Nazis.

'Hello . . .'

'Are you ready for lunch?'

'I certainly am.'

They set off for the local tea shop.

West End: Farrah Storr's phone is ringing non-stop, mainly from PRs wanting to meet for coffee, having seen the potential of *Women's Health*.

She receives a bouquet, so large it makes her colleagues gasp. It is from her husband. This is turning into a perfect day.

Then she looks at the clock and grabs her coat.

It's only a quick walk to the Soho Hotel, a boutique establishment favoured by media types. She steps past the 10-foot Botero cat sculpture on the porch.

She is shown to her table and is greeted by her host, the editor of Rodale Books. As the meal is served, they get down to business – discussing brand extension, and how *Women's Health* can become much more than just a magazine. For instance, it could promote gyms and fitness equipment, certain lines of food, sports and TV shows – anything which builds on its brand.

Tatler calls this place 'The Most Glamorous Hotel in the World'. But this is a serious lunch, not a food tasting, however excellent the menu.

Worcester: The *News's* deputy editor John Wilson is writing a blog, explaining to readers what his journalists do.

He taps: 'Every page we produce is proofread before being sent to the printing press. We check grammar and spellings, and make sure everything we write is accurate. The design of the page has to meet our own strict style rules, and we want to make our headlines as bright and as interesting as possible. Mistakes do sometimes slip through, but not because we haven't tried our very best to prevent them!'

London: Freelance talks to freelance. Jill Foster chats on the phone to a colleague who says she is having a quiet week. Foster laughs. Her friend has about five features on the go but, for her, that is indeed quiet.

Enfield: Greg Figeon, editor of multiple titles, lays out pages for *Pulman's Weekly News*, a Tindle-owned paper in the South West. He sends it to pre-press.

Rwanda: After taking his son to tennis coaching, Reuters' Graham Holliday sits down at the side of the tennis court and opens his laptop. He gets access using a 3.5G dongle and talks to Bosco Hitimana, a freelance business journalist. They discuss the press conference in Kigali this morning and the one tomorrow. Will there be a change of interest rate?

London: Robin Lustig is following Prime Minister's Question Time on the BBC News Channel. To his annoyance it switches to the Redknapp acquittal. He switches too, this time to the Parliament Channel, and watches Ed Miliband go in hard on the reform of Britain's National Health Service.

Lustig thinks that's pushed the NHS up *The World Tonight* agenda.

He leaves home and heads for BBC Television Centre.

Dorking: Already running an hour late, the *Advertiser* is hit again when the internet goes down. The subs call with a query about something on the council website.

Sam Blackledge tells them: 'Sorry, I've lost my connection . . . '

But they are resourceful and he proofreads the front page. They get their heads down and all push on and the internet is restored and they start getting on top of things.

As they do, a collective sigh of relief goes round the office.

When he has a chance to take a break, Blackledge refuses and just carries on and begins sending pages through for next week.

Bermondsey: Mark Solomons is wading through the marshy swamps of his email inbox and chasing up PRs, newsdesks and others who should have come back to them by now – one budget airline has taken the best part of a day to say why they charge so much for suitcases, while another took five minutes.

They've 'done up' their stories for the Sundays. All seems well and they are hoping that both get used.

Then he has a glance at the new *Private Eye* to see if they know anyone in trouble. In the past year at least eight of their former *Sun* colleagues – they left there in 1993 – have been arrested. Others are living in dread of the early morning knock of police officers from Scotland Yard.

Solomons looks again at the Redknapp verdict, just for reassurance. He's happy, for himself and all his fellow Spurs fans.

Bath: The *Chronicle's* Paul Wiltshire checks unique website users and sees they've reached 182,000. He's very pleased. It would be worth celebrating but he hasn't the time. He decides to skip lunch and crack on with the obituary page.

Sheffield: Having stepped off the London train, *Daily Mail* sub-editor Jayme Bryla is now addressing 20 students in Sheffield University's journalism department. These are informal seminars to give them the bigger picture.

He's young and they identify with him.

He tells them what the *Mail* is looking for – core skills, law, ideas, work experience, shorthand, writing, and expertise in audio and video recording and editing.

'The list grows and grows,' thinks his host Peter Cole, Professor Emeritus and former editor of the *Sunday Correspondent.* 'It is becoming absurd.'

But, for the moment, he bites his tongue.

Then Bryla talks to the students in pairs, giving them advice about CVs and interviews. He is making notes about who is impressing him.

Afterwards, Cole asks the students for their reactions. Some are worried about the emphasis Bryla put on national newspaper work experience. Where are students from outside London supposed to stay in the capital? It is so expensive.

It discriminates against them, accentuating the metropolitan bias.

Cole thinks how rapidly things have changed in the demands from employers.

A few years ago, his postgrads spent a year learning newspaper skills *or* broadcast skills, not both. Now employers want trainees who have all the traditional 'print' skills, including subbing and layout, *plus* the ability to make and edit videos, *plus* the skills to put stories, pics and videos, and links, on a website.

It is a big ask for the educators. But they have to rise to the challenge.

'This is the multi-skilled world,' Cole says. 'Students are paying a lot for courses and are entitled to demand that they are provided with the skills employers seek.

'It's a crude way of putting it, but they are buying an entry ticket into the media industries – only it doesn't guarantee them a seat. Can so much be learnt before starting the first job?'

He adds: 'And I've left out social media and, most important of all in the current climate, ethics and standards.'

The *Daily Mail* gets 1,000 applications for traineeships per year. Six to eight will be successful. Sheffield students took four of them last year; one of those is already working in New York – on the website, of course.

London: The *Daily Mail*'s training scheme has its own website. On it, some joker has written . . .

'Further to your advertisement for trainee journalists, please refer to my CV which I have attached as well as the six pieces of my work, which focus on Cheryl Cole at LAX airport, Cheryl Cole in jeggings and oversized glasses, Cheryl Cole in Heathrow Airport, Cheryl Cole walking in Louboutins, Cheryl Cole in JFK departure lounge and Cheryl Cole walking around in Dubai with a new Birkin.

'I do hope that these pieces parallel the criteria you seek in journalists who contribute to the Mail Online. Not only am I conversant in the cult of celebrity, I also am thoroughly polished in casual racism, sexism, homophobia and can feign moral outrage at benefits claimants at the drop of a hat. I look forward to hearing from you.

Dame Kitty Carryall'

It's funny but, in truth, the *Mail* is to be commended for setting up its training scheme.

London: It's one benefit of working from home. Being 37 weeks pregnant and still churning out stories isn't a problem for freelance Louise Baty because she can have a brief lie down on the sofa. So she does just that, then goes for a quick trip to the supermarket, telling herself: 'Sometimes it's handy being your own boss . . . .'

She's never worked so hard and loves it. She still gets a huge buzz when she sells a story – just as she did in her early days at South West News Service, Bristol. So the ups more than compensate for the downs.

In reality, although heavily pregnant, she usually ends up doing the washing up rather than relaxing when she has a break. Her flat has never looked so clean.

Twitter: From *Press Gazette –* 'Dorset Echo's Toby Granville named Newsquest Editor of the Year'.

Weston-super-Mare, Avon: *Suffering from melanoma, Alan Goode dies aged 72 in Weston General Hospital. The news spreads rapidly amongst many old colleagues. Goode was a former editor of the Herald, Plymouth, and chief executive of Bristol United Press, parent company of the Bristol Evening Post. Glowing tributes are immediately being paid to him online . . . 'a legend' . . . 'a brilliant newspaperman' . . . 'In the rough and tumble world of journalism, Alan Goode was the rough and tumble' . . . 'an inspirational leader'.*

Lincoln: At last ex-BBC reporter John Thorne is warming to his students, as they are warming to him.

Those who voiced the deepest concerns about broadcasting are now proving the more open, engaging and conversational interviewees.

Thorne's tales of journalistic bravado are enjoyed. Oh, how old he sounds and feels! Then they stop for a buffet lunch over trays of sandwiches and cream cakes.

Now it is his turn to wonder at the fabulous stories as the 'clients' let down their guard and start to tell him stories in return. He curses the ethics which demand they all must stay confidential.

Then he hears himself berating today's tabloid hackers while confessing to embarrassing demeanours in his own broadsheet and tabloid past.

In the back of his mind, three words continue to tap at his guilty conscience: *poacher turned gamekeeper.*

Tunbridge Wells: At the *Courier,* Sharon Marris sits with her fellow reporters and has a bowl of soup. She's worrying about a headline on one of her bylined Afghanistan pieces – *'14-year-old terrorist's face still haunts me'.*

It concerns a boy arrested while she was at Forward Base Shawqat. It took a lot of work to pull together, including interviewing a sergeant as she lugged her gear towards the helicopter landing site, ready to leave for Lashkar Gah.

But the headline makes her sound traumatised, unprofessional. She's not. She doesn't want readers to think she is. She's a *reporter*, the proudest title in newspapers.

Shepherd's Bush: The BBC's Frank Gardner is still editing his piracy film. Now he is looking at the footage of his recent maritime patrol flight over the

Indian Ocean and it makes him queasy all over again. He recalls that someone in that flight crew was called 'Chuck' – which is exactly what Gardner did.

Twitter: From Adam Boulton, political editor at *Sky News*, reporting from *Prime Minister's Questions* in the Commons – *'Ed Miliband having a good outing – but Sky News and BBC 24 have switched to Redknapp . . . '*
The People's 'Arry trumps the People's Dave and Ed.

By now, three big stories are running simultaneously -Redknapp, the Murdoch settlements and P rime Minister's Questions. Suddenly they are joined by a fourth – controversial blogger Paul Staines, aka Guido Fawkes, climbs into the witness box at the Leveson Inquiry, takes the oath and i s ready to give his evidence. He's expected to deliver a few shocks.

Delhi: Helen Roberts is checking UK newspapers. Then she cries out in horror. They have used another agency's photographs on a story she pitched to them weeks earlier.
She is disappointed, deflated. Why? She emails them. They reply quickly: *price.* The other agency was much cheaper.
She says to her colleague, Tanzeel Ur Rehman: 'The joys of being a freelance! Oh well, let's dust ourselves down and move on. You win some, you lose some . . . '
She gets a message from a media website offering her daily information on all celebrity movement in and out of India.
She says: 'It's pricey – but it could be worth it.'

KwaZulu-Natal: Travel writer Meera Dattani takes a break and watches lodge assistant Lacey bathe a corn snake, to help it shed its skin. It works a treat, peeling beautifully like school glue off fingers. Then the giant boas are served their lunch: mice.
Dattani doesn't get close.
By now it feels too hot to eat anything but she force-feeds herself Ryvita, cottage cheese and a mug of sweet coffee. She mounts the quad bike and sets off with Copper, the lodge's Staffordshire terrier, running at her side. She takes a quick tour around the property to collect washing and do other errands.
She returns to the patio to carry on writing but the heat is unbearable even with three fans whirring overhead. She retreats indoors, makes chocolate milk and watches half-an-hour of Harry Potter with the lodge owners' nine-year-old son.

Private Eye: *The magazine's new issue refers to the Mirror's campaign against Royal Bank of Scotland chairman Stephen Hester receiving a £963,000 bonus. The Eye perceives hypocrisy.*
It says: 'Okay, then. Perhaps the Mirror could start widening out the debate by considering the £660,000 bonus enjoyed last year by the boss of a m edia company which has seen sales of its products and share prices plunge since she

took over, and whose remuneration package was criticised by one of the company's biggest shareholders last week as 'just not tenable . . . it is out of kilter with the group's performance and current size.' The fatcat in question? Sly Bailey, chief executive of Daily Mirror publisher Trinity Mirror, which last week announced a further 75 job cuts on her national titles.'

The *Eye* is prescient. Three months later, Bailey resigns in the face of a shareholder revolt over her £1.7m pay package.

Walthamstow: Showbiz writer Nick McGrath stops for cheese on toast with his wife and two-year-old son. His broadband is very slow and he says, only partly in jest: 'I'm nearing breaking point.'

He uses his iPhone to access his email and sees a message from Lydia Bright's PR saying: 'Hi Nick, regarding your interview with my client, any questions about her recent relationship split are forbidden.'

What!

He mutters some choice expletives. Now even fake celebs are laying down conditions. What's the point of interviewing her, for God's sake?

His breaking point has just come one step closer.

Then, inexplicably, his broadband comes back to life. Hooray! He updates his website, emails several PRs, checks his bank balance for late payments (pretty much every major publisher), and goes on Twitter for the Redknapp acquittal gossip.

Next he streams Guido Fawkes live from the Leveson Inquiry, surprised to see this dangerous subversive looks like a provincial bank manager.

He's just relaxing when . . . *Aaagh!*

His internet crashes again.

London: Generally, the Redknapp story is being greeted warmly. He's a modern hero, an old-fashioned cheeky Cockney geezer. But there are some dissident voices, among them ex-*Sun* editor Kelvin Mackenzie, now a *Daily Mail* columnist and therefore a spokesman for law-abiding Middle England.

His thoughts are beginning to gel as he starts tapping at his keyboard . . .

'Perhaps I have lost my sense of humour but I do not share the joy . . . The idea of naming your bank account in Monaco after your dog is clearly odd. I tried to follow suit but my dog Paddy couldn't even fill a cheque in . . .

'But if you are a regular employee paying your tax by PAYE, this case was a shocker and I fear that the not guilty verdicts will encourage ordinary folk to start taking risks on their tax form. I don't blame Her Majesty's Revenue and Customs for going after Mr Redknapp. Clearly he had a case to answer and I would like to have seen the verdict had you or I tried to use his defence in court.'

Bedford: A newspaper war is being waged here every bit as bitter as that between, say, the *Mail* and the *Express*.

At the *Bedfordshire on Sunday (BoS)* staff discover that a reporter from a rival paper is to appear on Jeremy Vine's Radio 2 show. As if that's not bad enough, it is to discuss a *BoS* story – which they claim the other paper covered a week later.

So they switch the radio on and gather round grumbling. They listen in disgust to the competition.

BoS reporter Kathryn Cain is scathing.

She says: 'We are not surprised that she fails to sound like she knows what she is talking about. Journalists, even print journalists, should be able to speak well on TV and radio when required.'

Cain cheers up when the boss of a local chippy rings complaining about the council. He says they're telling him he needs planning permission to put an advert on a wall.

Cain and a photographer hurry off to visit the man. They do an interview and take pictures of him looking disgruntled.

But as they leave, Cain looks equally disgruntled. She's still disgruntled when she gets back to the office.

'He's a nice guy,' she says to the newsroom, 'but d'you know what?'

'What?'

'He didn't offer us any chips.'

A wave of horror sweeps through her colleagues' ranks.

London: For the *Independent,* its founder and ex-editor Andreas Whittam Smith is tapping out tomorrow's column, again picking on the day's most popular story so far. But his take is very different from Kelvin Mackenzie's . . .

'It was Harry Redknapp's misfortune to confront one of the most poorly organised activities of government . . . the fair and efficient collection of taxes is in the same wretched condition as control of our borders, care of old people in hospital and defence procurement . . . '

Task Force Helmand HQ: Press chief Gordon Mackenzie prepares an evening update for the Force Commander, including the latest progress of the BBC's Quentin Sommerville, still out on ops.

Hamitullah, Helmand: In convoy, Sommerville gets back to this military base without seeing any more roadside bomb explosions. The sun sets, darkness falls and the air temperature drops swiftly under a starry sky. He is shown to a tent and when he steps inside he's pleased to see there is a heater.

He attempts to have a shower, to wash away the layers of dust and sweat and oily fumes that have built up during the last eight hours. The water is mainly cold but he knows he's lucky to get even that.

Then he sits down to eat, his appetite prepped, unsure what he's going to be offered. His surprise verges on amazement when the food is brought in from the kitchen and served in front of him – freshly cooked steaks, with mashed potato.

A military miracle.

He digs in. Not bad at all.

Petersfield Golf Course: Ancient columnist Colin Dunne is seeking inspiration through a regime of rigorous exercise, self-discipline and modelling himself on P. G. Wodehouse. But as he traipses across the greens, swinging away and making a botch of it, he doesn't know which is worse, his golf or his ideas.

'Both,' he says to himself. 'They're equally rubbish.'

He recalls how Wodehouse did golf with comedy-writing whereas he, Dunne, does comedy-golf and no writing.

As he swings wildly to little effect, he tells himself: 'It is a heart-breaking waste of time. I must retire. I've no future in writing. Or golf. Or breathing.'

West End: After a hectic morning, *Reader's Digest's* Gill Hudson has arrived at the gym. She stretches her naturally fit body, does a few half-hearted weights, then a 20-minute swim. An irritating man is blocking the lane with his bizarre backstroke-cum-butterfly. Again.

West End: Having started to train her up, Helen Russell gets bad news about the new intern. She's just been offered a job elsewhere – a job rather than internship. The intern says: 'I'm sorry, I've accepted it.'

A stunned Russell says: 'Er, congratulations . . .'

But her smile conceals panic. Where can she find a replacement? As she sits there thinking, she sees some free samples of chocolate arrive and she eats some for consolation

She starts sorting through CVs and calling contacts to cover two other team members who will now be off during *Marie Claire's* busiest time of year. In effect it is 'fashion month' – New York *and* London – with hundreds of pictures coming in every morning, catwalk reports to write up and the awards season still chugging on.

She's also counting down to The Oscars in Hollywood, the biggest event of their editorial calendar. They'll need all hands on deck.

Right now she needs a keen, capable intern . . .

Here's what Russell advises people who want to break into women's magazines . . .

Take up offers of training. Whether it's online, in print, or on screen, training gives you an edge and makes you a more versatile (and attractive) employee.

If you say you want to work online, prove it! Show that you've made an effort to develop your experience in this area on blogs, Twitter and Facebook.

Adapt your style to suit different titles or sites. Always research thoroughly, from reading back issues to scouring the net and looking at the media pack.

Be comfortable at taking direction from editors and always welcome feedback. There's no room for ego!

Being genuinely nosy and fairly outgoing also helps. Good journalists are great at listening, finding things out and getting people to open up.

Cornwall: Editor Kirstie Newton finalises the front cover of *Cornwall Today*. She is pleased with it. It shows a beautiful sunrise over a cove – with a list of features from *Win a St Mawes Cookery Break* to *Cornwall Air Ambulance at 25*. It looks superb.

She pops home for lunch and chats to the man who is replacing her boiler.

'I recognise you,' he says. 'I saw your picture in the magazine.'

Fame at last.

Burma: The sun has sunk fast and now it is dark. Malcolm Moore and Adam Dean have crossed a time zone at the border. Burma is one-and-a-half hours behind China. With headlights switched on, they drive away from the KIA military recruits in Dabang Camp and look for somewhere to stay. They find a hotel, check in and sit down for dinner.

The fare is modest – fried rice washed down by Myanmar beer, but they didn't come here for the food.

They discuss what they've got.

Since June, the KIA has been fighting the Burmese Army, losing at least 100 soldiers – many, as they've seen, little more than kids. Over 50,000 people have fled their villages and are now living in camps dotted either side of the border.

It is a strong story although one largely being ignored in the West. And Moore will see that the *Telegraph* breaks it properly . . .

Camden Town: Agony aunt Katie Fraser is trying to think up a question for her weekly Facebook readers' poll. She needs something intriguing, to hook in her *Take a Break* followers at a glance.

After a few false starts, she has come up with one.

'Can a step mum be as good as a real mum?'

She posts it up on her website and waits. Five minutes later the first reply drops into her inbox. It's quickly followed by others. She loves to see the numbers mount.

Then she notices something alarming. There is an anxious discussion taking place on her Depression page. One of the regular contributors has disappeared. The others are worried. They know the woman's partner is violent. Has he done something to her?

Fraser tries to send the woman a message. She can't make contact. Even worse, her profile has disappeared.

It's been wiped out!

Some of the group fear the worst.

Camden Town: It is a spoof agony column – rather than a real one like Fraser's – that freelance Adam Carpenter has been working on. His first draft has gone down well, offering advice supposedly from the royal couple, Wills and Kate.

A fictional reader asks: 'What is the correct way to allocate domestic chores?'

Wills replies: 'Get the staff to do it, stupid!'

It's entertaining stuff if perhaps marginally unfair.

But then deputy editor Zoe Wright says: 'Adam, do you think you're going too far?'

'What do you mean?'

'Should we tone down some of the gags?'

He considers it. He hates throwing away a good joke. But he can see the point. It will work better if it's not just funny but *constructive*.

Carpenter starts to tailor it accordingly.

West End: At *Mother & Baby*, Kathryn Blundell studies her newest magazine cover again. It's flawed. Maybe it's the models. They look plasticky.

She puts it to one side and gets back to her proofs and emails and dealing with the stream of questions her staff keep putting to her.

But her mind keeps going back to the cover. It needs that touch of inspiration, a moment of magic, one cracking idea.

Manchester: Freelance Louise Bolotin takes a lunch break – no food, no lunch, just a break. It is interrupted when she receives an online editing test from a foreign news agency she wants to work for.

She stares at it, then starts to answer the questions and complete the assorted tasks. When she's finished, she presses *send.*

She does not have to wait long. A reply comes back giving her the result.

Thank you, Louise, you've passed.

Then it adds: 'And here's our fee rate . . . '

When she sees it, she does a little dance of joy.

North London: Health editor Lee Rodwell stops to have a sandwich, another coffee and to put a load of washing on. She reads sections of six health books. She is a judge for the Guild of Health Writer Awards and these are shortlisted. She is working through them methodically.

She transfers the washing to the tumble dryer and checks her emails.

West London: Beauty editor Liz Wilde has arrived at a salon to have her hair coloured. In her bag she's carrying some readers' questions in order to ask the expert opinion of the hairdresser, her friend. But when she sits in the chair, it's all too relaxing and she finds her eyes closing and the will to pick someone's brains ebbing away.

Mmm, another time perhaps . . .

Enfield: Editor Greg Figeon lays out the pages for the *Yellow Advertiser*'s Waltham Forest and Stratford editions. He wrote the content himself last night. Next, he checks pages for the Thurrock edition.

Twitter: From CourtNewsUK – *'Redknapp's co-accused Milan Madaric says, "I'm delighted I have today been cleared of the totally unfounded allegations of tax evasion".'*

Twitter: From Jon Slattery, media commentator, watching Leveson – *'Guido Fawkes tells Leveson that journalists are reluctant to speak out because of fears about their careers'.*

Tunbridge Wells: Radio Kent newsreader Jenny Barsby finds there's no sugar and declares: 'The day is now a disaster.'

She's a journalist. She likes to dramatise.

Luckily, she's brought some sweetener which she's guarding with her life. She says no coffee could mean a breakdown in her working practices. She discusses the merits of ordering a free Graze Box.

Barsby logs on and checks the latest headlines: *Harry Redknapp found not guilty.*

That'll be the top story for the one o'clock news then.

She rewrites cues to suit her own entertaining style and starts getting the bulletin ready.

She goes through the work inbox and thinks: 'Man, some real rubbish lands in here!'

Then she discusses shadow minister Andy Burnham's eyelashes. 'I'm told they are beautiful,' she says, 'like a cow's apparently.'

Wapping: *Sun* subs are already coming up with words to match the pictures the paper has bought of Victoria Beckham and her vomiting daughter at JFK, New York.

'IT'S POSH AND YUKS . . . Coochy, coochy goo!

Little Harper Seven had an upset tum yesterday -and left her famous mum looking more like Splosh Spice . . . Maybe Harper had eaten something Spicey . . . '

Notting Hill: At Talk To The Press, Georgette Culley books Meeka, the 17-stone pig, to appear on ITV's breakfast show, *Daybreak*, and the BBC's *This Morning.* But then there's a hitch.

The pig's owner says: 'It will be too stressful. Meeka won't be able to do all that travelling and she's never been to London.'

Culley: 'As a pig, she won't know it's London, will she?'

Owner: 'She's intelligent. London will be too stressful.'

Culley: '*This Morning* assure me you will both be welcome in the green room at the studio. She can relax there.'

'With all the other guests?'

'Yes.'

'Are you sure they'll like that, I mean, sharing it with a pig?'

'They'll be fine.'

'No, no, London's too stressful. She's sensitive.'

Undeterred, Georgette secures two magazine deals for the story.

Hollywood, Los Angeles: In her fourth floor suite, the star is probably asleep right now, her privacy shielded by the high security of the hotel on Wilshire Boulevard. But the paparazzi know where she has chosen to stay. She should rest now, enjoy her peace, because they won't let Whitney Houston rest when she wakes up.

New York City: *ProPublica* – a non-profit newsroom producing 'journalism in the public interest' – issues its daily bulletin of the stories it likes. They include:

'*The Minnesota Board of Medical Malpractice has consistently failed to disclose medical malpractice awards and discipline doctors (Star Tribune).*'

'*Current and former executives at Bain Capital and their relatives have given about $4.7 million to support Mitt Romney's presidential ambitions (The Center for Public Integrity).*'

London: '*Let's move the story along . . .* ' Every newspaper football writer is being given the same instructions by their sports editors as Redknapp receives saturation TV coverage. What's going to look fresh tomorrow morning? What's next? What's the big picture? How does it affect Capello?

The *Daily Mail* says Capello might resign but nobody else takes that seriously.

London: These days, Fabio Capello often prefers to speak to Italian football writers rather than British ones. That way he can use his native language and know exactly what he's saying.

He's never got on very well with the British press corps. He doesn't trust them. Targeting his comedy English, they pick on his linguistic imprecisions and turn them into a 'row' or a 'storm' and bury him with mockery.

He's a proud, cultured man with a history of success and he hates being treated like a national joke. He's even angrier with the FA for going over his head in demoting John Terry as England captain.

Capello's not telling anyone what he's going to do today when he keeps his appointment with his bosses, the Football Association, at Wembley.

But in his head he can sum it up in the tongue he's most comfortable with . . .

'*I giornalisti farebbero bene ad essere pronti con le penne ed i telefoni. I redattori anche. Sto per dargli il più grande titoli da secoli.*'

Anyway, it would be pointless saying that to the British football writers. They like to pretend they are a cut above the old-style hacks. Some of them think that having an occasional original thought and knowing where to put full-stops makes them a cross between an anthropologist and a playwright.

But most aren't really highbrow, not like Capello with his love of opera.

Yet they have the nerve to mock *him* when their Italian, if it exists, is a million times worse than his English. *Pah!*

CHAPTER 8

1pm-2pm
Lunch Al-Desko

'One of *Private Eye's* many contributions to Fleet Street's rich folklore is the invention of Lunchtime O'Booze as the archetype of the steam-age, pre-computerised journalist. Hacks just like him could once be found in all the pubs that lined the Street of Shame. He and his sort thrived on typewriters, telephones and beer. They have found the email revolution more challenging' – Ian Aitken, *New Statesman.*

Ask anyone to describe your average journalist, and they'll mention long lunches and heroic drinking. It does still take place. But journalism has changed. Some reporters hardly leave their chairs. They don't chat in the pub so much as email from their desk.

In some ways it's a generational thing. The older ones – raised in pre-computer days – still like to meet face-to-face. The younger ones act as if their computers were a ball and chain.

Yet if you look around the main media villages – the West End, Canary Wharf, Whitehall, Camden Town – you'll still see the art of lunching being practised by a determined minority. The best place is the Soho *quartier* marked by two exclusive clubs, Soho House and the Groucho, and two non-exclusive pubs, the French and the Coach and Horses. It is like a transposed piece of old Fleet Street, full of free-range journalists for whom *Private Eye's* Lunchtime O'Booze remains an heroic subversive, not a figure of fun.

But those are the lucky ones, and now a dying breed.

The others – the vast majority – are leading a much more humble and prosaic life. Suggest a glass of wine at lunch these days, never mind a bottle and you'll face a look of horror.

'Wine?' your companion will exclaim. 'I wouldn't dare!'

And for most, the old-style three-hour lunches are little more than an occasional aspiration, if not a capital crime.

West End: Farrah Storr is still dining at the super-cool Soho Hotel but it is hardly an indulgence. In reality it's just a posh working lunch. They even have an agenda (the antithesis of an old-style long lunch): helping *Women's Health* develop brand extensions.

Storr's giving herself one hour max. Two courses. No dessert, thank you. Water. To passers-by it might seem glamorous but it is substance over style, by working women too busy for the finer pleasures, eating against the clock, functional, serving a bigger purpose.

It's unfair to say so but it does seem a waste of a fine menu and wine list.

They can almost hear the call of their desks, summoning them to return soon.

West End: One of h er rival editors, Louise Chunn, hurries out to another favoured place, Mildreds. It's just a classy sandwich shop. She queues with the usual lunchtime crowd and doesn't have to wait too long, bringing back salad and soup to the office.

She eats over her desk, at last finding the time to study the first issue of *Women's Health* -so hers is a working lunch as well.

Chunn looks at the cover, then starts to flick through it page by page. How does it compare with her own magazine, *Psychologies*?

She identifies the obvious differences – it's younger, more about looking good and having great sex, less about deeper emotions and individual growth.

She also identifies the similarities – that they are both committed to women's personal development and therefore fighting for many of the same readers.

As someone over 50, Chunn firmly believes that looks are not – and never have been – the most defining part of being a w oman. The youthful self-confidence of *Women's Health* suggests otherwise, that womanhood is mainly about body, hair, teeth and skin.

She is thinking hard. It's not just her magazine that is under attack. At stake is its philosophy of female identity and worth.

It's California beach girl versus a walker on Hampstead Heath.

She has to defend not just sales but an idea.

An *idea*.

That's a big responsibility on her shoulders.

The Strand: Half a mile away, it is the *Women's Health* ideal of womanhood – not *Psychologies'* – that is being made flesh by Abbey Clancy, at the centre of another scrummage of press photographers.

She's a model. By definition, she is about body, hair, teeth and skin and now she has travelled from Wembley to Central London as the Lynx roadshow relocates to a prominent branch of Superdrug.

Clancy knows how to give a tabloid pose. She thrusts her slim hips forward, angles her legs asymmetrically. The cameras purr in appreciation.

A *Sun* reporter files copy to his Wapping newsroom.

'The mother-of-one stole the spotlight in yet another figure-hugging outfit, a clingy electric-blue body dress, which had temperatures soaring despite the sub-zero temperatures in the capital.'

Chunn's *idea* is under attack on all fronts.

By chance, Clancy is only a half-mile from the High Court where she and her husband, footballer Peter Crouch, have just been named among a fresh wave of celebrities who have launched legal action over the phone hacking scandal.

Tunbridge Wells: At BBC Radio Kent, Jenny Barsby makes her debut for the day reading the one o'clock news – leading with Redknapp's acquittal – and finishes with a nice bit of banter with the presenter. She likes the banter but this time it runs away with itself, with puns and *double entendres* rearing up unbidden. She fears it nearly ends up too smutty!

She starts writing up further stories from emails and discusses one about Gillingham Football Club with sport, the news editor and the 'drive' team, for later in the afternoon.

After her gym workout and brisk walk, she feels peckish and begins eating lunch at her desk. It's fajitas left over from last night. They're delicious even if they smell the place out. But before she can finish them, she is suddenly overloaded with work. She has to write up t hree stories, try for a police interview and speak to a man about his cat being shot.

She's just realised one story actually took place nearly two weeks ago. 'Police on the ball again!' she says.

She sees broadcasting legend Peter Sissons popping into the loo. He is using the studio because it has an ISDN line.

Brussels: Chris White walks back to the Place Luxembourg and meets another parliamentary official. The man pulls out an iPad and emails him a file as they stand shoulder to shoulder, then says: 'Can I buy you a drink?'

White says: 'I am not drinking.'

Official: 'One beer doesn't count.'

Not wishing to cause offence or seem unfriendly, White accepts and opens the iPad file. He starts to read it. It's about a well-known personality's business connections.

He raises an eyebrow. Is it another political set-up?

West End: For lunch, *Stylist's* Anita Bhagwandas meets the hairdressing kings, Toni & Guy, to talk about London Fashion Week.

She says: 'How can we work together, both on this and other projects?'

Again it's a business meal.

She doesn't stay long and when she returns to the office she tries to convince deputy beauty editor Sam Flowers of the joys of a Shu Uemura hairbrush – which Toni and Guy use.

Flowers hasn't tried it. She doesn't understand it. Bhagwandas calls the PR to have one sent over. She's positive she will convert her by the end of the day.

Twitter: From feature writer Amy Rowland, at *Bella* magazine in Camden Town – 'I need to buy lunch but it's TOO BLOODY COLD to leave the building.'

Twitter: From UK Media – 'Harry Redknapp trial. Police accused of leaking case to *News of the World*.'

Bath: Lunch is for wimps as far as deputy editor Paul Wiltshire is concerned. He's working through it. He is waiting for PR folk and a stray councillor to come back to them before wrapping up this week's paper. He Tweets to that effect and by magic the politician phones.

Then Wiltshire reassures a bereaved relative about the coverage of an inquest. He gets an update from the police on an armed robbery and thinks: 'Slowly getting there.'

Shepherd's Bush: After her constructive editorial meeting, Susan Watts eats a packed lunch at her desk while listening to a radio debate on the NHS bill – between campaigner Sue Slipman and politicians Baroness Warsi and Harriet Harman. For *Newsnight*, she is looking at the bigger picture. She is trying to identify the underlying arguments, to anticipate how she can develop them over the next year.

Camden Town: *TV Choice* editor Jon Peake has filled himself with too much free party food from Virgin and now he can only manage some Pret tomato soup. Olly Murs still hasn't called. No surprise there then.

West End: Lindsay Nicholson picks at a salad while reading proofs of the May issue of *Good Housekeeping* – three months ahead. Despite the snow around her home, and the cold outside the window, she is having to trick her mind into thinking *spring*.

Glasgow: At a local tea shop freelance Samantha Booth is listening over lunch to the 88-year-old man who once interrogated Nazis. It is fascinating. Everything is mentioned from lampshades made out of human skin to writing spy letters in lemon juice. It may make another feature.

Tunbridge Wells: Editor Ian Read dashes out of the *Courier* building and exclaims: 'Christ, it's cold!' He drops a suit at the dry cleaner's and gets a BLT sandwich from M&S. After the pace of the office, the queuing in the store seems interminable.

Don't they realise he's got deadlines?

During 15 minutes away from his desk, he gets hit upon twice by charity chuggers – people trying to sign him up for donations – including one youth trying to shake his hand to make him stop. Nice try, thinks Read, but he does that every day. The *Courier's* done front-page stories complaining about them.

Notting Hill: While Katie Evans is still hoping to secure the sperm donor story, the daily office discussion turns to where to get lunch. Portobello Road may sound glamorous but lunchtime options are slim. Tesco is usually the first choice, although a nice little sandwich shop has just opened in Ladbroke Grove.

Twitter: From *Press Gazette* – *'Sports reporters at Telegraph, Express, Standard, People, TalkSport, Guardian, breached court orders in Redknapp trial.'*

Petersfield Golf Course: OAP columnist Colin Dunne finishes a round of golf, thinking: 'By now Keith Waterhouse, his day's work done, would be opening champagne, having been at the keyboard since 5am. It's a very annoying thought. Guilt, my permanent companion, kicks in. I must get on with writing.'

He goes into the clubhouse and orders a sausage sandwich, saying: 'It's to top up my dangerously low cholesterol.'

When he's finished it, he returns home, plods down to the shed and forces himself to start on his golf column.

Hull: Jamie Macaskill has a sandwich at his desk and a flick through the *Sun, Mail Online* and the *Telegraph's* sports section – what he calls 'the ideal national trinity'.

He also catches up on work experience requests. They get a score a year. Last year he changed the system so they use journalism undergrads and students rather than school pupils. In his view, the youngsters don't adapt well to the office and it's hard to take them out on reporting jobs. The students are better prepared, keener and can contribute more.

Barnet: On maternity leave, *Take a Break* deputy editor Sara Ward is grateful her mum has come round to make lunch and help with the housework. Her family and in-laws all live in and around London and it's an absolute godsend. She knows colleagues – working for magazines and newspapers – who have a baby and find themselves having to move back home for family support.

Colchester: Having received 'divine guidance', Katy Evans, editor of *Soul & Spirit*, pops out for a brief walk which requires only earthly navigation along the rather ordinary route. It gives her time to consider more deeply the lengthy spiritual advice she received earlier this morning . . . *'Be inner-directed, self-referencing, and true to yourself.'*

She returns to the office and, divinely guided or otherwise, eats lunch at her desk.

Preston: As he ends his seminar, Kevin Duffy is pleased with the way the students have engaged with him. In part, he puts this down to having a good track record – he runs Duffy Media, and is making use of his 20 years as a staff journalist (including four years as a newspaper editor and two Newspaper Society awards).

Being a tutor is not what he set out to do but it has its satisfactions.

He tidies the lecture room, walks back to the admin building, files registers, does other paperwork, and prepares for the 50-mile drive back to Manchester.

Kingston: Freelance Natalie Dye is still battling with the space-time continuum and starting to feel as confused as a new Dr Who sidekick.

It is not easy to translate ideas like this into popular journalism. She breaks for lunch. She is vaguely tempted by the gym if only for a shower – she's still dressed in scruffy jeans and sweater – but fears it will be crammed with mothers of her age discussing 'Portia's likely GCSE results' while Portia is still in a buggy.

She tells herself: 'I cannot be doing with it.'

Instead she meets a girlfriend – a fellow scribe – for a quick coffee and a gossip, and tries not to dwell on her sudden pre-occupation with the paranormal.

Bristol: While others now take their turn for lunch, Heather Findlay has finished hers and is back at work and manning the ship. She interviews a woman about her experience adopting a child from abroad. It will make a feature pegged on a movie due to be released shortly.

Unemployed Ex-Murdoch Reporter: He has finished his tutoring session and now he arrives at the Job Centre, mildly traumatised by the experience and beginning to reveal his deepest fears . . .

'I'm unnerved by the excitement of the students, asking questions about celebrities I've interviewed, the most glamorous places I've travelled to, which gigs I got into for free: I feel ashamed, as if the way I exist now makes my life as a journalist a lie.

'It's how the long-term unemployed end up feeling. I avoid parties so I don't face the "what do you do?" conversations. While working on press agencies, I would lie anyway, make things up for my own amusement, tell people I was about to appear in Emmerdale, giving them the date of my appearance and a hint about my storyline.

'Now I mumble "I'm a journalist by trade". Now I want them to insult me, to say all journalists hack phones, just so I can stop talking about me; just so I don't have to use the word "unemployed". I worry that my future now will be unemployment or part-time work: it's a genuine concern that I might never work full time, in a permanent position again . . . '

He is having difficulty coping.

'If I end up back on the dole after my contract ends will I have to stock shelves in a supermarket to earn my benefits? My CV now has an injection of life because I can discuss recent work but will I again be told by Job Centre Plus to play down my qualifications and experience?'

Unemployed hack enters the Job Centre and eventually gets to see an adviser, sitting beneath a poster declaring, 'The job you want, the help you need'.

The man says: 'You need an interim job. You start from the bottom and just take off.'

Unemployed hack thinks (but does not say): 'I recall doing that 20 years ago when I was training. Now look where it's got me.'

Esher, Surrey: Freelance Robin Corry drives to Brooklands Radio, sits down in the studio and goes on air – or, in this case, the internet. It's an online community radio station.

Today, he enjoys the rare luxury of a broadcast assistant – the halfway stage to becoming a presenter – who takes care of the weather, travel reports and local information, and makes the tea. They represent the two extremes of a career – Corry, in his early seventies, and the assistant in his early twenties, in mutually beneficial symbiosis.

BREAKING NEWS . . . BREAKING NEWS . . .

Even at a local level, there is always a fresh headline and story and now Corry has a big one. He announces: 'Levi Bellfield, the murderer of local schoolgirl Milly Dowler, has been refused leave to appeal . . . '

It's a local story, and local people would be glad to see Bellfield's prison key thrown away.

Congleton: Editor Jeremy Condliffe starts pulling out subbed stories to go into their free newspaper. It's a mixture – items from the paid-fors, reinforced with some original copy.

The ad manager comes looking for a piece of lost type and says: 'Jeremy, you've seen it.'

Condliffe replies: 'I've not.'

Then someone from the Carnival Committee phones and asks: 'Jeremy, can we use your van on Sunday?'

He's on the Committee because he wrote an editorial having a go at them, so obviously they said, 'Well, you do better . . . '

Now he sighs and says: 'Yes, I suppose so.'

At least he doesn't have to write an editorial this week: one of the reporters has volunteered. It's about people objecting to planning applications on frivolous grounds, the council supporting them and refusing the plan, and then losing on appeal. It cost the local taxpayer £48,000 in costs last year.

That reminds him. He's got to email last week's editorial about phone masts to the US-based International Society of Weekly Newspaper Editors, of which he's a member (and former president). It's for its monthly newsletter, part of the global journalistic superstate which, for many hacks, overrides loyalty to mere nation states.

He has lunch: lentils, raw vegetables and fruit.

As he finishes, a reporter says: 'Jeremy, the police want us to run a page with appeals for information, photos of offenders, that sort of thing. Is that okay?'

Condliffe: 'Yes.'

Someone emails to ask if they want an agony aunt column.

Condliffe: 'No.'

He agreed to a gardening column yesterday. Free, of course, coming from a local bloke.

London: *Mint* mag's Marcus Harris looks at a few more submissions, including a scathing review of Cronenberg's latest movie. He starts arranging a fashion shoot.

He doesn't stop for lunch but finishes off a packet of biscuits he bought in Paris. He does some planning and research for the weekly podcast and tries to arrange the studio time.

Before lunch is over, the fashion shoot is finished, edited and published on the *Mint* site.

Cambridge: Cursing his lack of time, Society of Editors' director Bob Satchwell is becoming seriously overloaded. On the one hand he's been monitoring Lord Justice Leveson, trying to predict the way he is thinking. Concentration essential.

On the other, he has all his usual duties: phone calls, emails, reading.

He is trying to work through his to-do list but is repeatedly interrupted. Student journalists want interviews, conference organisers offer him invitations.

There has been no time to catch up with the national conference he is planning – only the dates are fixed at 11, 12 and 13 of November. He must announce the venue shortly.

Busy, busy, busy . . .

Shepherd's Bush: Frank Gardner goes to the BBC canteen. *Oh joy!* Its chicken korma, one of his favourites. He joins the queue with his friend Jonathan Beale, a defence correspondent. They take their plates to a table and start to eat with plastic cutlery. The fork snaps in Gardner's hand.

Damn.

The phone rings in his pocket. It's the chairman of the Ski Club of GB. As the Club's newly-elected president, Gardner sounds apologetic as he says: 'I'm afraid I haven't even seen the snow this season.'

The chairman asks: 'Frank, will you compete in the Men's Grand Slalom in Switzerland?' He adds: 'In a sit-ski, of course.'

Out of guilt, Gardner over-compensates and says: 'Yes . . . '

As the call ends, he wonders if he has made a mistake.

He checks emails and finds a press invitation to a private screening of *Act of Valour*, a new film about US Navy SEALs. It's the sort of thing he loves. He is tempted.

Rwanda: Reuters' Graham Holliday extracts his son from tennis and returns home. He catches up on emails, the latest news, but there's still not much going on from his end, although Somalia looks messy and Uganda is pushing forward with its 'anti-gay' bill.

He starts researching a malaria story for this week or early next. He has no confirmation that he'll be doing it for words, but Reuters TV want a report.

He goes on Twitter. The Rwandan head of the BBC World Service texts and they agree to meet.

'Tomorrow evening. Dinner and drinks.'

He helps his son with homework

Walthamstow: Headphones on, coffee drunk, showbiz writer Nick McGrath starts on the tedious task of typing up his Gregg Wallace transcript.

Bermondsey: Agency boss Mark Solomons nips out for a sandwich and a walk round the block and counts how many people own pit bulls. Where have all the soppy dogs gone?

West End: Having now left home in south London, freelance Chris Wheal is having a modest lunch with his 'apprentice' in Pret a Manger, next door to St Martin's. From there, people can watch the tourists in Trafalgar Square and the police preparing for this evening.

Barriers are being erected and the red carpet rolled out on the steps of the National Portrait Gallery. It's for a visit from the Duchess of Cambridge, Kate Middleton.

The pictures desks have been alerted. The photographers have been assigned. They will turn out in force. The barriers will keep them at bay.

Wells: Oliver Hulme has lunch on the run, gambling his health on a chicken pasty marked 'reduced to clear'. Back in the office, he spends the best part of an hour trying to get information out of the Patent Courts. It's hopeless. He gives up, has a coffee and turns to other stories, including one about a policewoman who has won two bravery awards.

He finishes off the nostalgia page by using a pre-First World War photo found during an office move. It was buried at the back of a cupboard. Now, a century after its creation, it will see the light of day again and perhaps triggers some old memories.

Cambridge: As Prince Charles starts his speech, a voice recorder goes off and starts relaying his words straight back at him, causing confusion. Is it a joker – or a protestor? No . . .

All eyes, including the Prince's, turn towards reporter Raymond Brown. He curses under his breath as he can't find the button to switch off his handheld machine. He backs out of the room leaving the Prince to continue in relative peace.

Brown feels embarrassed but the royal press officer says: 'Oh, don't worry.'

He returns and picks up where he left off.

He interviews education minister Michael Gove for video and print. The mischievous Brown asks him: 'Will you scrap Ofsted, Minister?'

Then he adds: 'What will be your legacy, Mr Gove?'

Gove laughs uproariously. As a former *Times* journalist, he knows the score.

Brown does a piece to camera, topping and tailing the video, and watches as Prince Charles finishes and leaves for his helicopter. The blades start spinning and it carries him off over the horizon as quickly as it delivered him.

West End: Salvation in human form arrives for *Mother & Baby* editor Kathryn Blundell, still seeking inspiration for her cover. It's in the shape of Mark Frith, the new creative director at Bauer Media. He's a legend, the man behind the success of *Heat* magazine.

They sit together and study the chromalin print-out. She says the model is too plasticky.

Blundell has been confirmed as editor for only three months and now she and Frith start to examine the coverlines . . .

53 summer baby health tips
Weaning guide
Your sex life -how to get it back.

They ask each other: *Are they as effective as they could be?*

They start to brainstorm, scribbling alternatives, trying different colours, testing them for size, shape and impact. Will they work on the W. H. Smith's shelves?

Manchester: On his trip from London, *Estates Gazette*'s Damian Wild has not stopped meeting and talking to people. Now he eats lunch at breakneck speed while chatting to a PR. He has pasta, which he can fork down quickly. She has strawberries, another posh fast food.

Shepherd's Bush: The BBC's Robin Lustig grabs a sandwich and logs in at his desk. Sure enough, *The World Tonight* team wish to go big on NHS reforms and see what they can get from Syria.

They also want to find an Argentine ambassador to talk about the Falklands dispute.

Lustig thinks: *They'll be lucky.*

Camden Town: As she tries not to drop chicken wrap into her keyboard, further nourishing the germ colonies flourishing on most office desks, *Take a Break*'s Julia Sidwell receives a story about someone finding a dead bird in a bag of salad. She says: 'Ugh, that's almost put me off.'

She moves swiftly on to the next email, hoping for something less unappetising. 'Oh no! This one's about a sex addict.'

As commissioning editor, she phones an agency to ask how the bidding on a story is coming along. Still no update. She'll have to wait.

She pops out to get some air – well, more like traffic fumes – with a stroll across the Regent's Canal and round Camden Market only to come back to lots more emails. She knows most will be useless but there may be the one gem.

On the desk opposite, feature writer Laura Brown receives a call back from someone she wrote to weeks ago.

'Thanks for ringing,' she says, trying not to sound too eager. 'I can be with you this afternoon. Yes? Okay, I'm on my way.'

She collects an office camera and heads out with a contract, to sign up the interviewee and get the story in the bag.

Leeds: Up to now his work placement has been busy and packed with interest, but today is proving quiet for student David Spereall at the *Evening Post*. He's seen the Redknapp news but it's being covered from London. There's not much he can do.

He writes up a few press releases – the dreaded 'churnalism' – then helps with proofreading.

He just wants to be involved.

Southbank: *Marie Claire*'s Helen Russell fetches soup from the shop at the foot of the Blue Fin Building and carries it back to her desk. She does a third sweep of her email inbox and checks the magazine's website for content, stats and ad placements.

She stays focused even during lunch.

West End: Having resisted some delicious desserts, Farrah Storr arrives back at *Women's Health* and finds she can't escape temptation that easily. A celebratory Bakewell Tart awaits her.

Their picture editor and in-house baker has made it for the team. The pastry is low-fat and the jam sugar-free, and Storr takes a bite and says, 'You'd never know.'

She gets congratulatory emails from two of her favourite fellow editors welcoming her elevation to their ranks: Alex Bilmes at *Esquire,* and Lindsay Nicholson at *Good Housekeeping* – who gave her a first job as a features writer.

Can the day get any better?

Worcester: As five crows scrap noisily in the trees outside, inter-departmental rivalry breaks out at the *Worcester News*. Head of content Steph Preece emails the sports desk: 'The sports list may be good – but the news list is better!'

To drive home the point, she adds: 'We've got murders, new high schools, high street revamps, Asda latest, and taxis failing spot checks – all in south Worcestershire!'

Well, sports can hardly match that.

Clutching her print-out, she marches in for the day's second editorial conference.

West End: Freelance Chris Wheal arrives at the office of *Post Magazine* – so-called because it was the first magazine ever sent by penny post. He is on maternity cover three days a week.

He shows his apprentice, Rhian, around and she talks to a reporter, the features editor and the online editor about their work. They describe how they got into journalism.

One says: 'I started subbing at the *Daily Mirror* as a 17-year-old in my school holidays.'

It's an eye-opener for everyone to hear that.

West End: Feeling saintly after her gym session, Gill Hudson follows up with a big mixed-salad at her desk in *Reader's Digest.* She brought it from home because it saves time nipping out to Waitrose, saves money and saves guilt from clearing rotting vegetables from the fridge at the end of the week.

Having finished the salad, she sits for a while, then notices she's still peckish. What to do? Ah well, she nips across to Waitrose anyway and returns with some chocolate.

Work resumes.

She gets first sight of the running sheets of the March issue. She thinks they look good.

She reads through an opinion piece for the next issue and decides it needs sorting, so she sorts it with some rewriting. She approves some more April spreads.

The City: Having been at his desk for four hours without moving, except to wash his coffee cup and fill it with water, Alan Burkitt-Gray reckons it's time to stretch his legs. He sets off on a walk – past St Paul's to Cheapside, then back along Newgate Street. He buys the new issue of *Private Eye* from a shop in Carter Lane.

It's not just humorous, it's full of inside gossip and business scandals which have not appeared in the major newspapers.

Back in the office, he checks emails. He's got dozens of requests for meetings at the Mobile World Congress, coming up in Barcelona, and files them away so he can select the best when he has time. He's too busy to do it now. He continues subbing more features while eating a sandwich.

He also checks stats for their new iPad app – Global Telecoms Business went live on the Apple app store two days ago, with 2011's two last issues and an annual already up there, free.

He will upload this latest issue as soon as it's done.

Hammersmith: At *Brand Republic,* Arif Durrani talks to two journalist/producers who are creating graphs and images to accompany his interview with the *Economist's* Andrew Rashbass. Two years ago these roles didn't even exist. Today, they're among the busiest journalists on the floor.

Now they are turning reams of data into an interactive graph and mocking up other images. It is impressive stuff.

He takes a lunch break.

He makes a quick visit to the gym opposite, then goes into Starbucks and buys a sandwich, fruit juice and cappuccino.

Enfield: Having laid out numerous editions, multiple title editor Greg Figeon tells his colleague he is dying for a cup of tea. *No reaction.*

He points out that he has made the most tea today. *Nothing.*

He says it's only fair that people take it in turn to get the tea in. *Silence.*

He waits and he waits, rather like the man on the beach in an old Guinness TV advert. His colleagues also wait, knowing from experience who'll be the first to crack.

Snap!

In the end Figeon can't stand it any longer. He gets up, stomps into the kitchen and makes tea again, slamming mugs down on desks, giving glares and saying: 'There's a serious lack of a round system in this place.'

Shepherd's Bush: Back in the edit suite, Frank Gardner thinks their piracy film for the BBC *Ten O'clock News* is coming together. He needs to get as much of it cut before the programme editor comes in to give his gladiatorial thumbs up . . .

Or thumbs down.

Santa Clarita, California: Lunchtime in Britain coincides with pre-dawn for BBC correspondent Peter Bowes who has just woken up on his ranch amongst the canyons. From his window, he can look out at the black shapes of the Santa Susana Mountains, outlined against a pale sky.

He begins by checking his emails.

He turns down an LA blogger's offer to cover the Grammy awards. Yes, Whitney Houston will be attending but at this point it seems a relatively routine assignment.

He has an exchange with a BBC editor over coverage of the TED (Technology Entertainment Design) conference in Long Beach next month.

There is no significant news breaking today. He takes a quick glance at local TV. All quiet, which is good, as he's due to drive down the freeway for an appointment.

He's got to go to Hollywood.

Brighton: Technology freelance Adam Oxford finishes his column for a South African mag, then has lunch as his desk. Again. He's no time for a break. He's straight into putting together an experiment with some hardware for an article tomorrow.

He chases two PRs for kit promised for a review and a photo shoot, also due tomorrow – both have let him down.

Then, as the US wakes up, it's time to check the news wires for breaking technology stories from the other side of the Atlantic.

Delhi: Helen Roberts has sent out another story proposal to newspapers and magazines, this one about an Indian child actor, Rubina Ali, a female star of *Slumdog Millionaire*. Rather fittingly, she has moved from a slum into a new flat.

Now the replies start to come in. Newspapers want to see her in residence and unpacked before they use it. But magazines, especially in Dubai, like the feature idea as it is.

Wapping, London: Inside News International, if you are taking the Murdoch shilling, it might seem churlish, even subversive, to snigger too obviously over *Private Eye*. Today's new issue supplies more gossip and jokes about the beleaguered News International empire.

Everybody reads it even on Murdoch's *Sun* and *Times,* if not always conspicuously.

And it's not just for the scandals exposed in the column, *Street of Shame*.

Whiling away their lunch, editorial staff indulge their secret pleasure, a piece of nonsense fiction about an octogenarian boss having a Leveson nightmare while snoozing in front of his young Chinese wife.

'*His beautiful young wife from the distant land of Ping Pong gently roused the multi-billionaire . . . 'Wake up, Lupert!'*

Dining al-desko – and with water not wine – has taken over journalists in a way which would have had the legendary Lunchtime O'Booze spinning in his grave 30 years ago. Here's an analysis of lunches of some journalists in this book.

Restaurant: *Women's Health*'s Farrah Storr (no dessert, back at desk at 1.45); Professor Peter Cole, three colleagues and the *Daily Mail*'s Jayme Bryla (at Iguana, Sheffield, one glass of wine each).

Salad: *Good Housekeeping*'s Lindsay Nicholson; *Psychologies*' Louise Chunn; *Reader's Digest*'s Gill Hudson (homemade, chocolate, gym); *Congleton Chronicle*'s Jeremy Condliffe (lentils, raw veg and fruit).

Soup: *Marie Claire*'s Helen Russell (from cafe below office); *TV Choice*'s Jon Peake (*Pret* tomato); Sharon Marris, *Kent and Sussex Courier*.

Sandwich: *World Tonight*'s Robin Lustig; *Kent and Sussex Courier*'s Ian Read (BLT from M&S, two Scotch eggs, Kit Kat, Vitamin C tablet); *Take a Break*'s Julia Sidwell (chicken wrap); *Brand Republic*'s Arif Durrani (Starbucks, with fruit juice, cappuccino and gym); Health editor Lee Rodwell (at home); Vienna's Mike Leidig (with bowls of cereal); freelance Colin Dunne (sausage, at golf club).

Walk and sandwich: *Hull Daily Mail*'s Jamie Macaskill (also a cigarette); *Global Telecom*'s Alan Burkitt-Gray; Society of Editors' Bob Satchwell; *Soul & Spirit*'s Katy Evans; agency boss Mark Solomons (counting pit bulls in Bermondsey).

Curry: BBC's Frank Gardner (BBC chicken korma); Delhi freelance Helen Roberts (chicken tandoori).

Dubious: Cambridge's Raymond Brown (crafty cigarette); *Mint*'s Marcus Harris (old biscuits from Paris); Stratford 's Matt Wilson (stinky battered sausage and chips).

Beer: Brussels correspondent Chris White (several, plus wines later 'out of politeness').

Coffee/tea: Freelance Natalie Dye (meets friend, gossips); *Yellow Advertiser*'s Greg Figeon.

Snatched: *Estates Gazette*'s Damian Wild (pasta); freelance Adam Oxford; *Wells Journal*'s Oliver Hulme (chicken pasty); BBC Radio Kent's Jenny Barsby (last night's fajitas).

Nothing: *Bath Chronicle*'s Paul Wiltshire (bacon sandwich earlier); freelance Louise Bolotin (lunch break without lunch).

Other: *Newsnight*'s Susan Watts (packed lunch); freelance Nick McGrath (cheese on toast); *Telegraph*'s Malcolm Moore (in China, three dishes, soup and rice for two, £2.40, and oranges),*Women's Health* team (giant Bakewell tart).

Considering they are a driven group of people, surprisingly few find time to go to the gym. The exceptions are *Reader's Digest*'s Gill Hudson; *Brand Republic*'s Arif Durrani; *Congleton Chronicle*'s Jeremy Condliffe; BBC's Frank Gardner (pre-work); freelance Natalie Dye (after work, fleeing from the space-time continuum).

CHAPTER 9

2pm-3pm
Game On

'Pip-pip-pip-pip-pip . . . BBC News at two o'clock . . . The Tottenham Hotspur manager Harry Redknapp has been cleared after a trial lasting two weeks . . . David Cameron has insisted there is widespread support for the Government's health care bill . . . The comedian Steve Coogan and the footballer Paul Gascoigne are among the latest victims of phone hacking to have settled their cases against Rupert Murdoch's newspaper group . . . '

Helmand: After steak and mash, Quentin Sommerville turns in for the night. Reporters get used to the best and the worst of accommodation, from a hayloft to a seven-star hotel. A military tent is tolerable, falling somewhere in between. It's early evening but he had a 4am start and it's been a long, demanding day. Tomorrow he will be up at the crack of dawn.

As he rests his head, he's unhappy with the material they've got up to now. It is not strong enough to make a radio or TV package. The Afghanis are too suspicious of the camera. He wants them to open up. He'll have to push them, deploy his charm, gain their trust.

A trip's productivity needs to be balanced against its risks. This operation is dangerous – the three explosions prove that – and anyone from the BBC is a high-value target, never mind Sommerville, probably the best-known name reporting from Afghanistan. There is no point in risking him for limited return.

Two years earlier a bomb killed *Sunday Mirror* reporter Rupert Hamer and seriously injured his photographer, Phil Coburn.

First thing tomorrow, Sommerville will discuss it with the Kabul bureau which will consult London and weigh up the pros and cons. Then a decision will be made as to whether he should carry on.

Tunbridge Wells: By now, the *Courier*'s pages are starting to be set and Sharon Marris looks with irritation again at the words over her Afghanistan piece – '*14-year-old terrorist's face still haunts me*'.

She says to editor Ian Read: 'I hate that headline.'

He wrote it himself and replies: 'It's brilliant – I'd read that.'

She says: 'But his face doesn't *haunt* me. It gives the wrong impression.'

In the end, Read tells her: 'Okay, you come up with a better one and I'll change it. Make sure it fits.'

Marris spends the next few minutes staring at the page. She's a reporter, not a headline writer, and she's struggling.

Then Oliver, the reporter sitting next to her, notices that one of her Afghanistan photos has been cropped badly. It's too tight. Now it's his turn to mention it to Read and it is sent back and someone zooms it out a bit so it regains its impact.

Marris is pleased for the sake of Sergeant Wes Calder, the Army photographer she travelled with from base to base, and she knows he'll be happy it survived the sometimes brutal page-laying process. He will see it online.

But she still can't think of a better headline.

Think, think.

Burma: Darkness has fallen over the town of Laiza but, undeterred, the Telegraph's Malcolm Moore climbs back into the car with photographer Adam Dean. They set off and the headlight beams cut through the blackness as they drive into the countryside.

Then they see lights and activity ahead. They pull up.

They have arrived at the first of three camps for internally displaced people.

He and Dean get out and while one starts interviewing, the other takes pictures of some of the people who have fled the fighting. Living conditions are terrible. They're sleeping in plywood boxes.

The journalists go to a military hospital, and there the scenes are equally shocking.

Moore notes: ' . . . The victims of the fighting lay on mattress-less beds. Four men, who had tripped enemy land mines and lost their feet, were waiting for prosthetic limbs.'

He wants patients' details, for authenticity.

'What's your name?'

'Kumbau Naw Mai.'

'How old are you?'

'Twenty-nine.'

'What happened?'

'I was peppered with shrapnel.'

With touching naivety, the wounded man tells Moore: 'The enemy uses its strength of numbers, advancing line after line and firing large mortars. Sometimes we creep up on them, shoot and run. Sometimes we wait for them to come to us and then open fire.'

Their tactics are primitive.

Moore and Dean return to their car and drive on and this time reach the Jayang camp, as big as a small town. Here they find 6,000 people living in huts woven from bamboo, surviving on two cups of rice a day.

Again he asks for full details.

Name: Maran Hkawn Nan; Age: 35. Children: three – 'they are always hungry.'

She left her home, a four-day walk away, after Burmese soldiers began arresting men in her village.

Moore listens as she describes the horror.

'They think we are all rebel fighters. We heard the men they took screaming and we do not know where they are now.'

Moore nods, scribbling further notes. Dean takes pictures. The *Telegraph* duo are gathering material which is not just powerful but of international importance.

Stratford-upon-Avon: Trainee Matt Wilson leaves the office and walks briskly down to the town's railway station. He is checking out work being done on an embankment by offenders sentenced to community service. They're supposed to be tidying it up.

On his way back, he feels hungry and is tempted into buying battered sausage and chips. He returns to the newsroom and, as he starts to eat it at his desk, his colleagues wrinkle their noses and say: 'God, that's disgusting.'

The smell pervades the atmosphere. They want to open a window but it's too cold.

Notting Hill: At Talk To The Press, a young couple contact writer Georgette Culley.

They explain that they are moving their wedding forward to this weekend so the bride's terminally ill mum can see her on her big day. Then, after the mum's died, they will look after the bride's younger siblings.

It is a story of ordinary people acting selflessly. During the interview, Culley is on the brink of tears.

She offers the story to real-life magazines.

By now all three phone lines are ringing at once. A newspaper wants to know about the sperm donor 'lesbian double impregnation' story. They're sounding impatient.

'Is it happening or not?'

Katie Evans tells them: 'We definitely hope so.'

Overseeing this frenetic operation, Natasha Courtenay-Smith isn't just a journalist but an entrepreneur and businesswoman. Now she checks Google analytics to monitor visitors to the TTTP website and see how much the daily advertising spend is.

After leaving the *Daily Mail*, she set up the agency. But while some of her competitors have since folded, she innovated and flourished.

She has self-published a book, *A Guide to Success in Real-Life Journalism*, and regularly addresses students and other audiences.

Bermondsey: Mark Solomons receives an email from a p al who has been arrested over phone hacking. It says: 'I h ope I ge t the same jury as Harry Redknapp.'

Solomons laughs.

He wonders if he should follow Redknapp's example and set up a Monaco bank account in the name of his dog, Dandy62.

Now it is paperwork time.

He starts to update cuttings, sends out invoices and reminders to late payers – notorious in the media – and goes through recent payments to update the books and VAT files, and check the bank balance.

How would he describe his day up to now?

In his colourful language, he says: 'We do the usual alchemy thing with a couple of science stories – turning crap into gold – and I turn round a release for PR companies who have us on a retainer. We've been trying to think of a pun about people who stop on motorways to have a wee. Some kind of link between peed and speed perhaps.'

Is it satisfying work?

He says: 'The Pulitzer Prize will have to wait for another couple of days. Between the two partners of Specialist News, we have five teenage children. We need the cash.'

He updates a client's Twitter and Facebook pages. It's a contract with a well-known online brand and it may not be why they came into journalism 30-odd years ago but it pays more than newspapers.

They also check Factiva, Google News and online newspaper sites to see who has used their copy either with permission or without.

They'll send invoices to what Solomons calls the TOGS (Thieving Online Gits).

Press Gazette Online: '*Sports reporters covering the Harry Redknapp tax evasion case are alleged to have breached court orders on six separate occasions – and the Attorney General's Office has confirmed investigations into two of those breaches.*'

Santa Clarita, California: As dawn breaks over his ranch, the BBC's Peter Bowes walks his dogs and looks at the sky. He reckons it will be a dry morning despite a wet forecast. That's good. The roads will be far better for the commute to Hollywood. Bowes thinks LA drivers can't deal with rain.

Shepherd's Bush: Robin Lustig arrives to take the chair at a seminar on Iran, which is being held by staff of the BBC College of Journalism. He is pleased to see familiar faces including Sadeq Saba, the head of the BBC Persian service, and James Reynolds, the Iran correspondent.

Will there be war over Iran's nuclear ambitions?

He listens as his two old friends give some fascinating insights into the current tensions.

This is the BBC at its most impressive, drawing on its deep resources, like a quasi-nation state.

Sheffield: With the student seminar at an end, Professor Peter Cole takes the *Daily Mail*'s young sub-editor Jayme Bryla for a late lunch. They go to a mid-market restaurant, Las Iguanas.

They are accompanied by three course leaders from the journalism department – Marie Kinsey, former BBC radio and TV financial journalist; David Holmes, former head of news at BBC Sheffield; and Bill Carmichael, former news editor at the *Yorkshire Post* and online news editor at the Press Association.

Over the Latin American-style cuisine, they talk about life on the *Mail* and Paul Dacre's prominent role in the Leveson Inquiry. Cole orders a bottle of wine. They have one glass each.

Cole is a liberal, not a natural fan of the *Mail*'s right-wing attitudes, but he is diplomatic and polite, and an unspoken truce is usually sustained on these occasions.

Bryla explains that this is part of a bigger trip he is making. Tomorrow, he is due in Preston, to speak to more journalism students, this time at the University of Central Lancashire.

It is like a *Daily Mail* ambassadorial tour.

Stedham: Sprightly columnist Colin Dunne has returned to his small cottage overlooking the village green and is esconced in the garden shed, at his keyboard, forcing himself to write. Suddenly, the muse overtakes him and the words start to flow.

Tappity-tap, tappity-tap.

He is working on his golf column for older people. He's even thinking up some new humorous images – about matching a four-hour game with a one-hour bladder, and picturing the golf course filling up with the sounds of whistling hearing aids, ticking pacemakers, and creaking tin knees and hip joints.

He reads it back to himself and thinks: 'Not bad . . . '

His fingers return to the keys, about to continue, when the telephone rings and he mutters: 'Excuse for a break – that's a relief.'

It's his friend and neighbour, John Dodd, another Fleet Street veteran who can't give it up. He's having problems with his *Daily Express* column.

Dunne says: 'It's obvious what this call is, Doddy.'

'What?'

'Distraction technique.'

'Oh?'

'Yes, writers hate writing. You're trying to put it off.'

'Am I?'

'Yes.'

'Really?'

'Yes. See, you're doing it now.'

'Doing what?'

'Putting it off.'

'Am I?'

'Yes, stop it!'

'Stop what?'

'Oh, it's pathetic.'

'What is?'

Having continued along these lines for some time, Dunne finally ends the call. He goes back to the keyboard but the muse has flown and he blames Dodd. He decides he needs tea to lubricate the creative cogs. He goes up the garden path to the kitchen, drinks two mugs, then has to trot to the loo.

He thinks: 'Gawd, I'm now locked into tea-wee loop. I could be trapped in it for years.'

He tips a third mug down the sink, and rings his friend Andrew, a columnist for the *Radio Times.*

'Hello, Andrew.'

'Hello, Colin. Trying the old distraction technique, are we?'

'Er, er . . . you swine!'

The call ends sharply and Dunne gets back to the keyboard.

Hull: At the *Mail*, the executives file in for the afternoon editorial conference. It's a quick run through the news list because editor Neil Hodgkinson already knows the main stories. They have two splashes lined up, one for Hull and one for the East Riding edition.

The first is about the number of parking tickets handed out in the city, almost 2,000 a month. Traders say it is scaring shoppers away.

The other is about e-fits of two well-heeled crooks targeting the elderly in Beverley.

Assistant editor Jamie Macaskill says: 'They are okay, but not earth-shattering.'

They've had a run of strong stories recently – a man is still missing after a night out in town; a high-profile murder conviction; and an 11-year-old boozer which made the *Sun* splash.

Camden Town: Agony aunt Katie Fraser is growing more worried. The depressed woman is still missing. No one can get in touch with her. Imaginations run riot and some fear the worst.

Meanwhile, Fraser gets a volunteer willing to befriend the other depressed woman who emailed her.

The woman, Laura, says: 'Katie, I'd be delighted to help out. I know what a terrible illness depression can be and how frustrating it is when nothing seems to work. When I was at my lowest I could have done with someone to talk to who would listen without judging. Friends and family were supportive, but I didn't want to burden them with my thoughts. Please give this woman my email address and tell her I am here for her whenever she wants me.'

Fraser loves working with such warm-hearted, caring people.

But she is still anxious about the missing woman.

Tunbridge Wells: Courier editor Ian Read scrutinises a story and reckons it's libellous. It defames a local nightclub. He rewrites it. Then he sends through the splash with his favourite headline of the day, The Million Pound Drop.

The council will hate it but it is fair without being deathly dull. He's got newspapers to sell.

When he puts through his fifth front page, he looks up and says: 'Now we're rolling . . . '

Just to be polite, a reporter asks: 'Anyone want a coffee?'

Everyone, including Read, replies: 'Yes!'

There is much glee as he is lumbered with a huge round and plods defeatedly into the kitchen.

Enfield: The injustice of tea rounds is something familiar to Greg Figeon but he is trying to move his life on. He mustn't be bitter.

He selects and lays out the letters page for the *Barnet Press* and signs off some other pages. He fancies another tea but keeps it to himself. He's playing his colleagues at the waiting game. It's someone else's turn. He must not expose his weakness again. Ever.

Task Force Helmand HQ: While Quentin Sommerville is having an early night in his tent, press chief Mackenzie is just sitting down to dinner in relative comfort. He's got a good appetite and, like Sommerville, he's impressed when the meal is served up.

He tucks in and says: 'The food here is great!'

Bristol: Medavia's Heather Findlay sends out two story teasers to the real-life magazines – the woman stalked for her knickers, and a woman disfigured by a bacon sandwich.

Will there be any takers?

She resists the temptation to call too early to chase them up. Instead, she stares at the phone, willing it to ring, and impatiently keeps clicking *refresh* on her email.

She waits. And waits . . .

Camden Town: Jon Peake is working on cover lines for *TV Choice*. It is the UK's biggest selling magazine, shifting 1,304,000 copies a week. But he's not complacent. Its lead over rival *What's on TV* is down to 53,000.

They are at each other's throats, the frontline of a war between two multinational giants – the German company, H Bauer Publishing, and IPC Media, a subsidiary of Time Inc, based in New York.

Both Bauer and IPC claim to be the UK's biggest magazine publisher. As it depends on how you add it up, both are right.

It seems quaint, even odd, that people still buy TV listings magazines these days when you can get one free in a newspaper or on screen. But people do buy them, and in *TV Choice*'s case – at 42p – it is mainly a female, working class audience who don't bother with newspapers or computers.

With their tastes in mind, it focuses on the soaps.

Because of the cover's importance – it is absolutely crucial – Peake works on it with his publisher, Liz Watkinson. Then the managing director David

Goodchild drops by, as does the head of marketing, Julia Toni. They all make suggestions.

They agree on the main story – *EastEnders*, in which a gangster called Derek hires a hitman to kill Roxy Mitchell.

But how should they tell it? Finally they go for a less in-your-face version. They see it up on screen.

It looks strong.

'Okay.' says Peake, 'we'll go with that.'

Oh, he is still waiting for Olly Murs.

His manager promised a call. Peake looks at the clock and sees this one going to the wire.

Daily Star: At their Thameside headquarters, editor Dawn Neesom and staff have come up w ith a cracking wheeze. It combines scandal, football and a picture of a hot woman in a slinky dress.

They are already designing page one with the blurb ABBEY AND CROUCHIE'S PHONE HACK HELL.

They are linking Abbey Clancy's Lynx launch with today's High Court proceedings regarding her and her husband, Peter Crouch.

Reporters Gary Nicks and Aaron Tinney are tapping out the copy, saying that the couple *'fear their most intimate secrets were hacked by the News of the World . . . They were named among a fresh wave of celebrities who have launched legal action over the hacking scandal . . . James Blunt, footballer Kieron Dyer, UKIP leader Nigel Farage, Eimear Cook, ex-wife of golfer Colin Montgomerie . . . it means 56 cases are now outstanding . . . '*

Neesom likes that. It's tailored just right for her male, working class readership.

Is sensationalism a good or bad thing?

Back in the late 1940s, *Mirror* editor Silvester Bolam was asked that question and gave this response: 'We believe in the sensational presentation of news and views, especially important news or views, as a necessary and valuable public service in these days of mass readership and democratic responsibility. We shall go on being sensational to the best of our ability.'

Arthur Christiansen, then editor of the *Daily Express*, put it lik e this: 'We have always got to tackle the news emphatically, with boldness and confidence . . .

'Make the news exciting even when it is dull. Make the news palatable by lavish presentation. Make the unreadable readable. Find the news behind the news. Find the news before it has happened.'

These principles still hold true.

Unemployed Ex-Murdoch Reporter: Leaving the Job Centre, he blogs: *'Bus home. I bought an all-day bus pass because it saves £1.10 so I can buy Chaplin some cat food: not the stuff he likes. I make a reminder on my disconnected mobile phone to sign on tomorrow.*

'I've no idea if I'll receive any more money after my benefits were suspended but I have to find out.'

He is starting to sound defeated.

'I used to visit the Job Centre as I would approach an interview, dressed smartly, feeling or feigning confidence, and with the expectation of being taken seriously. Within weeks I'd arrive with unkempt hair, an anxiety that would only pass once I'd signed on and be acutely aware that I was going to be patronised and even insulted.

'I was asked by a Job Centre adviser if I hack phones. This adviser, it turns out, ran a pub frequented by journalists on my first paper, when I was an eager trainee with a bright future of school fetes and amateur theatre reviews ahead of me.

'I remember this time with fondness. I remember myself with fondness, how I thrilled at seeing my byline, celebrated with a pint after my first splash, stroked the wax seal on my National Certificate Exam (of the National Council for the Training of Journalists) qualification with ridiculous pride.

'My adviser remembers things differently. "Some of those journalists were right up themselves," he says, as I take his pen to sign on. I don't even carry a pad and pen anymore. Over the nine months of unemployment my confidence has taken a kicking: I've argued with politicians, done a thousand death knocks, convinced hesitant interviewees to tell me the most intimate details of their lives but now I listen and nod as I'm shown the sort of contempt people assume is aimed solely at those supposedly unwilling to work.

'Unemployment is a great leveller.'

Delhi: It is evening and darkness has fallen across the Indian capital although the streets are still full of life and noise, people and traffic. Helen Roberts is starting to wind down. But the UK newsdesks don't give a moment's thought to the time difference and her convenience.

They are just getting into top gear and dropping emails into her inbox: 'Can we see more pix of the conjoined twins? We like it. Send all you've got . . . '

West End: With London Fashion Week only two weeks away – as well as the New York one next week – *Stylist's* Anita Bhagwandas is attempting to get ahead with her work. But her efforts are being thwarted by ringing phones and last-minute tweaks to copy.

She looks over page proofs with beauty director Joanna McGarry and makes a couple of amendments. Then the beauty team meet with their publisher and ads team. Top of the agenda is their Skincare Awards and they discuss their plans.

Bhagwandas looks uncomfortable.

'I'm unbearably hot,' she says. With it being arctic outside, the heating is on full blast.

'Should we open a window?' she asks.

Open a window? On a freezing day like this? She feels them staring at her as if she is slipping into madness.

Lincoln: The two training teams swap over. Those who've spent the morning learning about radio interviews now enter the wham-bam realm of the television news studio.

John Thorne warns them first. He tells them to beware the dangers which lie behind the superficial glamour of lights and cameras.

He says: 'It's like Hollywood. This is where image reigns over argument and understanding.'

They look both thrilled and apprehensive.

They do more role-playing and he watches their confidence grow. Shrinking violets start to debate the most controversial of ideas – National Service-style regimes for teenage offenders; shielding youngsters from the public cry for harsher sentences.

Thorne is impressed by their eloquence.

They've jettisoned the management-speak and jargon, and he says: 'Most of these discussions are good enough to broadcast.'

Everyone is looking pleased.

He tells them: 'You are breaking down the mythology that television and radio are all-powerful and untameable barriers to effective and open public service. Now you see that media interviews can be survived, even controlled, if you are properly prepared, and willing to share your knowledge and understanding.'

His audience nod and smile. Their trust has grown and they are learning a lot.

Canary Wharf: After all the good news about the *Mirror*'s sparkling new website – people said it was a ' vast improvement' – editor-in-chief Richard Wallace is suddenly told the bad news.

'Sorry, boss . . . '

'What?'

'It's crashed.'

The site is turning into an embarrassing, public disaster. He is dismayed. He is horrified.

It had been carrying their dreams, that they could establish a stronger presence on the internet. Now his tekkies are struggling to make it even work.

Disappointment hardly describes what Wallace and everyone feels.

In the end they switch to Plan B, reverting to their old website for several hours.

The launch momentum has been lost.

MediaGuardian: The Mirror's embarrassment has not gone unnoticed. Roy Greenslade, the UK's no. 1 media blogger – and an ex-*Mirror* editor – has been keeping his expert eye on the day's developments.

He tells his large media audience: 'The new-look site, which is certainly a vast improvement on the old one, went live early today.

'And then, sadly, it c rashed. Doubtless, it's merely a h iccup – though an irritating and embarrassing one, of course. Anyway, before it reverted to its old site, I managed to get a long look . . . '

It may be 'merely a hiccup' but figures will later show the *Mirror* suffered a 31 per cent month-on-month fall in average monthly unique browsers, down to 13m in February – a fraction of *Mail Online*'s 91m; the *Guardian*'s 69m; the *Telegraph*'s 46m; and the *Sun*'s 24m.

Five months later in an internal shake-up, Richard Wallace is fired, along with Tina Weaver, editor of the *Sunday Mirror*, as the two newspapers are combined in a seven-day news operation.

Daily Express: Editor Hugh Whittow follows an old Fleet Street adage: keep it simple. It is one definition of the popular journalism he practises so deftly, and nothing could be simpler than looking out of the office window at the people beetling below, wrapped up against the biting cold.

He is deciding on the front-page splash.

Not Redknapp. Not politics. Definitely not Syria.

What he's got in mind is cheap and easy and you can't get sued for it. The worst the *Express* will suffer is a few elitist comments on the BBC's *Today* for being a tad alarmist. He gets touchy about that but those snobs don't bother the self-acclaimed 'World's Greatest Newspaper'. They're not his readership.

Yes, he's made his choice . . .

He will splash with the nation's favourite conversational opener.

The weather.

Again.

It was Whittow who helped spread the allegation that Princess Diana was murdered by other royals. He's immune to sceptics. In fact, he chortles at them in a rather jolly manner – he's a lookalike for *Downton Abbey's* Lord Grantham – and champions the most populist of causes, on Europe, crime and foreigners.

Now the weather copy is being prepared and when it's ready he's got just the headline to grab the attention of his ageing, undemanding audience:

8 INCHES OF SNOW IN NEXT 24 HOURS.
Mmm, that'll work.

Congleton: At the Chronicle, page 43 has vanished into cyberspace. Editor Jeremy Condliffe taps at his keyboard and is relieved to recover it from the backup.

He starts putting stories through to the subs for next week's free paper.

Then another page goes missing. Two in a week is unusual.

An undertaker calls and asks: 'Can you fit in a late death for me?'

The deadline was noon yesterday but they have to be flexible with funerals, what with people not knowing they're about to die. So Condliffe says yes.

Then a switch goes in his head and he thinks: 'I've had enough for now.'

He tells himself: 'I've worked solidly since 5am this morning so that's nine and a half hours already and more to go. Time for the gym.'

He's getting his kit ready when the late death arrives and he hangs back to sort that out.

Right, now the gym, really. Hope the pool's quiet.

On his way out he notices some more pages need signing off and he doesn't want to hold things up. He checks and signs them. Now he's really, really going to the gym.

West End: Kathryn Blundell runs from her meeting with creative director Mark Frith and jumps into a car. It takes her to Knightsbridge and the five-star Berkeley Hotel. There she is greeted by PRs for Lego who want to show her the company's new launch for *Duplo*, a construction toy for small children, an ideal subject for *Mother & Baby*.

She asks: 'When's it going on sale?'

PR: 'March.'

Blundell: 'You've missed the deadline.'

'Oh dear, have we . . . ?'

Brussels: Chris White is walking briskly to the European Parliament but arrives too late for the press conference on 'EU Citizenship, Homelessness and EU Free Movement'.

Someone says: 'You should have been there, Chris, because the way things are going, we'll all be homeless soon.'

They go to the press bar where White, again reluctantly, has a small beer.

Then he bumps into an official from Sinn Fein who says: 'Would you like another beer?'

White says: 'Against my will, yes.'

It turns out to be a useful sacrifice because, not surprisingly, the man has strong views on the UK's Human Rights track record.

Next White goes to the parliament's Mickey Mouse bar – that's its nickname – looking for an MEP he needs to talk to. There are none to be seen.

Mitchelstown, Co. Cork: Nicola-Marie O'Riordan notices that the newsroom at the *Avondhu* is getting busier, louder and more animated. People are rushing about, photocopiers humming, phones ringing.

She is working on several stories at once – including a literary competition and a food waste inspection initiative. She tries to follow-up some more leads but no one is answering her calls. Her to-do list begins to run out.

As it whittles down, she panics.

Walthamstow: Nick McGrath is in the middle of typing up his Gregg Wallace interview – what he calls 'transcript hell' – when a PR calls and says: 'I want to offer you an interview with one of Scotland's best-known actresses.'

'Oh yeah?'

He gives a name.

McGrath: 'Never heard of her.'

'She's going to be big.'

'How come?'

'She's playing the title role in the new Susan Boyle musical.'

It's a valiant hard-sell from the PR but McGrath says: 'I still don't fancy it.'

121

He has a strong coffee, then a quick glance at some more Leveson tweets and ponders on the punning potential of *Essex* and *ethics*. He may deploy it at some point.

He's had some good news.

Despite an overprotective PR, TOWIE's Lydia Bright is more than happy to talk about her ex, as well as personal matters such as her special subject, fake eyelashes.

Hull: Reporter Kevin Shoesmith arrives back in the *Mail* newsroom from London. He's been on a quick visit to the Afghanistan Embassy collecting a visa. He's off to join the local battalion, 1 Yorkshire, serving in Helmand. It will be his second trip there and he's excited about it.

He's also picked up his body armour today and shows it to assistant editor Jamie Macaskill.

Macaskill: 'What's that bit?'

'Ballistic underwear.'

'Ballistic underwear?'

'Yes, special protection.'

Macaskill wastes no time in sharing this technological snippet with the newsroom.

'Kevin's got ballistic underwear.'

It triggers guffaws and unseemly comments.

Shoesmith can't wait to get on that plane.

Tunbridge Wells: BBC Kent newsreader Jenny Barsby is working through a list of stories for her bulletins. She calls the police and asks for an interview on this morning's metal raids.

The press officer replies: 'It's too late.'

Next, she rings the man with the shot cat but he doesn't answer, so she texts him instead.

Then she queries the pronunciation of *Mandaric* -the man cleared with Harry Redknapp. She wants to get it right. She argues with the sports guy over it.

All the time she is looking at the emails which have piled up in the inbox. She discusses what she's getting rid of, saying: 'I'm deleting as I go and flagging up the important ones.'

'What are those?'

'The ones that don't involve penis enlargement.'

She's also having trouble with the central newsroom 40 miles away and explains: 'The big boys in London haven't sent down the top clip and I'm having to scrabble about rewriting and changing the top story! Ooh, I hate that!'

Shepherd's Bush: During the video editing of his Somali piracy film, the BBC's Frank Gardner is keeping half an eye open for other events in his specialism, international security. A report from Kabul says the US has ruled out a Taliban office in Qatar until they divorce from Al-Qaeda. He tweets it.

While on Twitter, he notices there's a bunch of tweets addressed to him from both sides of the Bahraini sectarian divide.

A pro-monarchist declares: 'Look how thugs attack Bahrain's unarmed policemen and are called peaceful!'

A rebel one says: 'The sky is raining toxic gas. This is the crimes of Bahrain regime.'

He doesn't respond. If he did, he would trigger a torrent by return and he is too busy.

Bath: Paul Wiltshire has one more story to send through for this week's *Chronicle*. Already his colleagues are tweeting about the best stuff in the paper and he's even compiling next week's news list.

Then, the last story is sent. Hooray! He can lean back in his chair and take a breather. But not for long . . .

He approves letters for next week and discusses a supplement on the Bath Blitz of 1942 when, in retaliation for RAF bombings, Hitler targeted England's most picturesque city.

West End: At *Marie Claire*, Helen Russell holds a me eting with the commercial team to discuss a new advertising campaign. They have just secured a major fashion brand in an exclusive deal, and she plans to interview the designer next week.

Truro: With most of the editorial work completed, Kirstie Newton is able to have a quieter afternoon at *Cornwall Today*. She spring cleans her desk, returns photos to owners and answers letters. She gives a polish to their award – *Press Gazette*'s Magazine of the Year. She and her staff are rightly proud of that.

London: Freelance Jill Foster asks her interviewee: 'So you believe in angels?'

The interviewee replies: 'Yes, I do.'

It is for a feature for a national newspaper and Foster finds the subject fascinating.

She says: 'The main reason I love my job is the sheer variety of people I get to talk to – one day a forensic scientist, next a famous chef, next an angel-believing hypnotherapist. It's never dull.'

She sets up a photo shoot.

What are the qualifications of a typical freelance?

There is no such thing as a t ypical freelance, but Foster is an interesting example. She won *Cosmopolitan*'s journalism scholarship in 1997 and trained at London's City University.

She worked on the *Mirror* and the *Mail* before going freelance. She now writes regularly for several publications including the *Daily Mail, Mail on Sunday, The Daily Telegraph, Red, Fabulous, Look, Glamour* and*Weekend*. She specialises in real-life/human interest stories, lifestyle and health features.

Leveson Inquiry: The fearless Paul Staines, aka political blogger Guido Fawkes, is relishing his spell in the witness box and proving rather more successful at explosive detonation than his namesake 400 years earlier.

He does not disappoint the many journalists and politicians who have tuned in, some nervously, fearing they might get an unflattering mention.

Boom! He says the *News of the World* paid him £20,000 for pictures merely to take them off the market and curry favour with a leading politician.

Bang! He condemns the parliamentary lobby as 'an obedience school for journalists'.

Blast! He names journalists he says should be prosecuted for illegally accessing personal data.

Sizzle! He accuses one Sunday newspaper editor of personally authorising hacking and blagging.

Staines is a tease and a showman, in the flesh as well as the blogosphere. His evidence sets Twitter ablaze.

When it ends, it feels like an anti-climax.

Twitter: From Tom Harper, a young *Mail on Sunday* journalist – *'Paul Staines turns to the press gallery, winks, and says: "Enjoy" as he departs Leveson.'*

Twitter: From Selkie, of the Hacked Off campaign – *'That was entertaining.'*

Twitter: A former Westminster political aide – *'The News of the World paid £20k for a photo of me at, er, my mate's birthday party? I think somebody's having a laugh . . . '*

Bristol: Trainer Caroline Sutton fears her workshop audience is suffering from the usual early-afternoon slump. She tries to get everyone buzzing again.

She asks them: 'How would you get your stories onto the BBC's *Today* programme or *The One Show*? Come on, let's list your ideas . . . '

Defying the postprandial inertia, she prods them to come up with strategies, stimulating argument which drives the lethargy away.

She thinks it's going well.

Twitter: Freelance Clare Swatman, who works from home – *'Seriously, trying to work with four-year-old looking over my shoulder and a 20 -month-old kicking my arm, is not easy.'*

London: Mum-to-be Louise Baty opens an email, starts to read it and feels gutted. She's been working hard on her money-saving feature and thought it was good.

Now she's just got a message saying: 'Sorry, Louise, we're dropping it.'

She's more than disappointed and, alone at home, there's no one to reassure her except the faces peering from the TV she keeps switched on for company.

She tells herself: 'No point in dwelling on it – I'll try to sell it elsewhere.'

At 37 weeks pregnant – her husband, Chris Smith, is a magazine designer – she is trying to get as much work done as possible before the baby arrives.

She bucks herself up and speaks to the features editor at *Pregnancy & Birth* magazine. She writes a monthly column for them and is waiting for the go-ahead on the latest ideas she's sent over.

Then she moves on to her other feature – mums addicted to designer labels – and finishes the copy.

Leveson Inquiry: When the anti-establishment Guido Fawkes steps down from the witness box, he is replaced by an authentic establishment figure, Keir Starmer, Director of Public Prosecutions.

The DPP's evidence is eagerly awaited. It is expected to be pivotal.

Starmer says that in future there will be new guidance on the prosecution of journalists, and this will include a public interest defence for the uncovering of a miscarriage of justice.

It will be balanced against whether the journalist used threats or intimidation, or put criminal proceedings in jeopardy.

Starmer tells Leveson: 'It seems to me that it would be prudent to have a policy that sets out in one place the factors that prosecutors will take into account when considering whether or not to prosecute journalists acting in the course of their work as journalists.'

Twitter: From Ben Fenton, *Financial Times* – 'DPP announces he will publish a new interim policy on prosecution of journos & public interest defences within weeks.'

Cambridge: Society of Editors' Bob Satchwell takes careful note of the DPP's promise. It's crucial: to what extent can journalists defend their own law-breaking on the grounds of serving an overriding public interest?

Now Starmer will try to define it.

Hollywood, Los Angeles: At her Wilshire Boulevard hotel, Whitney Houston is asleep in her suite. Dawn has yet to break over the Hollywood Hills.

CHAPTER 10
3pm-4pm
Space-time Continuum

Santa Carlita, California: A white Landrover LR4 bounces down a mile-long dirt track between the walls of a canyon. At the wheel is the BBC's Peter Bowes setting off from one world, the tranquility of his ranch, to join a different one, the morning rush-hour into Los Angeles.

It's a vehicle he's chosen because it's rugged and has space for the tools of his trade: cameras, tripods, editing equipment. And, at the weekend, it can carry his bike and triathlon gear. He always buys white. The dust and dirt doesn't show as much.

He is allowing 90 minutes for the 30 miles to Universal City studios, Hollywood. The sun is up and as he turns onto the freeway he sees the traffic is heavy. But at least it's moving.

Good.

Enfield: As Greg Figeon checks pages for the *Yellow Advertiser*'s Redbridge edition, reporter Mary McConnell returns to the office from a visit to 10 Downing Street. She was accompanying the mother of Gary McKinnon, a hacker facing extradition to America.

They were lobbying the Prime Minister and she's pleased with how it went.

But if McConnell thinks everyone is going to be overly impressed, she is about to learn that the newsroom has more important issues on its collective mind: the politics of tea.

Tentatively, Figeon says: 'Who's making us all a cuppa?'

Innocently, McConnell says: 'I will.'

Figeon feels a wave of pleasure wash over him. As she serves a full round to everyone, he says: 'Mary, you're a trooper.'

Task Force Helmand HQ: After an excellent dinner, Gordon Mackenzie returns to his work. His is a 24/7 job and now he sits down for an update with his Media Operations Team. Then, over live video, he has a discussion with colleagues at the Ministry of Defence in London.

126

They talk about the BBC's new project, *Our War 2*, based on soldier headcam footage. It is a follow-up to the first series which was made, in effect, by the soldiers themselves about their constant battlefield companions – maiming and death, trauma and tears.

Journalism has many begatters.

Bristol: At Medavia, Heather Findlay is negotiating a deal for her psychic lady. An agreement is reached and she will appear in a magazine.

Bermondsey: Mark Solomons is asked to do a quick rewrite of some corporate copy for a client and bill them for an hour's work. He sets about it straightaway. It will pay the same as a newspaper page lead. Good money.

He also writes up a story ready to put out tomorrow.

Bedford: A reporter for *Bedfordshire on Sunday* heads off to court to cover the sentencing of a couple in an RSPCA dog neglect case.

West End: Lindsay Nicholson has her regular monthly meeting with *Good Housekeeping*'s other important elements – the publisher, the marketing department, the advertising and circulation teams, and, of course, the *Good Housekeeping* Institute.

They exchange commercial data and discuss issues, ideas and strategies. But, in the end, they all know it comes down to editorial, which is why her job is the most important and her voice the most powerful.

In the end, what she says probably goes.

Camden Town: At *that's life!* magazine, Adam Carpenter is editing a story about a woman who was almost killed by her brute of a husband.

He tells his colleagues: 'It is these stories that anger me the most. The guy looks a scrawny little thug. The attack is appalling – head-butting, biting, then he nearly strangles her.'

He adds: 'His sentence? Twelve months, meaning he'll be out in eight.'

Carpenter has an idea.

He says to editor Sophie Hearsey: 'Why don't we do a campaign? When someone commits a sexual assault, they are put on a register. Why not have the same thing for violent offenders? Or better still a website where women can just go on, tap in a name and see whether or not their new boyfriend has ever pummelled their ex to a pulp.

'I'd set it up myself but I don't want any of these scrawny little thugs turning up on my doorstep. Maybe there's mileage in it.'

Hearsey replies: 'Good idea, Adam. Let's think about it.'

She knows that a good campaign gets talked about and pulls in new readers.

One of her best was her Bras for Africa a few months earlier – recycling readers' bras – which got widespread praise and publicity.

Could this repeat that success?

Tunbridge Wells: After a delay, the top clip – or lead item – for Radio Kent's news arrives and prompts newsreader Jenny Barsby to utter an ironic 'Well done!'

How did Barsby build her career?

She says: 'I'm principally a newsreader at the radio station – though the job tends to involve interviewing, writing, editing and also deciding on what to run where in the bulletin.

'I did a degree in Broadcast Journalism at Nottingham Trent Uni (came out with a 1st) and started out working as an early newsreader on Invicta Radio – also down in Kent.

'I approached Radio Kent with a demo in 2000 and was offered a job pretty much straightaway – I was their Canterbury district reporter for a year and then brought back to the main office to be a principle newsreader and also stand-in presenter.

'I left the station for a year's sabbatical in Latin America in 2005 – then took redundancy. I came back and did a quick spot of freelance at Radio Cambridgeshire before becoming a press officer at the League Against Cruel Sports. Six months later, I went freelance full time and now work for four BBC local radio stations . . . London, Kent, Berkshire and Oxford. I have worked for 7 in all and also Smooth Radio London for a year too. PHEW!

'It's been a while since I did a shift that didn't start at 4am, to be honest!'

Glasgow: After a pleasant lunch with the 88-year-old anti-Nazi, Samantha Booth returns home and sits at her computer expecting this to be the busiest time of the day.

The silence is deafening.

She's dealt with a stream of questions about one of her stories and now hears absolutely nothing more from them. Do they like it? Do they hate it? She is left not knowing. She sends an email asking the question straight out: 'Do you want my story?'

No reply.

She feels ignored, exasperated.

Stedham Village: In the shed behind his cottage, septugenarian funny man Colin Dunne receives an email from a publisher who has just read the outline for his latest book: *How I Made Sex the Popular Pastime It Is Today, with the Help of Maureen Ashton.*

The publisher says: 'Hi Colin, it's definitely filthy . . . '

Dunne gets his hopes up.

' . . . and it's funny . . . '

Dunne gets his hopes up more.

' . . . but it's not for us.'

Bastard. Hateful know-nothing people.

Dunne is the author of a bestselling Fleet Street classic, *Man Bites Talking Dog.*

Still, his old golfers piece is going well – about old chaps being sent out by doctors and wives for their health, who end up eating sausage sandwiches in the club house. It's based around a golf club which flies it's flag permanently at half-mast in memory of all the members who now lie in the bunker of no return; where the survivors play for the Al Z. Heimer Cup.

He rings his son who says: 'Shouldn't you be writing, Dad?'

Serpent's tooth, son.

He gets back to work and finally completes the column. After sending it off, he takes a wander into the garden overlooking the green, hoping for casual conversation with passers-by. There are no passers-by.

Bastards.

He goes back to the keyboard. Checks emails. Four from friends. Two deaths, one memorial service, one divorce, one going into a home. About average.

It gives him a good idea to finish his old golfers' piece with a bit of dialogue.

He taps it out . . .

'Still on them statins, Charlie . . . ?'

'Aye, how's your wife's chemo going, Jack?'

Leeds: It's turned unusually quiet for student David Spereall at the *Evening Post* and after finishing the press releases, there is nothing for him to do. So he leaves early, a bit deflated.

On his walk back to Leeds station, he realises he's forgotten to bring a copy of the newspaper with him. He buys one and starts to leaf through it.

He almost gasps out loud. He wants to leap up and dance in the street. There it is – his name! Not once, but twice.

It's his first byline in the paper. Okay, so it's press releases – text book examples of churnalism -but everyone has to start somewhere. Brilliant, another stepping stone, something for his cuttings book.

Congleton: At last Jeremy Condliffe escapes the *Chronicle*'s clutches and arrives at the gym. Then he realises he's forgotten his trunks. So he does some weights, cycles for half an hour – ten miles – and rows for ten minutes.

He used to cycle every day, out on the real roads, but got knocked off last summer and lost his nerve. A witness took photos of the accident in case he needed them – obviously he did, but mainly as a downpage news story about a cyclist getting run down. He didn't name himself but generously gave the *Chronicle* a full interview.

He finds that seriously heavy music is needed on the cycling machine so he listens to a me tal band he's got for review called 4Arm. No, he doesn't understand the name either.

Cambridge: Streaming it on his computer, Society of Editors' Bob Satchwell is paying even closer attention than usual to the Leveson Inquiry. He has just listened to Keir Starmer, the Director of Public Prosecutions.

Satchwell tells himself: 'He's a firm friend of freedom of expression talking about public interest defences and the considerations that might save journalists from prosecution.'

Afterwards, he takes a late lunch break coinciding with Lord Justice Leveson's mid-afternoon break.

Satchwell's administrator, Angela Varley, says goodbye and leaves for home – they can only afford her part-time.

He goes for a walk around the block and gets a tea and a sandwich.

Then he returns to his chair just as Leveson returns to his and they both watch the next witness raise her hand and take the oath.

Leveson Inquiry: The next witness is Helen Belcher, a campaigner against trans-gender discrimination. She believes that some newspapers deliberately mock trans-gender people.

She refers to a *Sun* article headlined *'Tran or woman?'* She says it implies transsexual people elicit horror and are frauds.

It's not just the *Sun*.

She explains: 'The *Mail* publishes six times more trans stories than any other paper in this country . . . Individuals rarely want to pursue cases because they become afraid of future harassment . . .

'I would love to hear the *Sun*'s public interest justification for disclosing the gender transition of a lorry driver . . . we're asking for basic human decency and respect.'

Manchester: Louise Bolotin has brewed tea, looked at her RSS feed again and fired off four pitch ideas to an editor. Now the editor has got back to her and wants to commission her next week. She does 'a happy dance'.

Shepherd's Bush: In the demi-monde twilight of the BBC edit suite, Frank Gardner sees a headline flash up on his computer screen: 'Suicide car bomber kills 9 in Mogadishu'. As security correspondent, he could get involved. Then he has second thoughts. He needs to get this film finished. He'll leave it to the Nairobi bureau.

Enfield: Having enjoyed the cup of tea made by reporter Mary McConnell, editor Greg Figeon feels refreshed and starts laying out pages for yet another of his many titles, this time the *Barnet Press*.

Southbank: With her trip to New York Fashion Week coming up, Helen Russell has a one-to-one with her deputy to update her on things she'll have to look after while she's away. She runs through the QR (Quick Response) codes, the May issue flatplan, filming, edits, staffing and important commercial projects.

Camden Town: A deluge of proofs is starting to bury Jon Peake's desk as they emerge relentlessly from the sub-editors, who are churning them out like a

Henry Ford assembly line. His is the last stop before posterity. For him, it is the busiest day of the week, the day the bulk of the features go to press.

He casts his experienced eye over them and then signs them off one by one.

This afternoon, he is reading about everything from *Upstairs Downstairs* to *Benidorm* to *Homeland* to Gaynor Faye joining *Emmerdale*.

And that's just *TV Choice*.

In his other magazine, *Total TV Guide*, it's a bit more of the same with some added class – Nick Nolte and Dustin Hoffman. It has to justify its £1 premium price, against *Choice*'s 42p. It was set up t o challenge *Radio Times,* a British institution.

While *Choice* has been a runaway success, *Guide* sells 123,000 against *Radio Times*'s 960,000.

Central London: The seeming invincibility of Jon Snow has been exposed by the 'flu bug and now Cathy Newman is preparing to present *Channel 4 News* without the iconic anchor at her side. She's relaxed enough to be tweeting the truth about her posh girl image – *'People seem surprised at my sarf London heritage . . . don't know whether to be flattered or insulted.'*

Sheffield: After lunch with the *Daily Mail*'s Jayme Bryla, journalism Professor Peter Cole returns to his department and holds a planning meeting with the course leaders. It is about the annual 'field trips' for the postgrads.

They confirm arrangements – visits to the *Guardian, Telegraph*, and BBC; and a tour of the House of Commons with *Prime Minister's Questions* and then invited speakers – journalists and politicians – in committee room eight.

These London trips are popular with the students. The speakers are usually engaging, entertaining and informative.

Those who have given their time include Ben Brogan (*Telegraph*), Danny Finkelstein and Anne Trenneman (*The Times*), Simon Hoggart and Michael White (*Guardian*).

Cole usually tries to include former students who have made their mark such as Michael Savage and Rhoda Buchanan (both *The Times*), Adam Gabbatt (*Guardian*), Neil Mann (*Sky*), Mark Duell (*Mail*) and Ben Hazell (*Telegraph*).

As he says: 'They give current students hope!'

Brighton: Technology freelance Adam Oxford, having been too pushed to take a lunch break, now finds his body overruling his mind. He dozes off in front of his PC. It's the first time he's done this.

He blames it o n a v isit to the National Theatre two nights ago, an event involving giant illuminated alien heads hanging from the roof bar. He had to run to Waterloo Station for the last train and was very late getting home.

He is still recovering.

He wakes up with a start, gives himself a shake and starts editing a piece for a corporate contract.

131

West London: *How do I hi de dark under-eye circles? How do I pl uck my eyebrows?*

Year after year, beauty editor Liz Wilde gets the same questions from readers – and today is no different. People's beauty worries don't vary much.

Right now, she is planning a step-by-step shoot to illustrate her answers. The problem is finding something fresh and new.

Meanwhile, she bags up products to give to a keen 21-year-old beauty addict to test.

'Unfortunately, as a 40-something,' Wilde says, 'I can't really wear marbled nail lacquer or baby-pink lipstick.

'One of the side-effects is I've become hugely low-maintenance. I take 10 minutes tops to get ready for a night out. I s uspect the 21-year-old makes an afternoon of it.'

Bedford: After writing up various stories, Kathryn Cain looks into crime figures at local hospitals and discovers a 'shocking' number of cases where the police didn't have enough evidence to prosecute.

She sends a picture of a German number plate for the *BoS*'s John Ball's Diary section of silly things that happen to them during the week. The plates read FUCK 101.

It is unlikely to be published.

Tunbridge Wells: The proofreaders are turning their attention to the *Courier*'s own pages, having got its sister titles on their way to meet their earlier deadlines.

Editor Ian Read phones through some changes and proofs the sports pages himself. He and the sports editor debate the merit of putting the word *'Team'* above the teams on a football table.

He says: 'It's pointless. It will confuse people.'

But in the end they decide they will introduce it from next week.

Camden Town: Agony aunt Katie Fraser remains worried about the woman who has disappeared off the website. She is still not making contact.

Meanwhile, Fraser has to consider the balance of her newest column. It needs a bit of everything – one juicy letter about, say, adultery; one uplifting letter one about, say, kindness; and then a controversial subject the readers can vote on.

It's the latter she is now turning over in her mind. Finally she comes up with: *'Should I tell him I aborted our baby -yes or no?'*

She sends the question out to her registered *Take a Break* 'buddies', readers who wish to participate.

Quickly, the replies start to come in, many giving their reasoning. She chooses the best, then emails back requesting more info and, if possible, pictures.

Stratford-upon-Avon: Trainee Matt Wilson sees that an application for planning permission has been submitted for a new wind farm. It's not a strong enough story for the paper, but he bangs it up on the website.

He writes some NIBs (news in briefs) to fill the gaps in tomorrow's issue.

Then he decides to offer the metal theft article – the one involving Shakespeare's sister – to a national newspaper. He will present it to them as an exclusive. He considers the range of titles.

What about the *Daily Mail* . . . ?

Cambridge: After Prince Charles has taken flight, Raymond Brown starts driving back to the *News*'s office. On the way, the newsdesk calls to tell him a woman's body has been found in the River Cam. So he diverts and heads down there instead.

He parks up and walks to the riverside, leaving a trail of footprints in the snow. He looks round for the police but they have already gone.

There's a pub nearby and he goes in there and chats to customers. Did they see anything? Anyone know who she was?

West End: Fashion journalist Charlie Lambros arrives to see *Women's Health* editor Farrah Storr. They talk through a fashion story for the summer issue.

Storr defines the magazine's editorial personality – how fashion needs to be presented as a 'style shape-up'. It has to reinforce the front-page motto: 'It's good to be you.'

Outside the window, as they sit there discussing summer clothes, they see it has started snowing. Both of them stare at the falling flakes and feel a sense of dissonance. They say: 'This is bizarre.'

London: At *Mint* magazine, Marcus Harris has used Facebook and Twitter to call in readers' photographs for their 'My Town' project, showing how private intimacy can be found in public places.

Already the response is huge.

He thinks he could use an intern to put it into a more digestible format – he hasn't the time to even read all the emails.

Kingston: In her war with the space-time continuum, Natalie Dye has come down with an attack of paranormal writers' block. She is trying to simplify the concept for ordinary people – her readers are the socio-demographic groups C1, C2, D and E – and sometimes they are the most difficult to cater for.

She sits there, her fingers parked motionless on the keyboard, and looks round for a displacement activity.

Ah, the kitchen sink!

Like her mind, it needs to be flushed, cleared and refreshed. She gets up and starts attacking it with a plunger. After a few minutes, the water begins to flow smoothly and she returns to her keyboard hoping the space-time continuum blockage will yield just as easily.

Tunbridge Wells: It's time for Jenny Barsby to get ready for Radio Kent's *Drive* programme. After 4 o'clock she will be on air every half hour. She checks the usual news sources on her computer: police, fire, Twitter and various websites.

She discusses whether Adele's *Someone Like You* is the most played song now on TV soundtracks. A colleague wants to change TV channel but there's only one remote between three TV sets, and they have to hunt round for it beneath the piles of notes.

To add to her challenges, her email crashes – but she has time to reboot.

Barsby deals politely with a p ointless phone-call from a media company wanting to run something past them for Friday. She thinks to herself: 'For Pete's sake, it's WEDNESDAY! Stop bothering me and send a ruddy email!'

Her email crashes again.

She liaises with sports about which clip to run on the Gillingham FC story. Then she writes the rolling news sequence for the *Drive* presenter.

Her email resumes, but she doesn't trust it.

Camden Town: At *Take a Break*, features writer Becky Mumby-Croft opens an envelope, pulls out some photographs and splutters into her mug of tea. They've been sent by someone with a medical condition.

She says to her colleagues, Sian Gregory and Punteha Yazdanian: 'Ugh, these are gruesome.'

Gregory looks and says: 'It's too soon after lunch for pictures like that.'

Alongside them, their colleague Izzy Janner tries to phone a woman and says: 'That's odd – she's not in.'

'Why's it odd?' asks Gregory.

'The story's about her being housebound.'

Manchester: Having survived the drive back from Preston, Kevin Duffy returns to the reassuring familiarity of home comforts – his desk, computer, tea and a fresh packet of McVitie Digestives, which he tears open.

He resumes editing a video for a corporate client, keeping one eye on the Leveson Tweets, his jaw dropping intermittently when he catches up on the earlier Guido Fawkes evidence.

From time to time, he hits the phone, trying to drum up other work.

Esher: Also back in his home office, veteran freelance Robin Corry is pleased to see he's got replies from two people he approached earlier for their stories. They have agreed to speak to him.

One story is reassuring, the other alarming.

The first is a p araplegic woman with a touching love story. The other is a woman who was stalked by a tradesman after he'd done work in her house.

Corry emails both again, asking when it would be convenient for him to phone to conduct the interviews.

Tunbridge Wells: With her police story through, the three pages of Sharon Marris's edition at the *Courier* are done. She has also completed three pages for the main Tunbridge Wells edition and another one for the Tonbridge edition. She's been busy, as has everyone.

It's meant she's not had time to come up with an alternative headline for her Afghanistan story.

As the clock ticks away, editor Ian Read says: 'It's too late now, Sharon. Sorry, it's staying as it is.'

She gives a resigned nod. She'll have to live with it.

Read explains why he has also changed the first line of her Afghanistan diary. He says calling a flight into a warzone 'exciting' didn't sound appropriate when soldiers were dying on the ground below.

Marris nods again.

She helps proof some pages. Most are okay. The letters page, however, has so many mistakes that it has to be sent back.

She is still wondering how she can return to the warzone of Helmand. She needs to find out which units are set to go there next. Maybe they will have a Kent or Sussex connection.

She tells Read: 'I want to go back.'

He doesn't dismiss it but says: 'You'll need to make a really good case.'

Vienna: Working non-stop, Mike Leidig has been surviving on bowls of cereal during the day. Now he enriches his diet with a sandwich. He's not complaining. This is the way he likes it.

It's one task after another.

The agency is involved in a legal action over a story for a British Sunday paper and he has been translating documents.

He's also spent an hour teaching a press officer how to write for their news website.

These have been interspersed with a series of small tasks: finding out why they were not invited to a Super Bowl party at the weekend: speaking to a Belgian lawyer about a copyright case against a Belgian website; applying for a journalism grant from the EU; signing up for two internet banner partnership schemes; asking a local supermarket for a reader promotion partnership; speaking to a Salzburg picture agency about a partnership for their Salzburg online news project; and contacting the Austrian embassy in London over an advertising banner offer.

Leidig is juggling a lot of balls.

Walthamstow: Nick McGrath's fingers are clicking away at the Gregg Wallace transcript. Now he hears his six-year-old daughter dragging her friends back home from school for a transcription-busting play date. He knows he won't be able to resist joining them.

West End: At *Reader's Digest,* Gill Hudson is meeting her website team to discuss how they can upgrade it. Recently it's been severely under-resourced but now she has a more permanent staff in place. As they make a series of decisions, she says: 'Hooray. Good discussion. We have progress!'

Next, she rejects some freelance ideas. Then she prepares a report for the board.

After that she sits down with the features editor and discusses an article which just isn't holding together. She comes up with a new approach, adopting an old format: *'That was then . . . this is now'*.

It gives it a framework. It works.

She takes a quick read of the final pitch being made by the ad team. In her view, it's not quite there. She sits with them and does a fast rewrite. They like it. They send it off to meet the close-of-play deadline.

Hudson is a Gill-of-all-trades.

She says: 'I feel like a one-woman full-service agency.'

Hammersmith: When does a gift become a bribe? It's an important question. Get it wrong and journalists can find themselves on the wrong side of the law.

Now it is being asked by Arif Durrani at *Brand Republic* when he sees a reporter returning from lunch brandishing a new phone.

It's courtesy of a telecoms company. He thinks fleetingly about a recent debrief they all received on the new Bribery Act. Does this cross the line?

Durrani thinks about it. He decides it doesn't and is happy to reach that conclusion. Apart from anything else, removing all perks would make for a very miserable and officious workplace. As he says: 'God knows, we don't actually pay them enough.'

Last copy is filed through to subs for the *Media PM* bulletin, including his own Andrew Rashbass feature.

Durrani is starting to suffer from a lack of sleep – with his two sick children at home – and now the two-hour return trip he's planned to Oxford is losing its appeal. He's not going to make it to hear the speech from the *FT*'s Ben Hughes. He's sure he will understand.

Shepherd's Bush: Frank Gardner has finished cutting the piracy film – well, the short news version at least. Now they need to cut a longer version to go out on *BBC World*, the international TV channel. Then there's the radio version for Radio 4's *PM programme* and finally the online print version, with high-resolution still photos.

He's lived through a lot of changes in media technology and finds the distinction between broadcast and print journalism becoming more blurred.

Twitter: From Press Gazette – *'The Sun launches paid-for iPhone and Android app at £4.99 a month.'*

Independent: Columnist Viv Groskop has finished a piece attacking the *Sun*: 'Page 3 should have been dumped 20 years ago. The only reason it limped on is because Rebekah Brooks wanted to make a statement about not being soft as a woman editor.'

Unemployed Ex-Murdoch Reporter: Having returned from the Job Centre, he blogs: *'Home and immediately check emails . . . I look in vain and hope I'll be offered work.*

'Then I open letters and I'm relieved to find there is nothing depressing.'

He is worried over having his benefits suspended.

'It is 37 days before my employers will pay me due to contract timings and, despite urging me to take the work, Job Centre Plus now acts as if I'm a benefit cheat worthy of a Daily Express splash.'

Daily Express: Columnist Virginia Blackburn has finished her musings for tomorrow and now her provocative prose is being set on page 14, beneath the headline: 'Underage sex should never get a green light.'

All tabloids have at le ast one female columnist, usually right wing, pro-family, often catty and personal.

They are satirised in today's new issue of *Private Eye* through yet another of its invented Fleet Street characters . . . 'Glenda Slagg, Fleet Street's Snow Queen'.

In her distinctive style Slagg writes . . .

'Ann Widdecombe!!?!! So reckon gays can be cured!??! One look at you Widdie darling and the entire population turns gay -no offence!!!'

California: As he drives towards Los Angeles, the BBC's Peter Bowes reaches the usual bottleneck at the meeting of two freeways, 14 and 5. There has been construction work at this intersection for as long as he can remember, back to the last big earthquake in 1994. That said, he thinks they are still far better than British motorways.

He does his usual radio station hopping – BBC World Service via Sirius Sat radio – to check on the rest of the planet, as well as local channels KNX1070 and KFI640. The news on the latter is dominated by the Miramonte School abuse scandal, which he has already started covering for the UK.

Traffic eases. He drives on towards Hollywood.

Twitter: From Arsenal fan Piers Morgan, ex-*Mirror* editor, sending a message from Stateside where he is a CNN anchor – *'Stop whining about Harry going to England, Spurs fans . . . '*

Falkirk: Press photographers snap Manchester United manager Sir Alex Ferguson in an unlikely pose. Hands raised, he appears to be rapping. He looks uncomfortable impersonating inner-city, streetwise youth.

But he is doing it as part of a football campaign called Kicking Respect Back Into the Game – to stop abuse of players and referees.

Sir Alex's presence means the photos – however out-of-character – will be widely published tomorrow.

Lincoln: Following the acquittal at S outhwark Crown Court, the role-playing has developed a life of its own for John Thorne's trainees. They've heard Harry

Redknapp being interviewed on the news and it has injected an element of reality into the lessons.

Thorne tells them: 'Making a short statement to a b attery of hacks and cameras scares everyone – except Redknapp perhaps.'

Thorne wants them to feel that sort of pressure. So he is introducing them to the worst kind of experience – the media melee, the press scrum. How would they cope with a crowd of reporters and photographers rushing towards them, pointing microphones and shouting questions all at once?

Having described the set-up, Thorne offers a solution – apart from running in the opposite direction.

'Management is the key,' he says and they nod at the kind of words they're familiar with. 'You need a s trategy to get in, deliver, and get out with your dignity intact.

'The unprepared get "ambushed" and answer a torrent of more and more cheeky questions despite having insisted no dialogue would be brooked.'

The people in his audience are learning. They are beginning to get it. If Harry Redknapp can do it, so can they.

London: Although revelling in his acquittal, a jubilant Harry Redknapp is now dodging the sports reporters and getting back to work. He's got a job to do. Spurs will be hosting Newcastle United in three days' time, a big match.

He knows enough about the press to understand that, in the end, the only thing that matters is results. His reputation stands and falls on winning.

London: Ignoring reporters' questions, England football manager Fabio Capello steps out through the gate of his home with its white stucco frontage. He has a man bag on his left shoulder and glances down at his feet when he sees the cameras.

He mouths 'hello' but nothing more and reaches a car where the driver rushes round and holds open the door. He climbs in. Reporters continue to shout questions through the windscreen. They might as well save their breath.

The car drives off towards Wembley and Capello's date with destiny.

CHAPTER 11

4pm-5pm
Heads Down

Worcester: *'Hold the front page..!'* It's long been Steph Preece's ambition to shout that time-honoured phrase across the newsroom, just like in an American movie.

Now the head of content jumps out of her chair and does exactly that in a voice loud enough to spread equal measures of alarm and excitement at the *Worcester News*.

The best story of the day – by far – has just come up on screen and reporter Liz Sweetman is assigned to do it. But first she has to be calmed down.

In the rush, Preece momentarily forgets to send a page 10 lead through. Then editor Peter John dashes out of his office also hoping to pronounce those four words – *'Hold the front page..!'* – until Preece tells him: 'Too late. I beat you to it, Peter.'

He looks disappointed.

By now it's going up on the website.

BREAKING NEWS . . . BREAKING NEWS . . .

*'**Queen Elizabeth II is coming to Worcester in July as part of her Diamond Jubilee celebrations.'**

Everyone at the *News* is thrilled and, of course, it is a big story for the paper. Worcester is an historic city which paid a heavy price for being a royalist stronghold in the English Civil War. This is its chance to lay on a huge welcome around the medieval cathedral and castle.

Four minutes later, a reader goes on the *News*'s Facebook page and tries to burst the bubble by giving an alternative point of view.

'The Queen is a parasitic old bag.'

Ah well, it's a free country. But free speech or not, this is neither the time nor place and the comment is promptly deleted.

Reporter David Paine is not so keen either. He sees the story he's worked so hard on being shunted off page one. He gives a mock sob.

As the royal coverage is put in train, a professional calmness returns to the newsroom.

Editor John goes back to proofreading his favourite page – readers' letters. Tomorrow's letters will discuss petrol prices, Scottish independence, war with Iran, fears for the English countryside, anger about knighthoods, praise for a charity fund-raiser, and Worcestershire Royal Hospital.

He says: 'The letters page is a brilliant and unique forum for local people to share their opinions.'

Tunbridge Wells: While Peter John loves the letters page, fellow editor Ian Read calls it the bane of his life.

He's looking at it right now. A libellous letter's got through so he cuts it back and puts another one in to make the page fit. He is eternally vigilant against unintended consequences, legal and otherwise.

Then he talks to a reporter just back from covering several inquests into suspicious deaths. She says one of them is a powerful, emotional story. Read listens and skim-reads her detailed copy. He agrees. It's very strong. But there's no room to tell it properly this week – it would be an injustice to put it on page 30, which is the only space remaining.

He says: 'We'll hold it back for next week.'

He adds: 'This will also give us time to approach the family for comment.'

Another reporter's been working on the partial sale of Tunbridge's historic Pantiles area. He's been talking to traders and says to Read: 'I've got some great quotes, Ian. Can I let them run on?'

Read's got space to think about. He shakes his head and replies: 'No, hack it back.'

How important are readers' letters and emails?

Extremely. A single letter may represent 10,000 people – the others agree but didn't bother to write.

They provide a free reader survey – *'rubbish!'* – *'brilliant!'* – and they are an entertainment in themselves, eccentric, witty, moving and inspirational. Often they develop into stories of their own or trigger new ideas and innovations.

Good editors pay a lot of attention to their readers' letters.

Delhi: Any hope she could wind down for the evening are being dashed for Helen Roberts. Emails are coming in from the UK and she is still at her computer, her right hand switching from keyboard to mouse and back to keyboard.

Then her phone rings and she answers it.

'Sorry, Mum,' she says. 'I'm really busy. I'll have to call you back.'

'Have you had dinner?'

'I'm getting a takeaway.'

Her mother, Gaynor, is making her daily call from their home town of Conwy, North Wales. She's on Facetime, so they can see each other.

'Mum. I know it's not good for my waistline. But here it's cheaper than home cooking. I'll ring you later.'

'All right, Helen.'

The call ends.

Helping Roberts is Tanzeel Ur Rehman, from Kashmir, a young journalist she met when she came to India. He has a degree in journalism and speaks the local language which has helped her secure many stories. He's now primarily her videographer, which he prefers. She also has a photographer, Shariq, and reporter Jalees. For now, the office is the front room of Roberts's flat but in time she hopes they'll hire something more suitable.

How did Roberts get this far?

Roberts: 'I started work at my local newspaper, *North Wales Weekly News*, after my postgraduate degree in journalism in 2000. I loved the excitement and being involved in so many stories and issues and current affairs.

'I then went travelling around the world for a year and caught the bug for exploring new places. I came back to the UK and got a job at South West News Service in Bristol before moving to London and working on *Closer, More* and *Look* magazine. But I still wanted to go overseas.

'So when I went freelance in 2008 I tried to re-direct my work towards international stories that would be of interest in the UK.

'I never wanted to be a travel writer but more of a journalist writing about foreign issues and stories. I eventually chose India because it's a huge country full of amazing stories, covering the shock factor as well as the emotional and the developing side. There are all kinds of stories brewing here of interest back home.'

Task Force Helmand HQ: Press chief Gordon Mackenzie takes a call from Rachel Thompson, a senior producer based in the BBC's Kabul bureau. She has a message for Quentin Sommerville.

Mackenzie agrees to pass it on.

He attends a meeting to get an update on Sommerville's progress. The British strategy depends on the Afghanis taking over when they leave. Sommerville's broadcasts – in Britain, and across the World Service – will be absolutely crucial, making him probably the most influential journalist in the field.

But at the moment it's not going well. Sommerville's frustrated over the lack of cooperation. He's even thinking about pulling out.

Notting Hill: At last, the Talk To The Press office falls quiet – relatively speaking – as the phones stop ringing and the writers get their heads down and do some copy. There is the reassuring *click-click* of keyboards.

After all her effort, Katie Evans finally secures the lesbian 'double pregnancy' donor story. Within minutes she's put it in front of a Sunday newspaper who snatch it up.

Hull: Editor Neil Hodgkinson and his deputy Paul Hartley have been pulling together the stories for the front page and page leads, with assistant editor Jamie Macaskill.

But they hold back from interfering too much in the newsroom. They don't want to get in the way. They prefer to let the newsdesk and subs crack on with the work before tipping in with their thoughts later on in the day.

Bath: With all the pages through at the *Chronicle*, Paul Wiltshire is a happy deputy editor and grabs his coat. Now he can stop being a journalist for a while and return to 'civvy street'.

He is taking his daughter to ballet.

Enfield: Greg Figeon rings *Chingford Times* reporter Matthew Stanton at the Basildon office for a brief chat before deciding on the running order for that paper.

London: A magazine emails freelance Jill Foster with a commission. It sounds interesting and she accepts immediately. Big mistake.

They say: 'We need 2,800 words – including three case studies and quotes from an expert.'

She says: 'That's a lot of work. What's the fee?'

They reply: 'It's £450.'

She's not happy. She always feels awkward haggling over money but it boils down to economics.

She says: 'I might lose out on a job that pays more money for less time if I take this on.'

She stands her ground.

In the end they give in and up their offer.

Camden Town: To pixelate or not? The deadline is *now*.

Editor Rebecca Fleming needs to decide about the picture she is using on *Take a Break*'s cover. She discusses it again with acting deputy Siofra Brennan. What exactly is its status? Brennan re-checks Facebook.

She says: 'It's still there as the woman's profile picture – so it is visible to anyone who wants to see it. So can she claim it is private?'

Fleming says: 'If everyone can see it, then I think we'll use it – unpixellated.'

At that, she signs off the cover and sends it through. It will undergo final processing before being sent off, in digitised form, to Bauer's giant press plant in Poland. There, it will be printed and trucked back for distribution across Britain and Ireland, where it tops the real-life magazines with 800,000 sales a week.

Rwanda: It's all peaceful for Reuters' Graham Holliday in contrast to the neighbouring states – a bomb has gone off in Nairobi, and there is more violence in Somalia.

At home in Kigali, he bakes a banana cake with Rwandan 'finger' bananas. As he slides the dish into the oven, he worries that it will be spoilt by one of the regular power cuts.

He checks Twitter. After a quiet day, it looks like a quiet evening.

There is no power cut and he takes the banana cake out, successfully cooked. He pours himself a glass of Chilean red wine feeling nervous about having a drink around this time in case of a grenade attack in the city. They've had quite a few, including two recently.

The attacks happen in the early evening, mostly Thursday, Friday and Saturday. Maybe he should relax a bit more as this is Wednesday. He re-heats leftovers of yesterday's homemade beef pie and slow-fries courgettes.

They all sit down for dinner.

During the meal, he receives a text message from a diplomatic contact inquiring about unconfirmed reports of various goings on in another neighbouring state, the Democratic Republic of the Congo.

It's not his area of expertise, but Holliday puts out some feelers.

He will chase them up tomorrow morning.

Bristol: She's been watching her phone and willing it to ring, and checking for replies on her email, but Heather Findlay has still not sold all her stories. The day feels incomplete and she's frustrated. After her early start, she tidies her desk and gets her coat. It is time to leave and she says goodbye and sets off home.

She will pursue her stories first thing tomorrow. Maybe she'll have better luck.

Unemployed Ex-Murdoch Reporter: After suspension of his state benefits, he blogs: *'I've got less than £20 to my name. I fret about bills, my rent, how much money I'll have for food.*

'The absurdity of poverty makes you laugh out loud: I boil the kettle to have a stand-up wash and leave the pots to pile up, knowing the taps will splutter freezing water; I sit under blankets, not wanting to put the heating on, using the halogen heater instead of a lamp; and I've eaten boiled rice with a blob of leftover tomato paste because I've nothing else in.

'I've tried my hardest to cut back but there is only so much one can do. I've also cried myself to sleep, desperately thinking about what I could've done to avoid being unemployed. I think back to my career: press agencies and newspapers I've worked for have closed. I believe leaving the industry was inevitable.'

He tries to sound more hopeful about the future but hankers after the old days.

'I hope re-training as a lecturer will eventually bring permanent work but part of me will always miss journalism. I remember the free stuff: I used to dine out regularly, spending in one evening what I now put aside for a week's food; I could go to almost any show in town but now spend evenings on the settee with Chaplin; I flew first class sitting amongst people far richer than me but with all the confidence of a millionaire.

'These days I copper-up or walk to sign on because £67.50 a week won't stretch to bus fares. I miss the glamour, the nosiness, the petty sense of power that comes from knowing everyone at the town hall but, mostly, I miss meeting people, seeing life in its many forms: before I found part-time work I could go a week without seeing anyone.'

Among other problems, he is lonely.

'I still can't bear to meet friends knowing they will have to stand my round again and again.'

Shepherd's Bush: Robin Lustig sits round a table with *The World Tonight* team and runs through the newslist: NHS top, then Syria, Falklands and perhaps Republican candidate Rick Santorum too.

They nod in general agreement.

It's six hours before he'll be on air and anything can happen.

Bermondsey: Mark Solomons is online looking to see if any of their stories are up on newspaper websites yet. He checks what else is around. The airline still hasn't replied to his enquiry about baggage charges. He thinks: 'If their planes were as late as this, they'd be out of business.'

Mind you, Solomons offered a story to the *People* newspaper at 9am this morning and they haven't come back either.

They write two more stories ready to put out in the morning.

West End: At *Good Housekeeping*, editorial director Lindsay Nicholson's face is displaying shock and horror for the second time today. She has just returned to her flood-damaged office to find a replacement sofa. Things are going from bad to worse.

It is too big and has been shoe-horned in. She recoils and says: 'It's hideous.'

Facilities are trying. They know she has to be kept in the style to which her magazine entitles her, and which her readers expect. This is not it. Before she can do anything, she sees a guest arriving.

She qualifies her greeting with an embarrassed apology.

Jerry Wright, chief executive of ABC, has come to discuss St Brides – the Fleet Street church – where they are both churchwardens.

He says: 'I don't think it's quite as disastrous as you do, Lindsay.'

She remains unmollified. Would that sofa get the *GH* Seal of Approval?

It's not even worth thinking about.

Tunbridge Wells: Jenny Barsby is cracking on with her four-thirty headlines. She just realises she's been writing about 'dawn raids' and 'this morning' and thinks: 'Ummmm, when else would they have been – silly cow!'

Her email crashes AGAIN!

Someone notices the two marshmallow cupcakes in her colleague's lunchbox and says: 'They look like Wonder Woman's breasts.'

Bristol: As the training day draws to a close, Caroline Sutton sits on the panel for a final Q&A session.

An audience member says: 'But how can we be creative when we are so short-staffed and lacking in resources?'

This is a FAQ – frequently asked question. Sutton has a FOA – frequently offered answer.

'There's never been a journalist,' she replies, 'who says they have too much money and too many staff.'

It is a universal truth.

Then she adds: 'Be creative over the constraints – and your work will be even better.'

Twitter: From Journalism.co.uk – *'Riots and phone-hacking coverage shortlisted for Royal Television Society Awards.'*

Leveson Inquiry: Another witness is now giving evidence – Pam Surphlis, MBE, who runs a charity for the families of murder victims. She has travelled from Northern Ireland and explains that her own father and sister were murdered.

She describes the behaviour of some reporters doing the so-called 'death knock' – trying to interview the grieving and the bereaved.

She tells Lord Justice Leveson: 'A lot of families give in to giving interviews in the hope it will stop press intrusion . . . '

Then she adds: 'Families don't want to know how to handle the media – because they don't want the media in the first place.'

North London: There are others who, despite personal turmoil, are willing to be interviewed in their grief. Pursuing *Take a Break's* organ donor campaign, health editor Lee Rodwell phones a mother whose son is on the waiting list for a heart transplant.

The woman tells her: 'I'd never thought of putting my children on the donor list until this happened to my own child.

'Now, if the worst happens and he doesn't survive the surgery, we want them to take whatever they can of him to help others.'

Rodwell says: 'That is extremely courageous.'

The interview ends.

Rodwell puts down the phone, staring at her notes and thinks: 'That woman is amazing. Thank God my children didn't need new hearts, or livers or kidneys.'

She will be an ideal figurehead for the campaign.

Rodwell writes up her notes, checks emails, looks at the clock and sends her Mac computer into well-earned sleep. She retrieves the washing (now creased) from the tumble drier and thinks about having a glass of wine. She looks at the clock again. Too early. She makes a coffee instead.

145

Twitter: From Jemima Kiss, Guardian media reporter now on maternity leave – *'Boob is the only word in English which contains full 3D view of the object. Top view: B. Front View: oo. Side view: b.'*

Twitter: From *Bella* feature writerAmy Rowland, having just looked out of her first floor office window in Camden Town – *'I'm booked in for a spray tan this eve but am well aware that in this weather I am going to look ridic . . . .'*

Twitter: From networking queen Julia Hobsbawm – we last heard of her parking at Heathrow after traffic hell – *'Here I am, in snowy Sweden.'*

West End: At *Psychologies,* editor Louise Chunn gets a quick visit from her publisher to discuss marketing money. They can see the threat from other titles – such as *Women's Health* – especially if they start buying up prime shelf space in the shops.

They need to get copies of *Psychologies* into more people's hands, to make it more visible. They think they have a good magazine and once people see it, they will become regular readers.

But this requires investment. How much can they spend?

Co. Donegal: Paddy Clancy arrives home and eats a very late lunch. He has got another story, this one about a beach-side hotel where Tony Blair spent his childhood holidays, and which is now up for sale. It's in the hands of the liquidators.

The reserve price is a rock-bottom €650,000 because banks won't give the manager a loan to buy it. As Clancy says: 'Banks are giving nobody any money in Ireland these days.'

He calls the Smithsonian Institution in Washington to check if they have anything on Titanic survivor Margaret Devaney, his other story.

London: *Newsnight*'s Susan Watts is on her way to a parents' evening at her daughter's school. It's being held to celebrate women's achievements through modern history – and is called, appropriately, *Her Story.*

Then her phone rings and it's the *Newsnight* editor on the line with an idea for this evening's progamme. She will need to get on with it urgently.

'Can you do a live two-way on the story about Lake Vostok in Antarctica – the largest lake below the ice that Russian scientists have drilled down to . . . ?'

Watts is familiar with it.

'Er, yes,' she replies.

She adds: 'It's a great tale – a feat of engineering with new science as the goal.'

She starts re-reading and suggests interviewees. US and UK teams are also drilling down to other sub-glacial lakes. It's a competition between nations. How can she simplify it in a few words? She thinks hard. Then she has a touch of inspiration . . .

The Earth-bound Space Race.

Homs, Syria: At least 27 people have been killed in the city today and now a desperate local man named Waleed Farah gets through on a satellite phone to a *Guardian* reporter.

'Tell me what's happening?'

'We are seriously dying here. You hear the rockets and explosions.'

'Can you describe it?'

'You feel you are at the front. The situation for civilians is pitiful.'

Camden Town: Story proposals are streaming in at *Take a B reak*. Commissioning editor Julia Sidwell sorts them out on screen, then discusses the best with editor Rebecca Fleming, only a desk away.

By keeping the top team compact, Fleming can talk through ideas at any time and make immediate decisions. They hardly need editorial conferences. Sidwell lists some stories.

'There's this married man,' Sidwell says, 'who had a tattoo of a buxom lady inked on his calf and has now had silicone implants inserted to give her a 3D bosom. Here's the pictures.'

Everyone has a look.

Fleming smiles, shakes her head and says: 'No, not for us. It's just a gimmick. There's no narrative.'

Sidwell pitches two further stories. They decide to go for one and not the other. Sidwell calls the freelance and offers a fee, then waits to hear back if it's accepted. It's an auction. Very good stories can go for up to £7,000 – most of which can kept by the freelance, some might say unfairly.

Meanwhile Fleming, a mother of three, checks a beauty page layout and sighs. 'How does anyone have time for skin-brushing?' she says. 'I certainly don't.'

Chelmsford: Editor Katy Evans has been working on the flatplan for the April issue of *Soul & Spirit*, particularly their *Psychic Special* section.

Now she is reading a book about angels and may ask the author to write a feature.

Some days it feels like she gets loads done, such as yesterday when she spent the morning on web-related tasks. But today has turned into a 'clearing the decks' day, tying up loose ends, largely because they went to press last Friday. It leaves her feeling dissatisfied.

Camden Town: All around Jon Peake, various feature writers are preparing to conduct last-minute interviews for *TV Choice* and *Total TV Guide* – with *EastEnders*, Tom Hiddlestone, Gareth Gates, Emilia Fox, John Sargent and Jeremy Irons.

Is it okay to pat a woman's bottom? Peake is amazed to discover just how many cuts there are on Irons's belief that it's fine.

They've spent the whole day waiting for Olly Murs to call. Now they hear why he hasn't. He's soundchecking on a stage somewhere.

Peake says: 'So he's on tour – and now they tell us!'

147

'Don't worry,' says his representative, 'he'll still phone you, he really, really will.'

Digging into his pile of proofs, Peake wouldn't bet on it.

Kingston: Ghostwriter Natalie Dye is still struggling to explain the 'space–time continuum' to ordinary women. Her column is coming along very slowly and she suspends work to collect her 15-year-old son from school.

She's late but, fortunately, he has long learnt not to complain, and plugs in his iPod at the mutually agreed signal, the first syllables of Mum saying, *'I am not a taxi driver'*.

Cambridge: Back in the newsroom, Raymond Brown discovers more about the man found frozen to death in the church doorway. By chance, he was a resident of the charity being visited by the Duchess of Cornwall – part of today's royal visit.

The death highlights the gap between the theory and practice of caring for the homeless.

The Duchess is informed and offers her condolences. She can do no more.

At last Brown slows starts to slow down slightly after a long day. He gives himself time to grab a coffee. He's not eaten anything except toast at breakfast, which is pretty normal for him, deadening the hunger pangs with the odd crafty cigarette.

Right now he is writing up stories on the Prince's visit, the two bodies found, and doing some NIBS and a picture story.

London: *Mint* magazine editor Marcus Harris leaves home, heading for the West End. He is tweeting and checking emails incessantly during the 45-minute journey.

He wants to hire a style editor and has arranged to meet someone.

As they sit and talk, he is more than won over by her enthusiasm. She also understands what they are trying to do. He makes a decision on the spot and takes her on, relieved to relinquish both workload and some control.

Knightsbridge: Kathryn Blundell leaves the Berkeley Hotel and shunts through the Piccadilly traffic back towards the *Mother & Baby* office. In her head, she is replaying the meeting with creative director Mark Frith.

When she arrives, she hurries to the art editor's desk with the new coverlines.

But then, at the last moment, she has a change of heart. She reckons one of the lines still isn't as clear is she'd like. What to do about it?

She decides to hold off, take it home and stick it on her kitchen wall and think again.

She hopes the legendary Frith will approve.

New York: An even bigger legend, Anna Wintour, editor of US *Vogue* and part of a British journalistic dynasty, is hosting a party for the very rich and extremely influential. It is to launch *Runway to Win* – a fashion-world fund-raiser for President Obama's re-election.

The most glamorous editor on the planet wears a Thakoon scarf and freezes briefly for pictures.

Her unblinking mystique makes her a news item.

The photos are immediately sent worldwide and particularly to UK newspapers where Wintour's reign over New York is followed with a chauvinistic pride.

With her $2m salary and $200,000 shopping expenses, she is one of a handful of journalists who carry such a combination of power and status.

Next week, she will be the uncrowned queen of New York Fashion Week, easily identifiable by her pageboy bob haircut and dark glasses when she slips into a front-row seat alongside the runways.

Wintour will perch in judgement, inscrutable as a procelain Buddha, reserving her precious opinions for *Vogue*'s priceless pages.

West End: Wintour is an aspirational role model for younger journalists such as *Marie Claire's* Helen Russell who now goes to pick up dollars for her New York Fashion Week trip.

She will attend some of the same events but will occupy a les s-elevated position in the industry's transparent pecking order.

Russell is exremely proud of her job. As a teenager in the late eighties *Marie Claire* was the first glossy she picked up. It had just launched.

'It felt so unique and really spoke to me,' she says, 'and treated me like an intelligent person who is interested in more than sex and handbags – although I'm obviously interested in handbags as well.'

Like everyone else from British magazines, she has to accept her place one rung below the American editors. But that doesn't mean she has to feel overawed by the woman whose aloofness has earned her the nickname 'Nuclear Wintour'.

Russell reminds herself to collect the clothes she dropped in at t he dry cleaners on the way to work this morning. Wintour, one imagines, doesn't have that kind of thing on her to-do list.

Glasgow: Trying not to feel discouraged, freelance Samantha Booth pitches two more ideas to editors, then waits, telling herself that things must improve. They really, really *must.*

Worcester: From the press bench at Worcester Crown Court, reporter Tony Bishop watches as jury members file back into court and take their seats. The foreman stands and announces the result of their deliberations. Bishop takes note and is immediately on to the *Worcester News* newsdesk, which is still excited over the Queen's visit.

'The Troughton jury's just given its verdict . . . '

'Yes?'

'Guilty of murder.'

He files copy about 74-year-old Roger Troughton who beat his cousin to death with a spade. It's a headline story to run alongside Her Majesty's.

London: Despite having had a feature dropped and being 37 weeks pregnant, Louise Baty is striking back strongly.

She's found a new story – a mum whose baby nearly died after being born nine weeks premature (pregnant feature writers are not spared). Even better, the woman's partner is a photographer so they have high-quality pictures to match the emotional narrative. It's ideal for true-life women's magazines.

She sends out a teaser and crosses her fingers. She hopes she will hear back either this evening or tomorrow morning. In fact an offer comes in straightaway. *Sold!*

Wells: An hour later than he'd planned, chief reporter Oliver Hulme sets off for home from the *Wells Journal*.

He checks Facebook on his phone and immediately feels annoyed – the *Daily Mail* has scooped his Kris Marshall wedding picture. A local news agency got wind of it and tracked down the bride. But he reckons the *Mail* picture won't affect their sales – and at least he got it.

Walthamstow: His email is back up and showbiz writer Nick McGrath receives a picture of the actress who is to play Susan Boyle. It's a very determined PR. Apparently she was in the Rab C Nesbitt comedy show.

McGrath calculates the chances of getting a commission for interviewing her and concludes: 'They are slightly slimmer than for Kate Middleton.'

He returns to working on the Gregg Wallace transcript.

West End: At *Stylist,* Anita Bhagwandas uses the back of her hand to try out a range of new lipsticks from Dior, Chanel and Burberry. Which will she recommend to the readers?

Then she regrets it, fearing she will end up wiping the colours all over her white top by the end of day.

She tells colleagues: 'This office is still too hot.'

When she gets little response, she says: 'I'll get dehydrated.'

She disappears and comes back with a pint glass of water which she downs to dramatise her point while writing up her feature about this morning's Fragrance Awards.

She is also working on a Kylie Minogue hair gallery for the webpages, matching Kylie's hairstyles to specific dates. It looks simple, but turns out to be fiddly.

She reckons the office is like a furnace.

Finally, she's had enough, gets up and opens a window herself, spurred on by fashion director Alex Fullerton.

Four minutes later she notices the window has been closed. Her heart sinks.

She pecks at her keyboard.

Then the subs desk staff say they are aghast as her use of the word 'inapprope' – short for 'inappropriate'. Someone tells her: 'It's tawdry East London terminology.'

Bhagwandas makes a mental note to finish her words in future.

The room is getting hotter, feeding her fears of being cooked to a crisp.

Lincoln: The training day is drawing to a close and John Thorne is pleased with the way the course has gone. It's been useful to have the Harry Redknapp story running in parallel.

They hold a final debrief and everyone says they have learnt something. It has been constructive.

The suspicion and distrust have vanished and they shake hands and exchange friendly farewells.

Afterwards, Thorne discusses it when he has a wind-down beer with an old BBC colleague Barnie Choudhury, now a principal lecturer in broadcast journalism at the university.

Thorne says: 'To a degree, the monster media image has been unpicked. But, poacher turned gamekeeper, am I still playing a legitimate part in the world of journalism?'

It's a question he thinks about on the return journey home to Yorkshire.

Enfield: Greg Figeon signs off m ore *Barnet Press* pages ahead of the 5pm deadline. No tea.

The City: At the *Global Telecoms* offices, Alan Burkitt-Gray is making good progress. All features in his inbox are now subbed and have been sent off with pictures to the designer, a freelance based 300 miles away in Cornwall.

It's time to write a couple of pieces of his own.

Ah! – he doesn't have the picture for one of the interviewees. He emails the man's head of communications in the Netherlands. There, an assistant puts one on a file transfer service within minutes, all 40 megabytes.

He thinks: 'Thank God for technology.'

Burma: Tearing themselves away from the desperate refugees, the *Telegraph*'s Malcolm Moore and photographer Adam Dean retrace their route through the darkness and find their way back to the town of Laiza.

They pull up outside their hotel. They have kept going knowing they wouldn't get a second chance but now they are reaching their physical limits.

It was the previous night that they set off on the 2am red-eye flight from their base, in Shanghai, and the lack of sleep is starting to catch up with them.

They've still got a lot more work to do.

Tomorrow they want to interview Sumlut Gun Maw, the Brigadier-General in charge of the Kachin Independence Army. It means another early start. They need to recharge.

They fall into their beds, making sure they don't oversleep.

Hollywood: Having judged the traffic well, Peter Bowes arrives 13 minutes early at t he gates of Universal Studios. He drives in, parks and greets his cameraman and the Universal publicist.

He is escorted inside to a hospitality area where he meets other journalists, mainly from overseas. He sits down and has a coffee. They talk about the weather. Everyone seems to talk about the weather to him. Visitors are jealous of the blue skies and sun. They think it's like this every day.

He tells them: 'Last year we had snow.'

He sees the shock-horror on their faces.

Coming from the North-east of England, he's the first to admit that the climate is one of the reasons he stays here.

Then he gets to work, interviewing and discussing Universal Studio's upcoming 100th birthday.

In his head, he's virtually writing the story already . . .

'Universal Pictures, the Hollywood studio known for classic films such as To Kill a Mockingbird, Jaws, Out of Africa and All Quiet on the Western Front, is marking its centenary by restoring and re-releasing some of its best-known titles . . .'

Dundee: The city's main newspaper apparently has a new fan – *'Mum-to-be Ann Curran's pregnancy has left her with a bizarre craving for a taste of her local NEWSPAPER. She can't go a day without munching on t he Dundee Evening Telegraph.'*

KwaZulu-Natal: *Danger!* A venomous vine snake is found in a garden near the Umkhumbi Lodge where travel writer Meera Dattani has been sitting on the patio, tapping at her laptop. Now there is a 'snake call-out' and she goes along out of curiosity. She doesn't get too close.

Expert Anton Roberts has been summoned. He catches the creature and lets Dattani take a look.

She says: 'It seems too small to do much harm.'

He replies: 'Never judge by appearances.'

She returns to the patio and resumes work. The sun is high and it feels as hot as a sauna.

What's Dattani getting out of this trip?

Dattani says: 'It's a break from routine. I feel more creative because I have more time and that's worth its weight in gold.'

Does she feel cut off?

Dattani: 'Isolated as it can feel out here, I am actually rarely physically alone – which I am more so in London.'

How important is the internet to you?

Dattani: 'It enables me to travel like this, working in the same way for the same clients and meeting deadlines. I'm online all day.'

What about distractions?

Dattani: 'As I'm abroad and my clients, friends and family know that, I receive no phone calls. I watch no TV out here – I don't have one in my room –

just the occasional film if it's an early night and the lodge owners Anton and Emma suggest we watch something. I'm reading more and writing more.'

How different is it from London?

Dattani: 'While I'm working, life doesn't feel hugely different other than the fact I'm outdoors and I have company.'

What's different?

'The biggest difference for me is what I do after work. Instead of playing tennis, which I do twice a week in London, seeing friends, attending work events, having a night in with the TV, seeing family, here most nights are the same. I head to the main bar and restaurant and chat to guests.

'Sometimes I'll pitch in and help behind the bar or even serve a dish or two, then I sit down for dinner with the lodge owners, their son and two other staff members. Conversation is always interesting.'

Why the Umkhumbi Lodge?

Dattani: 'I was in this exact same region for 10 days last year doing research for a travel feature for *National Geographic Traveller* magazine. I loved the area so much that I negotiated a long-stay working holiday.'

Stratford-upon-Avon: Matt Wilson is eagerly waiting to hear back from the *Daily Mail* newsdesk after sending them his story about the stolen Shakespeare pipes.

He reads proofs of tomorrow's pages, then fetches a round of coffees partly to make up for stinking out the office with his battered sausage and chips.

He wonders who's looking at his email at the *Mail* and what they're saying about it. Perhaps it's being shown to the editor-in-chief right now . . .

Daily Mail: Dedicated as he is, *Mail* editor Paul Dacre has a lot to think about and the theft of Shakespearean pipes, interesting in itself, does not top his agenda right now.

First, he's got another appearance at the Leveson Inquiry tomorrow. The *Mail* is still insisting it is just an over-elaborate probe into phone hacking – whereas others say it is a much-needed audit of British democratic processes.

Second, he's got to chair a board meeting.

And third, he's editing what some say is Britain's most influential newspaper – his most important role.

Right now, he needs to focus his attention on the splash headline.

Like his rival, Whittow, at the *Express*, he has considered – and dismissed – the Redknapp story for that slot. He'll leave that to the red tops.

But unlike Whittow, he wants to give his readers something more challenging than *8 INCHES OF SNOW*.

He's considering the alternative stories being offered by the newsdesk, bearing in mind the *Mail*'s large female following.

The one that catches his eye is: *BBC BOSS: I GOT IT WRONG ON OLDER WOMEN.*

Will that work?

London: In an address to an invited audience, Paul Dacre's ultimate boss Viscount Rothermere is warning about the dangers he thinks could arise from the Leveson Inquiry. He claims it threatens freedom of speech in Britain.

'What matters,' he says, 'is that we don't castrate our industry from doing our job.'

He makes additional points in his role as chairman of the *Daily Mail* and General Trust.

In particular, he criticises the Office of Fair Trading for blocking regional press groups – such as his own Northcliffe – from consolidating in the face of fierce competition from the internet.

He says the company is looking again at options after its revenues fell a huge 9 per cent in the last quarter.

This sounds ominous.

Tunbridge Wells: Editors like Ian Read at the *Courier* see reports of Rothermere's speech – and the severe drop in revenues – and wonder what it means for themselves and other dedicated Northcliffe staff. They might be producing great local newspapers, but competition from the internet is relentless. And no one seems to have the answer.

Will newspapers become extinct?

Leveson Inquiry: Pam Surphlis, MBE, has finished her evidence and steps down from the witness box. She is the last witness listed for today. Lord Justice Leveson rises and disappears through the door behind his chair.

Court 73 starts to empty. Lawyers and journalists trudge out of an opposite door, through the wide corridors and into the freezing-cold Strand just as the street lamps come on. When they appear, the array of photographers greet them and cameras pin them in dazzling bright beams and flashes.

It's been a day packed with sensational evidence.

Twitter: From *Hacked Off* correspondent Selkie, among those leaving Leveson and the latest to come down with the 'flu bug – *'Going home. Dying.'*

Wembley: With its own starry lights, the iconic metallic arch over the football stadium seems to be propping up a darkening sky while far below, on planet Earth, a silver car sweeps along the road, watched by reporters and photographers.

The vehicle halts and a tall figure levers himself out, grim-faced, giving nothing away, staying silent, thinking a lot. The Italian walks inside the entrance where two people are waiting to greet him, to shake his hand.

There is coolness underlying the encounter, a lack of assurance in the smiles and an uncertainty in the handshakes.

Capello tries to read the faces of the two men – David Bernstein, chairman of the Football Association, and FA general secretary Alex Horne – and they, in turn, try to read his.

What have the Englishmen got up their sleeves?

And what has the Italian got up his?

'I giornalisti farebbero bene ad essere pronti con le penne ed i telefoni. I redattori anche. Sto per dargli il più grande titoli da secoli.'

(Translation: The reporters had better be ready with their pens and phones. So had the editors. I am going to give them the biggest headline for ages.)

Capello, Bernstein and Horne go into a room and close the door behind them. They need to talk in complete privacy and confidence.

The reporters would give anything to be a fly on the wall.

CHAPTER 12

5pm-6pm
Dogs and Vajazzles

Darkness descends. Today the sun is setting at precisely 5 o'clock over Britain, applying its wintry lockdown.

In London, the national newspapers are starting their final editorial conferences. Most are settling on their page 1 splash.

At the *Daily Mail,* editor Paul Dacre leans back in his chair and goes round his circle of executives, asking what they've got, what progress they're making.

'Anything new on Redknapp?'

'Not really, not since this morning.'

Everyone joins in the discussion.

'It will be all over TV tonight . . . '

Harry's given a few quotes outside court.'

'You can't really beat that for now.'

'He's back at work, preparing for the Newcastle game.'

'What about Capello?'

'We're still waiting.'

It'a all down to Dacre. His staff watch him, wondering which way he will jump.

To some of them, he's as much a cult as an editor, a leader who dominates the decision-making. As a boy, he was virtually trained for the job by his journalist father, Peter, and combines his vast experience with a strong – some say alarming – presence.

Now the *Mail* is faced with a familiar problem. Print newspapers cannot compete for speed with TV, the internet, even their own webpages. The Redknapp story's been up on Mail Online for six hours. They have to find another way, something different to attract, charm and seduce readers.

Dacre is the master of this art and he turns his mind towards the alternatives. There's always the weather, of course. The newsdesk is putting something together on frost and snow. But for him, it is not a splash.

'Leave that to the Express.'

He's more interested in the confession from the BBC's Director-General Mark Thompson.

He likes it.

The *Mail*'s TV correspondent Paul Revoir has written the copy and Dacre looks at it and makes a bold decision.

Page 1. Present it big.

He can already visualise the headline . . .

BBC BOSS: I GOT IT WRONG ON OLDER WOMEN . . . There are too few on television, he admits.

Dacre approves in part because it is about a cultural powerhouse he polices relentlessly. He is in two minds about the BBC. He sees it as brilliant British institution. He also believes it is a sanctuary for a liberal metropolitan elite, the kind who patronise the *Mail* and it's readers – and this story exposes their hypocrisy.

The *Mail*'s readership is 53 per cent women yet critics say it is misogynist, which infuriates Dacre, and he likes to expose the double-standards of media outlets which dare to espouse it.

The BBC boss has offered his head on a plate. It would be rude to refuse.

As for the Redknapp acquittal, the *Mail* will suffice with a front-page picture and a partisan headline: *HARRY HOUDINI.*

Over at the *Express,* similar thoughts are running through the mind of Dacre's counterpart, Hugh Whittow. He doesn't see Redknapp as the splash either. Not everyone's interested in football.

On his pad, the canny Whittow is also visualising the shape of his front page, forming beneath a bold headline: *8 INCHES OF SNOW IN NEXT 24 HOURS . .*
.

Then, just to give it more punch, it's sharpened up with a further ten words . . . *And it will be too cold for grit to work.*

The copy has been put together by his regular weather reporter, Nathan Roe.

It was Roe who authored another splash: *-20°C TO HIT US IN WEEKS.* It was published five months ago and heralded an October which turned out to be one of the warmest on record.

Doh!

Do readers care? Do they even remember? Probably not. They are very forgiving on weather stories. It's low-cost, no-risk editorial.

But for the red tops – the *Sun, Mirror* and *Star* – the Redknapp story is still top of their agenda. They can combine it with a new poll showing most people want Redknapp to take over the England team.

Right now the editors know that Fabio Capello is in a meeting with the FA at Wembley. But hardly anybody expects much to come out of it. They toy with headlines such as:*CAPELLO BLOCKS REDKNAPP.*

It's all hypothetical. Really, the nation will have to wait for the accession of King 'Arry. Maybe soon, maybe never. Who knows?

As for other stories, everyone is going big on the pictures that SWNS photographer Adam Gray took this morning of the burnt-out cookery school run by Hugh Fearnley-Whittingstall – he's still in the Antarctic and looks like being the last to know.

Whitehall:
Breaking News . . . Breaking News . . . Breaking News
The press office at the Ministry of Defence is putting the final touches to a press statement. It is about Prince Harry, Princess Diana's younger son.

It is more in the form of an announcement. It says that today he qualified as a front-line Apache attack helicopter pilot.

The result – he is to return to Afghanistan. He won't be hiding away in a bunker. He's a co-pilot gunner. He'll be flying in and out of the battle zones, getting stuck in, supporting troops, and being exposed to enemy fire.

Realistically, Prince Harry will be in the business of killing people and in return he could get killed.

The MoD media bods press *send* and the statement appears instantaneously on newsroom screens across the country.

Executives see it and weigh it up.

Daily Telegraph: The implications of the Prince Harry statement are immediately grasped by editor Tony Gallagher. He doesn't want to tuck it inside. He says it's front-page, maybe the splash. It is assigned to his own top guns – chief reporter Gordon Rayner and defence correspondent, Thomas Harding.

Gallagher's been making other decisions, designed to attract the kind of readers he wants to draw from rival newspapers, especially from his old boss and mentor, Paul Dacre at the *Mail.*

He is looking at pictures of *Vogue* magazine editor Anna Wintour, in a Thakoon scarf, taken in New York a few hours earlier today. Power, money, fashion – she is an aspirational role model for his audience, present and future.

'Page 2. Use her big.'

Notting Hill: At Talk To The Press, boss Natasha Courtenay-Smith leaves to pick up her son from nursery.

West End: At *Mother & Baby,* Kathryn Blundell returns to her desk to find the pile of page proofs has grown during her absence. She considers whether she can deal with them now. Then she decides she will read them at home and sticks them in her bag.

She talks to the production editor about what pages are outstanding and where they are with sending the issue to press.

She's told a box is missing on a feature so she agrees to do it. She approves three new layouts for subbing and chases some copy she commissioned last night. It turns out the writer is ill – that 'flu bug again – but she promises to do her best and complete it overnight.

Glasgow: Still waiting for editors to get back to her, Samantha Booth looks at the clock and tells herself: 'Enough is enough. Time to go and do something less boring than just sitting here staring at the screen.'

She abandons her computer, pulls on a heavy coat and heads out for a brisk walk in the cold, crisp early evening.

Task Force Helmand HQ: Press chief Gordon Mackenzie opens a bottle of beer and takes a swig, feeling it wash down the fine Afghani dust. It is non-alcoholic but still a welcome reminder of the higher refreshments awaiting him when he gets back home to Edinburgh.

He is celebrating the promotion of a colleague to the rank of captain. It's late evening and he decides to knock off for the day. He's been busy and he is still wondering how the Quentin Sommerville reports will turn out.

They are important. Despite its independence, the BBC's influence makes it a quasi-political force. What it says, counts.

He relaxes and watches TV.

He's not so keen on the popular junk that is preferred by most of the troops. In work as in leisure, he is drawn to the nexus between power and the media and chooses an appropriate programme: an episode of the Danish political series *Borgen.*

As it ends, he falls asleep.

Salford: The BBC's Rebecca Pike – on her trip north from London – is now broadcasting live from the Lowry Hotel. She is reporting for Radio 2's *Simon Mayo Show* and is offering an eclectic mix.

She's covering a performance by Don McLean and the Dubliners and mixing it in with other stories.

She interviews someone about cracks in superjumbo wings, then switches to the redevelopment of the Manchester Ship Canal.

Then – as part of the show's daily 'confession' slot – she admits she once believed that *Blockbuster*'s Bob Holness was the sax player on *Baker Street,* a story put about by music writer Stuart Maconie. She was young and journalism had yet to nurture her hard shell of scepticism.

Pike says: 'I forgive you, Stuart.'

Manchester: Not far from the Lowry, *Estates Gazette* editor Damian Wild is also on a trip from London to the Northern capital.

He and his audience have spent the afternoon in serious mode, discussing the Greek debt crisis, retailer carnage and the importance of transport nodes.

Now it is time to relax.

Wild leads the way to the drinks reception he is holding at Manchester's fashionable Epernay Champagne Bar.

He's the host and wants everyone to feel welcome. He decides he will make a speech.

But first he looks round. Corks are popping and the champagne is flowing. He can see everyone's had a long day. He tells himself not go on too much.

Congleton: After his gym workout, Jeremy Condliffe returns to his desk and signs off the last few pages of the *Chronicle*.

Although it is the busiest time of the week, a casual staffer stops by for an idle chat, undeterred by the pile of pages on the editor's desk.

Shepherd's Bush: Robin Lustig is listening carefully to the *PM* show, BBC radio's teatime news programme. He needs to ensure they don't end up repeating too many items on *The World Tonight*, only four hours later.

At the same time, his team are busy assembling their own material.

Producer Anna is on Skype and gets through to a man surviving in terror in the beleaguered Syrian city of Homs. There is gunfire in the background and fear in his voice as he paints a grim but vivid picture of death and bombardment.

The call ends.

With that in the bag, Lustig wonders whether Syria should go top of their running list instead of the NHS.

Stedham Village: In the shed, which he ambitiously calls 'Canary Wharf', veteran columnist Colin Dunne decides it's time for tea, and also time to ring friends and family.

Then a voice in his head starts nagging. It says: 'No, no, no, stop it, no distractions. Get writing. Tap those keys. World is waiting. Now, let's tackle that piece. Publishers gasping for it, I expect. Squadron of airborne pigs pass overhead. Ha ha.'

After a pause, he asks himself: 'Why do I do this? Right, I shall retire – tomorrow.'

Essex: Speeding home on the electrified commuter train from London, agony aunt Katie Fraser asks a reader by email: 'Can you please send me a picture of yourself?'

The woman replies: 'Sorry, I haven't got a picture of myself. Can I send a picture of my dog?'

Fraser: 'No, I don't want your dog. I want a picture of you.'

Woman: 'I only have dog picture.'

Fraser: 'Can you get a picture of you?'

Woman: 'No, only dog.'

Fraser looks at her fellow passengers and wonders if they suspect the existential drama in which she has been plunged. She decides to move on. So she checks how her readers' poll is going, in answer to the question she posed two hours ago – *Which uniform turns you on?*

She notes her own suggestion of traffic warden has received little support. The most popular so far is the most predictable . . .

West End: At *Psychologies*, editor Louise Chunn reads chromalins and proofs that have piled up over the day, then discusses changes with the chief sub. It's tweaking mostly, but still vitally important. This attention to detail will strongly influence how the finished magazine will look and read.

WestEnd: Although she has been summoned back to the studio, *Newsnight's* Susan Watts is at school at the moment. She is listening to her daughter acting as advocate on behalf of the Frenchwoman Marie Curie, urging others to recognise her importance. Watts is gratified that her child's hero is a woman and a scientist. She is following in her mother's footsteps.

The debate finishes and Watts boards the tube back to BBC Television Centre, clicking from mum mode to work mode and thinking *Earth-bound Space Race*. She uses the journey to draft questions and outline a script

She's due to pre-record an interview with the British Antarctic Survey at seven-thirty.

Bermondsey: Agency boss Mark Solomons is sending a few final Tweets. As he reaches for his coat, he says: 'Heart FM is playing f****ng Adele yet again. That's it. I'm off.'

Twitter: From MediaGuardian – *'Phone hacking: News International faces more than 50 new damages claims.'*

Unemployed Ex-Murdoch Reporter: He blogs some more about today's activities and thoughts: *'Read Manchester Mule and Salford Star online before checking websites of mainstream newspapers.*

'I've not bought a newspaper in a long time: gone are Sundays surrounded by broadsheets and t abloids because I s imply can't afford it. Two pounds for a broadsheet is a one-way bus fare to sign on, or a loaf of bread or toilet roll that won't leave ink stains.

'Still, I find myself editing as I r ead online, fighting the urge to email corrections. I'm on the outside now. I r etain all the pedantic fury of an experienced journalist but none of the escape.

'I wrote to NPower about the excessive cost of gas and laughed at the illiterate letter I received from the "executive" handling my complaint. I watch BBC subtitles or read its digital output and tut with pompous indignation. I read Tweets from journalists and envy their attempts to seem casual as they add a link in celebration of their article.

'I fear ending up like the readers who used to send me letters with clippings attached telling me kids were goats not children.'

He's been following stories about the Anfield Cat – a homeless tabby which ran on to the pitch and held up the game between Liverpool and Redknapp's Tottenham Hotspur – a so-called *paws in play* while scoring a *cat-trick*.

'I thrill and feel envy,' he says. *'Oh, why couldn't I have been paid to write these puns?'*

Kingston: At long last, Natalie Dye conquers the space–time continuum and completes her column. She feels the relief of a *Dr Who* girl finishing off a Dalek. She emails it in and now starts to revel in space and time of her own, to think of something other than journalism.

'Thank goodness, that's over,' she says.

Uh-uh, she's spoken too soon . . .

An email comes back from the features editor saying: 'Natalie, can you do a short news-style story based on this book extract we've just bought?'

Dye: 'When?'

'Now. It's urgent.'

Dye: 'Yes. I'm on it.'

She starts to bash it out while re-heating a microwave meal for her son who has long since abandoned hope his mother will ever take up proper cooking.

West End: You can almost feel pity for Lindsay Nicholson's replacement sofa. It is now being inspected by the Expert's Expert – *Good Housekeeping*'s legendary interiors editor, Marg Caselton. She casts a withering eye over it and ill-conceals her horror. Her verdict is damning.

'Lindsay, it has got to go!'

To Nicholson, furniture is what clothes are to fashion commentators such as Anna Wintour. She is a guru of home style and she needs to reflect the readers' aspirations.

She can't be caught with anything this naff.

She makes a pleading call to Facilities who, despite it being the end of their day, nobly come to her office. At her request, they lift up the sofa and carry it away.

Nicholson, an astrophysicist by education, thinks: *'Nothing is better than something.'*

She finds a table in a meeting room and commandeers that. By now it's too late to call Facilities again so she recruits two editorial males – the creative director and the head of the *Good Housekeeping Institute* – and they carry it down the corridor for her.

They shift it into place and she steps back for a better look. Well, it's an improvement.

Cambridge: Bob Satchwell starts catching up on the work he's missed today because of the bug going round the media industry – no, not the 'flu but Leveson Addiction.

He is returning calls and responding to emails.

He completes checks for next week's meeting of the Society of Editors' parliamentary and legal committee. It will be with Lord Hunt, the new chairman of the Press Complaints Commission, the self-regulatory body fighting for its life.

He finalises emails announcing the Regional Press Awards and sends notes to the judges.

He makes more calls.

West End: It's been one of the best days ever for Farrah Storr and it is not over yet. She has another quick check on Twitter to see what people have been saying about *Women's Health* and thinks: 'So far so good.'

163

Then she gets a call from reception. She's got a visitor – her personal trainer Cathy Brown, the boxing champion. She wants to talk through some ideas. Can she come up? Yes, of course.

Okay, I'm on my way.

But when the ultra-fit Brown walks on to the editorial floor, the first thing she sees makes her eyes pop.

Good God, client has terrible eating disorder. Lives on huge Bakewell tarts. And she's editor of Women's Health!

Storr can imagine the thoughts reeling through her trainer's head and quickly explains.

Brown nods, hoping it's the whole truth, and starts talking serious training strategies.

KwaZulu-Natal: After the excitement of the deadly vine snake, Meera Dattani is struggling with a feature. The heat seems to have melted her brain. Then the evening breeze kicks in.

Suddenly the terrace goes from sauna to perfect office and she feels invigorated. Her mind clears, her fingers tap-dance on the keyboard and one thousand words are reeled off almost effortlessly.

London: A national newspaper emails Jill Foster asking if she can take on a feature. She agrees straightaway. She has a good relationship with them and, just as importantly, it sounds an interesting job.

She sets up a couple of interviews and checks Twitter.

She gets an email from a friend at another newspaper to inform her one of her features is being published tomorrow.

Foster wishes all offices were that courteous.

Then she looks at the time and turns off her laptop. She goes into the kitchen.

She starts preparing dinner for her husband. She is not always this domesticated but he has been away for a few days so she wants to make the effort. It's one of the benefits of working from home.

Enfield: The pre-press manager asks editor Greg Figeon when he will receive the final eight pages of *The Press*?

Figeon doesn't want to admit the truth, that they are still being laid out and will be a little while yet.

So he says: 'We are just sending them.'

It's a little fib to oil the cogs.

Meanwhile, he checks the pages for the *Yellow Advertiser*'s Barking edition. It's fine. He feels a surge of glee. All *Yellow Advertiser* titles are now complete for another week.

Michelstown, Co. Cork: Nicola-Maria Riordan is not sure whether she has finished for the day or not.

She is looking at her diary and sees she has an out-of-office event pencilled in. It is a local group's annual general meeting. Despite it being her birthday, duty comes first and she sets off.

When she arrives, she takes some photos and drinks some tea. The meeting begins and is going well but in the end she gets up, saying: 'I'm sorry, I have to go. I'm 29 today and I've got some dinner reservations.'

At that point the chairman says: 'Well, happy birthday – and I wish to thank you for all your coverage in the past.'

Then, before she can protest, other members of the board stand up and thank her for her help with various initiatives.

One says: 'You have helped boost the local economy.'

'Thank you,' says Nicola-Maria, feeling slightly embarrassed. 'It's like getting an extra birthday present. Thank you.'

Hull: Two complaints drop onto assistant editor Jamie Macaskill's desk.

The first is a letter about an article exposing a man who claimed to be a military officer – and wasn't.

Macaskill is confident it was accurate and sends the standard reply: 'We stand by the story.'

The second is trickier. It is from a local head teacher about a report on redundancies at the school. It's not black and white.

This requires more thought and Macaskill wants to give himself time. He marks his diary to remind him to deal with it tomorrow.

Next, he goes into the newsroom and finds himself hovering around the newsdesk and subs while they put together the last pages, tops and front-page plugs. All looks okay to him.

Then a tip comes in to the newsdesk . . .

'A bus driver has had a heart attack. He was at the wheel. The bus careered off the road and crashed into a restaurant.'

'Where?'

'Bridlington.'

That's just up the coast and reporters hit the phones.

'The bus was empty,' one says, replacing the receiver.

'What about the restaurant?'

'Empty too.'

'And the driver?'

'Recovering.'

It is still a story but is pushed back to page six.

Brussels: Chris White heads over to the Coco Bar in search of a n EU Commission official. The man has offered him a briefing on issues that need to be addressed on 'The Island' – as he and others are starting to call the UK.

He is not there but Olivier, the owner, says: 'Have a beer.'

His tone insinuates that refusal will cause offence and White relents.

Afterwards, he sets off for the train station to go home but on the way bumps into UKIP leader Nigel Farage, whom he considers one of the more personable of British MEPs. They have their differences but they put them aside and Farage says: 'Can I buy you a pint, Chris?'

According to today's High Court, Farage is one of 50 public figures preparing fresh phone-hacking cases against Murdoch's News Group.

White says: 'I'm not drinking, Nigel.'

Farage replies: 'I'm celebrating being given the Freedom of the City of London. I'd like you to join me.'

White thinks it might seem rude not to drink a toast and, out of politeness, says: 'All right, one small beer.'

West End: At *Stylist*, Anita Bhagwandas is ploughing through emails which stream in as fast as she deals with them. She is momentarily distracted by the art and features departments donning comedy headgear and she thinks: *'I love my job.'*

She discusses news stories and potential exclusives from New York Fashion Week.

West End: As she prepares to fly to New York Fashion Week, *Marie Claire's* Helen Russell edits a colleague's flipcam video in iMovie so it can be linked to a QR code.

Cornwall: Editor Kirstie Newton discusses sales promotions for *Cornwall Today,* ones which will appear in their sister newspapers. She chooses half a dozen stories to appear in different sections – health, antiques, gardens – and covering a wide spread of locations.

She finishes and leaves the office. For once she gets home on time, wondering how her husband and baby are, with their bad coughs.

Delhi: At Helen Roberts's agency, her colleague Tanzeel goes home after a long, busy and productive day. The clock is approaching midnight. They have already started planning for tomorrow. They've got a story about a family so large they could be a new Guinness record breaker.

They are trying to get them all together for a family photo. But that's easier said than done. It is turning into a nightmare.

Camden Town: At *Take a Br*eak, deputy chief sub Ben raises his head from proofreading to ask an innocent question. Unfortunately it coincides with a lull and he uses a voice which carries to more ears than he intended.

'What's a vajazzle?'

Stunned silence while all eyes turn towards him.

His many female colleagues explain that it is a style of bejewelled grooming below the waist evolved from the *Brazilian* and the *Hollywood,* and much favoured by women from Essex. He wishes he'd never bothered.

The features team decide they will hold a pet wedding. They think it will make a great picture spread. They tell the picture desk, who are not so sure. Animals tend not to cooperate with photographers.

Stratford-upon-Avon: 'Fantastic!' thinks a young Matt Wilson as the *Daily Mail* gets back to him on the stolen Shakespeare piping.

He's sent them 400 words and the *Mail* newsdesk says: 'Can we have 600 words – and more from the cops.'

Wilson starts getting on with it – fast – because he has another job coming up shortly. He calls the police press office. No reply. It's after 5pm, and he cannot get an alternative number. He calls local police officers but they're not much help.

He phones the *Mail* newsdesk.

Someone tells him: 'You need to send copy earlier if you want to get it in the paper. Anyway our Midlands man is onto it.'

It's useful experience for Wilson, who has been on the *Herald* for only five months. He's plugging himself into the wider journalistic network.

Tunbridge Wells: The shot-cat man finally gets back to Jenny Barsby and agrees to do an interview for BBC Radio Kent. But the interview studio is busy and she has to wait until after news and sport. Finally, she gets the space and does the recording.

Having failed to finish her fajitas, Barsby has a banana while getting the 6 o'clock news ready.

Her colleague, Chris, sneezes – that bug is getting everywhere – and some of his colleagues send him an email saying: 'Bless you.'

A local news agency tweets an interesting story and Barsby checks it with a local police inspector, the press office having gone home.

He says: 'I know nothing about it. They're probably scratching around for ideas because it's so quiet today.'

Barsby puts her coat on, not that she's leaving yet. The heating's been turned down and she says: 'It's bloody freezing in here!'

Bedford: Kathryn Cain browses through the agenda of Bedford Borough Council's executive meeting for this evening. She turns the pages without anything capturing her attention and decides to use her time more pleasantly. She heads home.

Manchester: After the long drive to Preston and back, Kevin Duffy feels he's had enough. Time to relax and recover after his teaching sessions and other work. He reaches for the Chinese takeaway menu while eyeing up the wine rack. Red or white? But before he can do anything, his eyelids droop and he falls asleep, right there on the sofa.

West End: At *Reader's Digest,* Gill Hudson is trying to put together her entry for the PPA magazine awards. She keeps getting interrupted and can see a late-night looming early next week in order to beat the deadline. Her partner emails through some property details and she makes a quick call to an estate agent. Both are in full-time, full-on jobs and they find it difficult fitting in the personal stuff.

She looks at the time and starts packing up.

Gotta go.

Wells: For once, there are no Wednesday night council meetings to occupy Oliver Hulme's evening. He's got home and is already putting his feet up. He's looking forward to watching the BBC Folk Awards. One of the winners was a star at last year's Priddy Folk Festival, just outside Wells – that's got to be worth a nib for the paper.

He'll write it tomorrow.

Coffee. A fag. He pours himself a vodka. This is the life. He leans back and relaxes.

West End: It is home time for Kathryn Blundell at *Mother & Baby*. But even as she clears her desk, two new pieces of copy come in, and the features editor wants her to check something else.

Blundell says: 'Can you email it all to me so can read it tonight.' She already has page proofs in her bag. It looks like a busy evening.

She pulls on her fur coat, switches into heels and heads out the door.

Brighton: Adam Oxford drafts out a story for tomorrow, one he will post to another blog he writes for. Then he sets off home, having promised to cook supper for his wife and child.

Sheffield: Journalism Professor Peter Cole boards the train to London. He is one of three trustees of the Press Association Trust and they have a formal meeting tomorrow morning.

Tunbridge Wells: At the *Courier,* editor Read and his staff are up against the clock and the newsroom is feeling the pressure. The stresses and tensions of the day keep erupting as he keeps them hard at it.

They've still got some editions to finish.

An argument starts between the news editor and the subs, sufficiently so that editor Read has to stop proofreading and step in.

A few minutes later there is more trouble, this time an embarrassing muscle-flexing standoff between the news editor and a reporter. It's over a tiny detail in a story and again Read intervenes, saying: 'Calm down.'

The atmosphere remains tense.

In a way, it shows how much people care about the job. They want to get it right. Sometimes the passion boils over. Read, who was in before dawn, knows he can hardly blame them for that.

Walthamstow: Transcript finished, Nick McGrath cannot resist the call of the kids downstairs. He joins them for pre-bathtime CBeebies on TV and to read his new copy of *Time Out* magazine.

He casts a professional eye over the listings. What's on? Who's appearing? Who can he interview and profile?

He is planning his next few days' work.

Cambridge: Reporter Raymond Brown is another journalist who is still hard at it after a non-stop day. He's making calls trying to identify the dead bodies that have been found. They're suffering the final indignity of death: anonymity.

No one is even missing them.

It's not only about two sad endings; it's an important social issue which is highlighted by another story he's following. That's a court trial taking place about a homeless man beaten to death and dumped in the Cam. Brown is asking police for the CCTV and pictures. Can they release them for publication?

He's waiting for a reply.

Brown – who describes himself as 'relentless' – has yet more stories on his plate. With the ones he's writing, he is adding new information as it comes in, tying up loose ends and double checking. He is also helping to edit the online video of Prince Charles's visit.

Tunbridge Wells: In the cauldron that is the *Courier* newsroom, Sharon Marris is getting the latest update on her story – The Mystery of the Edenbridge Loyalty Card Winner.

The head of the Chamber of Commerce calls her to say he has a plan. Tonight he is going to door-knock along the street which he thinks he has identified from the card. Maybe that will get a result.

Marris makes notes.

Tomorrow, she is driving up to RAF Halton in Buckinghamshire to return some of her Afghanistan equipment – body armour, helmet – so she tells her colleagues she won't be in first thing to deal with any last-minute page changes.

On any other day most of the *Courier*'s staff would be finished by now. But Wednesdays are much more demanding.

Half of the team remains to keep proofing pages. Others are still working on stories. Marris has had a busy week and wants to get out by 6 o'clock.

'I'm knackered,' she says.

Co. Donegal: Paddy Clancy is well plugged-in to the local network of news and gossip and now he hears that an Irish TV chef and his wife – who live about a half-hour away – had twins earlier today. A couple of quick calls, checks on Twitter and Facebook, and he has the story written and on its way to the newspapers before six o'clock.

A contact phones him and says: 'Paddy, I want to tell you about this illegal garbage dump. It needs writing about.'

'Okay,' replies Clancy, 'can you get me more details? Then I can do something.'

'Will do, Paddy,' says the man.

Clancy returns to his Titanic feature and rings Margaret Devaney's 86-year-old daughter, living in the American city of New Jersey. Despite her age, she is good for quotes. He'll write it up tomorrow

Twitter: From freelance Clare Swatman – *'Dear weather, please don't snow again this weekend. It's boring now. Thanks, love Clare.'*

Hollywood: With his cameraman alongside, the BBC's Peter Bowes is being taken deep inside the Universal Studios lot.

He is ushered into windowless editing suites and allowed to record skilled restoration artists at work. They are re-mastering classic Universal films – such as *Sting* and *Jaws*. It is an incredible task. They are doing it frame by single frame.

Peter Schade, in charge of the project, says to camera: 'Our main concern is to maintain the film-maker's vision.'

Bowes will put together a TV feature to run at the end of April.

Hollywood: Most of Los Angeles is wide awake by now and Wilshire Boulevard is chock-a-block with limousines. But it's still too early for some of the big stars to be out and about, to have got further than breakfast in bed or maybe the sun terrace. Yet the paparazzi are taking no chances. They're keeping an alert eye on Whitney Houston's hotel.

She's unpredictable, which is what makes her worth tracking 24/7. Is she up yet?

It's Whitney Watch.

CHAPTER 13

6pm-7pm
From Bottoms to Beauty

Notting Hill: The culture at Talk To The Press is not to work late unless they think it is absolutely necessary. Natasha – having collected her son – Katie and Georgette shut down their computers, switch off the lights, lock up and clatter down the winding staircase back into the early evening bustle of Portobello Road.

In the milling crowd, they part and go their separate ways, their duties done for the day.

Shepherd's Bush: One mile away, at the BBC, Frank Gardner's mobile rings. It's his daughter asking him for a lift home. He glances at his watch, reckons he's spent enough time in the twilight world that is the editing suite and says: 'Yeah, go on then.'

Camden Town: Methodically, page by page, editor Jon Peake has worked his way through the piles of pr oofs rolling off the *TV Choice* and *Total TV Guide* production line and now he looks proudly at his empty desk. He has cleared it bang on time. He's pleased with himself, and his staff.

The much-desired Olly Murs still hasn't called. No surprise there then.

Peake gets his coat, says goodbye, descends from the fifth floor and walks through the bustle of Camden High Street to the tube station.

As he hops onto the escalator, he considers his plans for tonight, not quite as glamorous as those of the stars he has been reading and writing about. He is a journalist, not a showbiz personality, and his aspirations are modest.

He intends to spend the evening with his wife in front of the TV, catching up on all the shows he both wants and needs to see – *Alex Polizzi The Fixer*, *Masterchef* and *Law & Order*.

In his TV watching, he doesn't need to distinguish between work and play. It's where the personal meets the professional.

172

Tunbridge Wells: Thoroughly tired, Sharon Marris is out of the door at the *Courier* and walking home along cold pavements. Will she sleep any better tonight? Or will Afghanistan continue to invade her thoughts and disrupt her rest? She doesn't know.

Sydney, Australia: Ex-*Daily Mirror* editor David Banks has just rolled out of bed. He feels groggy but has an excuse which has nothing to do with late nights or whisky. It's called jet lag.

He looks out of his hotel window. He's on the other side of the world.

It's 7am and Banks, now a media commentator, is a long way from his home in Northumberland. He is using the trip to look up old mates from the time he spent working in Oz.

He is travelling with his wife Gemma and it's more than just a pleasant break. It's research and a journey back to the 'old days' and a life he loved; sun, sea and service as one of Rupert Murdoch's top lieutenants.

Banks is a diabetic and starts by taking a blood sugar reading. It's good. So he goes downstairs to stoke up on breakfast while Gemma pops along to the Cronulla pool with old Aussie girlfriends and does aquarobics.

While he eats, Banks scans the Sydney *Daily Telegraph*, a paper he edited 20 years ago. He's jealous of the way it looks, reads and sells today.

His mobile pings and he sees a text message: *Let me buy you lunch.* It is from an old colleague Chris Mitchell, now editor of the *Australian*.

Excellent. He accepts.

It will be Banks's last chance to get a quote or two on the impact that the UK hacking scandal is having in Murdoch's own backyard.

He can use it in his *Press Gazette* column back home. He's got a deadline to meet. It's due the day he and Gemma get off the plane back in Britain.

Melbourne, Australia: Nearly 550 miles down the coastline, Dame Elisabeth Murdoch is waking up to another beautiful morning on Cruden Farm. She is still glowing from her 103rd birthday celebration.

She is full of appreciation for the good things in life that comes with such advanced years. It was a splendid evening even if her son, Rupert, and grandson, James, were absent.

It will be Rupert's 81st birthday in four weeks time. Perhaps they can make up for it then.

Dame Elisabeth can think back to his birth in 1931 and admire at all that he has achieved, and is still achieving, in a remarkable life and career.

United States: Another dark cloud has been cast across the Murdoch family reputation with the multi-million pound phone-hacking settlements made seven hours ago in the London High Court. Everything was agreed beforehand, through lawyers, so it did not come as a complete shock.

Yet it still felt like a public humiliation to Rupert and James Murdoch, an admission of serious fault inside their company, under their stewardship.

The relentless pressure is taking its toll.

But now father and son have a rare glimmer of good news and it is time to counter-strike.

Their riposte will come tonight in a way which matters most to them, and to their board and their shareholders.

The bottom line.

Murdoch & son have seen the Wall Street forecasts for News Corp's profits. Huh, what do the financial scribblers know? In six hours' time, the real figures will be released.

And they will be a surprise.

As one of their own tabloids might have headlined it: *The Empire Strikes Back.*

It is one means of lifting the cloud. But, for the Murdochs, will the sun ever shine as brightly as it once did?

West End: It has been a wonderful day for Farrah Storr as *Women's Health* continues to draw compliments from journalists, PRs, advertisers and – most importantly – readers. She is at her desk when she gets a call from Morgan Rees, her big boss, to see if she and the team are still in the office.

'Yes,' she says.

'Right, don't go anywhere. I'm popping over.'

'Okay.'

Hmmm . . . she has mixed feelings. Is there a problem? Is a good day about to turn bad?

Five minutes later she looks up and exclaims: 'Oh my God!'

Brandishing bottles of champagne, Rees is leading in the entire *Men's Health* team. They are all grinning as they take it in turn to congratulate Storr and her colleagues. Corks pop around the room. Glasses are raised. A toast is proposed.

'Great job, Farrah.'

'Relish your success.'

'It's celebration time.'

'Thanks.'

She enjoys it but, in the back of her mind, a little voice keeps nagging away, saying *'Now we just have to sell lots of copies.'*

West End: In the same building as *Women's Health*, but on another floor, Lindsay Nicholson knows that this is when she would normally get down to reading articles for the next issue of *Good Housekeeping.* But there may be heavy snow again tonight. She's got to get on her way before the weather deteriorates.

She sticks a wad of pages into her bulging bag, puts her snowboots back on, says goodbye and sets off in the direction of Hertfordshire.

She's glad to see the back of the Sofa Crisis.

Tomorrow it will dealt with.

West End: Louise Chunn is still at her desk, this time looking at potential April cover pictures. She is talking to her art director, Andrea Lynch. They need exactly the right face to convey *Psychologies'* strengths, to project its subtlety while making it leap from the newsagents' shelves.

That's quite a challenge. Subtlety and impact? They are not natural partners.

Now Chunn studies a selection of shots. She scrutinises them in turn and discusses them with Lynch.

'She's too old . . . '

'This one?'

'Hair too big.'

'This one?'

'Too glam.'

Chunn and Lynch know that this decision is as important as any they make each month.

Magazines use faces to broadcast subliminal messages about content – through eyes and mouth, hair and accessories, angles and inclinations. In many cases, the requirement is relatively simple. But the needs of *Psychologies* are more complex, like its editorial.

It has to emphasise why it is different from *Women's Health*: more cerebral, more upmarket, older but not staid, and not at all girly. It has to say all that in a nanosecond of a glance Chunn can compare the two magazines by placing them side by side on her desk.

Women's Health is in-your-face, with coverlines promoting physical assets – a flat, sexy stomach, a hot yoga body, perfect weight, great sex. It shows movie star Kate Beckinsale, her athletic figure enhanced by a clingy dress. It is positive, with a self-praising narcissism which is summed up in the mantra, *It's good to be you.*

Psychologies' coverlines are different – *stress less, make friends, parent better, promote wellbeing*. As for sex, it is mind over motion. It lingers more on imperfection, on reality rather than the unrealistic.

Its current cover displays the less well-known actress Anna Chancellor, in her forties, looking thoughtful, even unsure, beneath an untidy mop of hair. It shows just her face, not figure, saying this magazine is about the mind. Its slogan is *Know more, grow more.*

One is a bit *Daily Mail,* the other more *Guardian.*

Chunn and Lynch continue to discuss the cover pictures.

In the end, Chunn cannot make up her mind and says: 'I'm going to go home and think about it.'

She packs up and leaves.

Eventually she does decide. Her final choice is very different from Anna Chancellor. It is another actress, Kristin Scott Thomas, but wearing bright-red lipstick, better groomed, looking more confident. The main coverline has moved from the negative – *Stress less* – to the positive – *Kick start your creativity.*

At this point, Chunn has steadied a fall in circulation to 131,000. Her success – or failure – will be defined not only in her figures but in those of Farrah Storr.

They are as locked together as the conjoined twins in Helen Roberts's version of India.

Delhi: It's real conjoined twins that Helen Roberts is dealing with and even now, as the clock approaches midnight, she sees another email appear on screen asking for more details. It is from an Irish paper and they like the story. She replies. As it turns out, it is the last email of the day.

Her screen falls quiet and darkens, and now she makes the call she promised.

'Hi, Mum.'

'Hello, Helen. You sound as if you've been busy.'

'Yes, it's going well.'

They can see each other on Facetime as a sultry night in Delhi sits alongside a freezing-cold teatime in Conwy.

They continue to talk as if they were sitting over cup of coffee.

Enfield: Greg Figeon signs off and sends the final pages of *The Press* and finishes planning the running order for the *Chingford Times*. He leaves the office, locks the door behind him and gets into his car. He's been at work nine hours, with only an irregular supply of tea to keep him refreshed, but he's not finished, not for hours yet.

He starts driving. It is a 30-mile journey and he finds himself caught in the middle of the evening rush hour.

Essex: Agony aunt Katie Fraser is on the train when she gets an important email: the missing woman from her Depression Support Group has reappeared just as suddenly as she disappeared.

She is sending out messages to all those who were worried about her.

'I'm fine. Sorry for causing a scare.'

At least she's not been murdered.

South London: Back home in his box-room office, Chris Wheal tries to work on an AOL feature but is distracted by phone calls and the demands of an internet forum. To his irritation, PRs have not replied with answers to apparently straight-forward questions.

Belatedly, he realises his favourite comedy half-hour has started on Radio Four and so he leaves his desk and hurries down to the kitchen. He begins to cook dinner while his son does Morgan Freeman impersonations.

Twitter: *'Guido reports the Jimmy Saville scandal will be exposed shortly by The Oldie magazine, edited by former Private Eye editor Richard Ingrams.'*

Having finished his evidence to Leveson, the irrepressible Paul Staines – aka blogger Guido Fawkes – is showing he still has lots up his sleeve.

Camden Town: While most of the staff are going home at *Take a Break,* a small hub of feature writers remains behind. They want to discuss weddings – both pet and human.

Glasgow: Samantha Booth returns from a b racing walk with her appetite sharpened by the cold. In the kitchen, she knocks up a quick meal, worrying about her slow working day. Why on earth can't people get back to her? It's just a matter of common courtesy. Ah well . . .

She sits down with a plate of pasta. The first forkful almost makes it to her lips when the email pings. She looks.

Can we have copy please. NOW!

It's from an editor. There is no alternative. The fork clatters to the plate. Forget eating. Start working.

Ten minutes later another *ping,* this one from a PR client asking her to update their Twitter feed.

Booth looks at her pasta growing cold, and her screen getting hot, and is grateful, if hungry.

She thinks: 'Hooray, going to be a busy evening.'

Tunbridge Wells: Jenny Barsby is reading the news when she feels the urge to burp. She does so, disrupting her usual smooth flow. That will teach her to eat a banana in the run-up. She explains this on air to the presenter and then, as she finishes the weather, he plays the Flumps music – short trumpet sounds.

Barsby is alarmed, in a comical way.

Off air she says: 'People across Kent will think I have the farts!'

She's completed three clips regarding the shot cat. Now she's sorting out the headlines and sport for the 6.30 bulletin.

Hammersmith: Despite flagging a bit, Arif Durrani makes a trip into London's West End. He is with reporter Maisie McCabe. They attend an event called the Future of Television.

It is being held by Walker Media, one of the big agencies.

The speaker is *Thinkbox*'s Tess Alps who Durrani knows is always good value, with original thoughts and controversy guaranteed. It also provides him with a chance to catch up with some of the media agency fraternity.

Worcester: Sub Mark Halliwell sends through the final page for this week's *Berrows Journal* and blogs: 'So rest assured, the world's oldest newspaper will once again appear this week, continuing the tradition started in 1690.'

That is 322 years of journalism.

Elsewhere on the editorial floor, Steph Preece puts through the front page of the *Worcester News.*

She says: 'It's been another struggle to get everything in, but I think we've managed it. Another jam-packed *WN* hitting the press tonight.'

Subs are putting the final touches to pages one and two right now. Most of the staff have left and those remaining are nearly done.

Deputy editor John Wilson checks the pages a final time. He is full of enthusiasm, his love for the job shining through.

'Everything looks good,' he says, 'but we'll try to do even better tomorrow. It's been a hectic day. It's great to work with such a tremendously talented team of people.'

He looks at the time. He's got to go. He was expected home half-an-hour ago. He flies out the door.

Bristol: The training day has ended and Caroline Sutton has a quick drink and chat with Andy Marshall, group managing director at Immediate. She's pleased with how it went. Then she heads to the station to catch the train. She clambers aboard, finds a seat and relaxes as she heads back towards the south coast and home.

Vienna: Mike Leidig's working day has been 14 hours, which is normal for him. Lunch was a sandwich at three o'clock and bowls of cereal at sporadic intervals. He is not complaining at all. He still loves the job after 20 years in the business but says: 'It's a lot different from what it used to be.'

He sets off home.

Barnet: New mum Sara Ward has just sent a video of her with baby James to her colleagues at *Take a Break*. She misses her workmates but they keep in touch regularly.

Right now, she is looking at *Mumsnet* to see how other new mums are getting on. Their posts remind her of the issues they've covered in the magazine and now they give her ideas for some new features. She jots down a list . . .

Mums made to feel like failures because they can't breastfeed.
Short-staffed maternity wards.
Tired, sore new mums trying to fend off amorous husbands.
Families at war over, or brought together by, the new baby.
Post-traumatic stress syndrome after a difficult birth.

Ward stops. Right now, James is crying and needs her attention.

Manchester: At the jam-packed champagne bar, *Estates Gazette*'s Damian Wild is playing host and wants to say a few words of welcome to everyone. He is undeterred by the rising babble of voices and stands up and starts to speak.

'Thanks for coming . . . It's been a brilliant day . . . '

He's brave but that's not enough. The drink is flowing and it's tricky trying to prise the crowd of 100 or so of the city's great and good away from topping up their champagne flutes.

He continues, hoping against hope. But who's taking notice? After a few minutes getting nowhere, he decides if you can't beat 'em, join 'em. He cuts his losses and heads to the bar, refilling his glass.

There is wall-to-wall chatter and banter.

Stratford-upon-Avon: Having been delayed by the demands of the *Daily Mail*, Matt Wilson looks at his watch and jumps up like the White Rabbit declaring he's going to be late.

He runs out of the office.

178

It's lucky he's fit as he now sprints along the pavement, past the dawdling crowds of Shakespeare tourists, all the way to the district council offices. He arrives breathless, bursts into the council chamber – and sees there is no space left at the press table. It is filled with rival hacks and they are not giving way. He is ushered to a desk by himself in the corner, as if he's been a bad boy. He sits at it feeling both excluded and exclusive.

There is more than normal interest this evening. This is the planning meeting for a controversial cinema proposal. The debate kicks off and the arguments begin. It gets heated and passionate, and Wilson taps away at his keyboard, providing a live Twitter feed.

Multi-tasking, he still hasn't finished with the *Mail* story either and texts them extra information.

Stedham Village: In the shed behind his cottage, veteran columnist Colin Dunne's next article seems to be coming along well. He's writing about a fictional author called Ross Thomas.

'Fascinating guy, Thomas. Marvellous writer of sharp, funny thrillers. Took no crap from publishers. Told that words like Chinaman and Dwarf were forbidden, Thomas immediately wrote "Chinaman's Chance" and "The Eighth Dwarf". Ex-journo, PR man, political campaign manager, speech writer for politicians. And one book a year. Must've known the string-around-leg trick. Probably hawser-round-leg to write 26 books. Damn him. Here in Canary Wharf (shed's grandiose nickname), it's pretty good to read one book a year, never mind write one.'

He taps away as the moon peeps between dark clouds.

Camden Town: Adam Carpenter has left the offices of *that's life!* and rides the down escalator into the underground and is grateful to get a seat on the tube. As the train moves off, he hits the BlackBerry again, this time to write his weekly blog for *Working Mums* online.

'Okay,' he murmurs to himself. 'I'm not a mum. Live with it.'

Instead he is the controversial *Grumpy Dad.* It's an unpaid column which he started 18 months ago as a favour for a friend and he has kept it going. He says he's against professionals writing for free but he enjoys this, a regular rant about the pleasures and pain of parenthood, just letting off steam.

He taps: 'How come, after four years of ballet lessons, my daughter still dances like someone from Madness?'

In recent weeks he's covered the teachers' strike, the effects of video games and Tesco selling smoky bacon cocktail sausages.

'Are women writers better than men on women's magazines?'

Carpenter: 'Yes, usually.'

'Why?'

Carpenter: 'First, these are consumer magazines – that means they deal with women's clothes and other women's products. As prime users, women are more expert.

'Second, many articles focus on women's personal relationships, both good and bad. Women are more relaxed being interviewed by another woman, especially about intimate details.'

'So men shouldn't apply?'

'No way. This does not stop men being effective as editors, subs and designers.'

Southbank: *Marie Claire*'s Helen Russell secures freelance cover for the next fortnight and breathes a sigh of relief. She is beginning to wind down and is looking forward to the evening. She won't go straight home. She fancies a glass or two of wine over dinner with an old friend.

Tunbridge Wells: Libel alert! Editor Ian Read is alarmed as he reads some copy. He reckons it is inflammatory and dangerous.

The story is an inside downpage story – so why invite unnecessary trouble?

He has a quick chat with the reporter and explains the problem. He rewrites it so it is safe. This is common sense, not cowardice. Read doesn't want to spend next week dealing with last week's problems.

He phones through a few more changes before the proofers leave.

Then he pauses long enough to think back over a very busy day. He loves his job, loves seeing all the different editions come together as they have done, even if it's been a struggle. It's not just exciting, it's a privilege.

Today has had its humorous moments and he smiles to himself at some of the corrections he's made. He can't decide which amused him more – the line implying a crash victim lived with the coroner, or a nib suggesting a community litter-pick tidied up the litter rather than removed it.

Leeds: After arriving home early from the *Evening Post*, David Spereall is wearing his other hat now, as editor of the Leeds Trinity University's magazine. He's got a lot of submissions from fellow students to read through.

He gets busy, emails writers back, proofreads and edits down where necessary.

He needs everything ready.

Tomorrow, he will send the magazine off for printing.

As he's forever telling his flatmates: 'It's the best job in the world.'

Rwanda: There have been no terrorist explosions reported in Kigali to interrupt Reuters' Graham Holliday's evening. He reads his son a bedtime story, a mythical tale about pandas in China. Then, after wine and coffee, he gets into a nostalgic mood with his French other half Sophie and explores *YouTube* for the worst and the best of eighties pop.

The internet connection is fairly good tonight although sometimes the videos stall.

Hull: It's all fine on the front and back pages of the *Mail* and a late lead is coming together nicely.

Assistant editor Jamie Macaskill checks out the last emails of the evening and peruses tomorrow's diary, so he can prepare himself. He's getting ready for going home. Then he's shown a picture of a naked bloke playing darts. Someone says: 'What do you think, Jamie? Should we use it?'

It's a story about a Facebook page featuring Hull blokes in the buff in the snow. It is attracting thousands of hits.

'Let's take a vote,' he replies and everyone in the office is quickly polled.

Macaskill makes the final decision.

He says: 'On this occasion, a smallish picture of a big bloke's arse won't offend the readers – so put it in.'

At that, he leaves for home, thinking: 'All in all, a fairly straight-forward day.'

Holborn: After a 10-hour day at *Reader's Digest,* Gill Hudson just won't stop, or can't stop, living up to her reputation as a bit of a human dynamo. Now she arrives at a meeting of Women in Journalism, a networking group set up to combat sex discrimination, among other things.

Although women's numbers in journalism are equal to men's overall, they get fewer top positions.

They discuss various items including their recent lunch with shadow minister Yvette Cooper, a forthcoming seminar programme and a contacts book.

Hudson agrees to hold a session entitled 'How to pitch in a digital age'.

The meeting runs on. She has two glasses of wine and munches tortilla chips and concludes: 'My nutritional status is dire.'

Westminster: In the world of beauty journalism, it is headline news: *New product from Nivea. Please come to our launch.*

It's not in some bland conference centre on an industrial estate. Not at all.

The location has been selected to lure and to flatter: the ultra-fashionable new Corinthia Hotel. And right now *Stylist's* Anita Bhagwandas is heading towards it, power-walking across Trafalgar Square and into Whitehall Place.

She swirls through the revolving doors precisely one minute late.

As she steps from the cold into the warmth, she is greeted with a lot of excited chatter from her many working friends. The hotel is spectacular, a conversion from British Empire days. No expense has been spared as they are ushered into a dining room to find their table cards.

Dinner is served.

There is seafood and wines, white and red, and the service is smooth and splendid with a Mediterranean charm which defies the frost on the pavements outside. This is a place where a raw fish starter costs £19. Everything is on Nivea.

On their modest wages, few beauty writers could afford to indulge like this. This evening the only price they pay is to sit quietly during the Nivea presentation.

Nivea receives polite attention.

After that, they resume their excited chatter.

Is this usual?

One beauty writer says: 'I was at a lunch recently and had the misfortune to sit at a table of 20-somethings from the glossies, probably all on very low salaries, and every girl spent the dinner name-dropping, which spa was best, New York of Los Angeles or San Francisco.

'When I'd lifted my head out of my plate where it had sunk through sheer boredom, I realised the girls were just totally spoilt because they get SO much. I've heard lots of "don't you know who I am?" stories from these posh trips when someone doesn't get as good a room as someone else. It amuses me that they probably fly easyJet when they go on holiday themselves.'

Congleton: All *Chronicle* pages have been sent via FTP (File Transfer Protocol) and now Jeremy Condliffe and his editorial colleagues wait to hear that they have arrived safely. Finally, the printer replies.

Received okay.

Two little words which mean such a lot and Condliffe gives a sigh of relief and proffers his thanks to those around him. *Well done, everyone!*

Work completed, people pull on their coats, say goodbye and head out the door. The office empties and suddenly Condliffe finds he is sitting alone, as solitary as he was when he first began working in his pyjamas at 5.30 this morning.

The buzz has evaporated. But, though the room has drained of bodies, it still retains its newspaper heart and soul.

He's not ready to leave yet. He glances round. His emotional attachment runs deep. His father John, then editor, bought the newspaper in 1988 and Jeremy is only the fourth person to occupy the editor's chair. It's a privilege, more than a job.

He gets on with some editorial maintenance – backing-up the week's work, updating the computers, leaving the subs some copy for the morning.

While the back-up's running, he practices on his drum kit. He's got an electric one in an office and a real one in the room where they used to print. He has a punk band and they still rehearse on the spot where the old Cosser printer stood when he was but a lad.

Brussels: After a beer with UKIP leader Nigel Farage, veteran correspondent Chris White makes his way to the station. He boards the 19.41 train and soon arrives home. He tells his wife it has been a productive day and adds reassuringly: 'I am glad I am not drinking.'

Manchester: Louise Bolotin downs tools although she is still checking emails and reading her RSS feed.

Kingston: Having completed and sent off her urgent commission, Natalie Dye collects her husband Gino from the train station. He is returning from his job as art director of *Take a Break* 'specials'.

She says: 'You look a tad jaded.'

He agrees.

She says: 'I blame it on a combination of things – lateness, sub-zero weather, a vile commute, and a day stuck in an office when you would rather be up Everest.'

He agrees with that as well.

He asks what she's been doing.

She says. 'Just the space-time continuum.'

Paris: A woman at the medical charity *Medecins Sans Frontieres* takes a call from across the Channel. An English voice introduces herself as a journalist for BBC Radio's *The World Tonight.* Can she discuss the deaths and violence in Syria? Yes, the woman says, and the interview begins . . .

Shepherd's Bush: Robin Lustig and *The World Tonight* team listen as the woman from *Medecins Sans Frontieres* describes the killings and atrocities in the city of Homs. It's a powerful interview, just what they need.

Once it's finished, they reconsider the programme's running order.

Lustig thinks Syria's now definitely top. That means the NHS discussion will be later in the programme, which is a problem, as the participants have also been booked by TV's*Newsnight*. The two programmes almost overlap.

Mmm, what can they do? They call the interviewees and explain.

'Can you come in early so we can pre-record at nine-thirty?'

'Yes, of course we can.'

KwaZulu-Natal: Travel writer Meera Durrani looks at the clock and thinks: *quitting time.* She abandons the patio and stands in a cold shower. She puts on fresh clothes and walks up to the main bar/restaurant for a much-needed G&T sundowner. She's carrying her laptop with her – she's still some features to work on – but ends up ignoring it and talking to some guests who have just checked-in.

Then she sits down, picks up a fork and starts to eat a plate of pasta.

Breaking News . . . Breaking News . . .

Trafalgar Square: The red carpet has been rolled out on the steps of the National Portrait Gallery and some metal barricades are penning in the news photographers and film crews.

It's a big occasion in every sense.

A black limousine sweeps up and draws to a halt. A man pulls open the rear door and a slim, angled leg appears and triggers a surge of excitement. Motorised cameras whirr at 40 frames a second as the rest of the leg's owner emerges into view. She flashes a s mile, super-white dentistry reflecting the dazzle of the popping flashlights.

Behind the photographers, a mixed crowd of royalists and celebrity stalkers emit a cheer.

The Duchess of Cambridge – Kate Middleton – is on her first solo engagement.

Her husband, Prince William, is 7,500 miles away in the South Atlantic, serving with British military forces in the disputed Falkland islands. How will she cope without him as she attends a preview of the paintings of Lucian Freud?

Whirr-whirr, whirr-whirr.

Some of the best shots are taken by Rebecca Naden, of the Press Association, and she starts sending them straight to her picture desk, who are ready and waiting.

A motley crew of reporters are in attendance, straining alongside the snappers.

The *Mirror*'s Victoria Murphy, their royal specialist, is backed up by Dinah Turner, from fashion, and they start to file copy . . .

'Understated and elegant, our style icon wows again . . . '

Currently, it is red-top policy to support Kate and – at least for now – she cannot put a pedicured foot wrong. She's on a media honeymoon. Yet Palace advisers, and the royal family, remain wary. They know how quickly the newspapers can switch from friend to foe, and turn a heroine into a villainess in the public's mind.

For years, Prince William hated the press, both before and after the death of his mother, Princess Diana, but he is an intelligent realist. The Crown's future depends upon it 'being relevant'. That means being visible, not living behind high walls.

Kate has become the new lead in the eternal drama that is the royal soap and is playing her role as if born to it.

Wembley: With a high level of drama, another kind of soap opera is being played out at the FA headquarters. Behind closed doors, the England manager Fabio Capello is saying his piece to chairman David Bernstein.

He's angry.

As on the football pitch, there is a contrast between the expressive Italian style and the more reserved Englishness.

Outside, football reporters are monitoring the meeting but it's private and they can only indulge in speculation. Few are speculating correctly.

Tunbridge Wells: For her next broadcast, Jenny Barsby takes a new clip from TV, one about metal theft.

Overall, she thinks it's been very quiet today. She has a last look at Twitter, websites and emails and then four pips start the countdown to 7 o 'clock, precisely.

In a calm, steady voice she begins her shift's last bulletin .

CHAPTER 14
7pm-8pm
Breaking News

Pip-pip-pip-pip . . .

Tunbridge Wells: The pips end and Jenny Barsby launches into her final news reading of the day.

She's been updating and reading the bulletins for seven hours now, since she came on duty at noon. She's had coffee but not much else apart from a banana and half a stale fajita.

Now her voice travels over the airwaves to the loyal listeners of BBC Radio Kent who are familiar with her well-modulated Home Counties tone.

She is an experienced broadcaster, doing a job she thoroughly enjoys. She moves from item to item, adjusting her tone to the content, and then finishes with the wintry weather.

'Wrap up warm everyone.'

The bulletin comes to a close. Her microphone is silenced and she relaxes and steps away from it.

Another shift is over.

Then it is time to wrap herself up warm and she pulls on a coat.

She says her goodbyes and is out of the door and walking briskly towards home.

Unemployed Ex-Murdoch Reporter: He is saying he's traumatised by his visit to the Job Centre, still depressed about his future and sounding like he's losing hope.

Now, to recuperate, he is settling down with his cat, Chaplin, for an evening of telly viewing, with a hot Vimto spiked with whisky at his elbow. It's a recipe he stumbled upon when ill and unable to afford Lemsip. He finds it vaguely medicinal and comforting.

Delhi: Helen Roberts's call to her mum over Facetime has been quite a long one. Well, it's free if you both have iPhones.

She says: 'It's been a fab day, Mum, working in the best job in the world in a crazy country like India.'

The call ends.

Now, in her modest flat, Roberts moves from desk to bed to get some much-needed sleep, knowing she's got to do this all over again tomorrow.

London: Susan Watts is at Baker Street tube station on her way back to BBC Television Centre. Then she gets a call from the *Newsnight* producer. There's been another change of plan.

'Oh . . . ?'

It has affected her Antarctic drilling story.

Just to clarify, Watts speaks to the editor-of-the-day and for a moment there is an air of uncertainty as circumstances alter yet again. The news is is in flux.

' . . . *hold on, Argentinian/Falklands interviewee is just pulling out . . . you may be back on . . . can you hold . . . ?*'

'*Yes.*'

She waits a couple of minutes while a decision is reached. Then she gets the final answer. Dropped. Definitely. Her story is out.

She turns round and heads in the other direction. Forty minutes later, she arrives home in Hertfordshire. Just in case, she still runs through the Vostok two-way interview with her daughter. You never know when it might be needed.

Essex: Agony aunt Katie Fraser counts up her readers' poll about men in uniform. Who's the sexiest? She emails the copy to her editor.

The winner is big, strong and protective, trained to carry women in their arms, like medieval knights rescuing princesses from turrets. Fraser ponders on the biological basis for the predictability of female lust.

Why do women fancy hunky firemen?

Cambridge: Having finished off his many pieces of copy, one-man story machine Raymond Brown brakes to a halt. His fingers stop tapping. He comes to rest. He turns off his computer and heads for the exit. At last.

He arrives home and back to normal life, to dealing with two children. He doesn't know which is harder, work or the kids!

His wife, Lisa, is a psychiatrist and they start to talk about their day, sharing their little dramas. He describes his Prince Charles cock-up. She laughs. She asks about the body found in the church doorway. He tells her what he knows and says: 'Just another normal day!'

Walthamstow: Freelance Louise Baty has been contacted by a PR acting for a breast cancer charity, who tells her about a woman who is 'a twenty-something survivor'.

'That sounds interesting,' says Baty. 'Will she talk about it?'

'Yes, she's very keen. She wants others to know, to give them hope.'

'Okay, I'll call her.'

She will pitch it to a woman's magazine tomorrow.

The Sun: *'The Kate pictures are here.'* A voice from the picture desk tells anyone within earshot that they have received the photos from outside the National Portrait Gallery.

The executives gather round and look at the images. She's a nice well-groomed girl but without the enigmatic glamour of Princess Diana. Her appeal lies in her ordinariness. She's modest in manner, background, even clothes. Readers can identify with her, sharing her extraordinary elevation from girl-next-door (a posh one). She is Duchess Everywoman. Maybe that is a good thing for modern times.

Editor Dominic Mohan and his senior executives evaluate the pictures.

In the old days, with Diana, they'd have been page one. Guaranteed. Now, they've a slot waiting for Kate on page nine. That's the difference.

Anyone got a headline, to suit her first appearance without her husband? She's in a shiny dress and someone says: *'Kate can glow solo,'*

It's a pun. The *Sun* is one of the last resorts of punning. Most newspapers have largely abandoned the practice because bad puns outweighed good ones, and looked desperate. But the *Sun* persists and – despite a few clunkers – its sub-editors pride themselves on being the acknowledged masters.

Say it again.

'Kate can glow solo.'

It fits. That's it. Well done, matey!

The Kate headline is workmanlike and falls far short of some of the paper's classics:

SUPER CALEY GO BALLISTIC, CELTIC ARE ATROCIOUS
TOM AND THIERRY
CELEBRITY BIG BLUBBER
and, of a George Michael toilet incident, the most famous of all . . .
ZIP ME UP BEFORE YOU GO-GO.

Daily Telegraph: Copy has been swiftly knocked into shape on the Prince Harry story by chief reporter Gordon Rayner and defence correspondent Thomas Harding. They've got lots of extra detail about what's been happening this very evening . . .

'He was told that he had been declared the best co-pilot gunner of his class of more than 20. Captain Wales was presented with a trophy . . . '

Editor Gallagher likes it. The words 'best co-pilot gunner' explain the reality. It won't be a sightseeing tour. It's not about rescuing people, like his elder brother. Essentially, he's been taught to do one thing above others.

Kill.

Not all the other papers have latched onto this.

Right, Gallagher says, that's the front-page splash, and now the headline and sell are being written and rewritten until they are exactly right. It looks easier than it is. Finally, they are satisfied . . .

Headline: *Prince Harry to return to front line.*

Sell: *Prince is likely to have to kill insurgents in Afghanistan as Apache helicopter co-pilot.*

There's the key word again. *Kill.*

West End: Mint magazine's Marcus Harris arrives for dinner and a catch up with his former arts editor, who now works at a South London gallery. She gives him ideas for new editorial features and how to make progress with the photography project he is pursuing.

Wine flows.

He thinks: 'This is getting very liquid.'

City: It's been a long day but now Alan Burkitt-Gray gazes with satisfaction at his flatplan. It shows most of the 90-page issue is ready for the press. His associate editor – a freelance who comes in for two weeks – clocks off and leaves.

Burkitt-Gray just has his own interviews to write up and a few pages to check, and the contents pages and cover to do. Oh, plus he needs to think about an in-house advert – one from inside the company – to promote their new iPad service.

So he's not quite finished yet.

London: Freelance Jill Foster is back to staring at her computer screen and compulsively pecking at her keyboard, having started to get some food ready for her husband. She's on Twitter. She can't leave it alone.

She's sure she's got better things to do. She's read about users becoming addicted. Maybe she's crossed the line and it's happened to her. Perhaps that's her next story – technological enslavement of women home workers.

Channel 4 News: The show is on air right now, being broadcast without its star anchor, Jon Snow, who is down with 'flu. It is in the equally capable hands of Krishnan Guru-Murthy and Cathy Newman. They're not big names like him yet but both are popular with its upmarket viewers. By now it's been on the air for 25 minutes.

BREAKING NEWS . . . BREAKING NEWS . . .

Almost mid-show, Guru-Murthy sees the script reshape itself in front of his eyes and hears an insistent voice explaining why into his concealed earpiece. His eyes flicker.

It's a bombshell.

He takes it in, thinking on his backside. Then he shakes his head and adjusts his posture like a man physically steering a hurtling spaceship, changing course from one moon to another with a deft sway of his body.

Keeping his tone steady, he announces . . .

'We have just heard . . . '

There is a slight pause as he makes sure he is getting it right. He knows – as the BBC learnt earlier today with Redknapp – how a mistake turns into a joke to be repeated on loop as an internet sensation. He doesn't want that.

We have just heard that Fabio Capello . . . '

A slight pause. Gotta be sure.

' . . . has resigned as the England football manager . . . '

Another hesitation. Then he repeats it more confidently.

'Fabio Capello has resigned during his meeting with the Football Association. He has been at their headquarters in Wembley. We'll bring you more as we receive it.'

BREAKING NEWS . . . FABIO RESIGNS.. .BREAKING NEWS . . . FABIO'S OUT

The news is dropping everywhere, bursting out of every UK media channel with the velocity of a Didier Drogba penalty shot. It is being screamed and shouted across newsrooms, from sports desks to backbench executives to editors-in-chief. People rush into rooms and shout it. People rush out of rooms and shout it. There is an instinctive human pride in being first. Yes, it's just a football story. It is not religion, it is not war. In Britain, it seems much more important than either.

People are dying in Homs. Nobody's shouting about that, even on the posh papers. But they're all shouting about this.

Fabio's quit. Fabio's gone.

And, at the same time, other newsroom voices are asking: 'What about 'Arry?'

What about 'Arry?

With every mention of Capello, there is the inevitable ryder . . .

Since his happy release from the Crown Court dock eight hours earlier, Redknapp has retreated into his real world. Spurs have a big match coming up, against Newcastle United on Saturday. He's been working, overseeing team preparations at White Hart Lane stadium.

Capello's gone.

Football reporters who've spent years cultivating Redknapp's friendship jab at their phones. Get 'Arry. It's time to call in the favours. Got to get 'Arry. He must have heard. What's he saying?

Somewhere Harry Redknapp sees his phone light up. Non-stop.

Every editor gazes again at his front page. There's some ripping up to do. That's the easy bit. Then it needs putting back together again. That's the hard bit.

Tick-tock, tick-tock.

The clock is without mercy. Time is slipping away. Big ideas are needed. Now, this instant. This is when editors show their mettle.

Twitter: From *Telegraph* football writer Henry Winter, recently rated Britain's top sports journalist – *'D.I.V.O.R.C.E . . . End of a loveless marriage between*

Capello and England. FA must appoint somebody to inspire/unite players. Harry Redknapp.'

Wembley: Right now, the FA press office is releasing a statement . . .

'The discussions focused on the FA Board's decision to remove the England team captaincy from John Terry, and Fabio Capello's response through an Italian broadcast interview.

'In a meeting for over an hour, Fabio's resignation was accepted and he will leave the post of England manager with immediate effect.'

That's all folks.

Enfield: Arif Durrani is on the train home when he sees it on Twitter. *Capello resigns.* He thinks: *unbelievable.*

Twitter: From ex-*Mirror* editor Piers Morgan, now a C NN television interviewer in the US – *'Bye Fabio. Hello Harry!'*

Shepherd's Bush: Robin Lustig sees the news flash. *Capello resigns.* They don't do football on *The World Tonight.* It is a programme of heavyweight foreign news and politics.

But he's thinking again and says: 'This is a must.'

The production team go into overdrive and start hitting the phones.

Tunbridge Wells: Calm has returned to the *Courier's newsroom.* All the reporters have gone now and Ian Read sits with the news editor discussing the strengths and weaknesses of this week's paper. There's a TV on behind him and he senses something is happening on screen and turns round in his chair to look at the screen.

BREAKING NEWS . . . BREAKING NEWS . . .

Unbelievable.

Read is as shocked as anyone. As a Spurs fan, he says: 'That's terrible – Harry will leave us for England.'

No one really expected Capello to quit.

But there's nothing he can do about it. Read puts it aside for the moment. He forces his mind back on his job and sends an email thanking the subs for their efforts in catching up with the workload.

As the news editor leaves, Read says: 'Are you okay for tomorrow morning – seven-thirty?'

The news editor replies: 'Yes, Ian, see you at seven-thirty.'

They've got a new paper to produce. All six editions. They've got to do it all again. The pace is remorseless.

Walthamstow: Nick McGrath opens a bottle of wine. He's chosen a red from his modest collection, something with depth and flavour. His internet is down again and he has to use his phone to check the day's final emails.

He stares in shock.

Capello resigns!

His phone screen won't suffice so he tries his computer again. Still down. He decides to dial the number he's been putting off all day: time for the Dreaded Call Centre Battle.

He gets through.

'Hello,' says a voice. 'How can I help you?'

Hmmm, it sounds like India.

Basildon, Essex: In the rush-hour traffic, Greg Figeon sees the lights of a Tesco store up ahead and pulls over to make a couple of swift purchases. Then he continues to the offices of the *Yellow Advertiser*. He puts his newly-purchased chilli con carne in the microwave while making a cup of tea. He's had a long day. Time to treat himself. He opens a box of mini cookies.

Sydney: Having breakfasted, UK media commentator David Banks changes into shorts, pads down Cronulla Beach and wades into the surf. He crests a wave and starts to swim.

The water is great. If only it was this warm off the coast of Northumberland.

As he crawls away from land, he can't help thinking he'd make either a good snack for sharks or a fine target for tsunamis – this is the South Pacific after all.

What a headline for the Newcastle *Journal* – Our Columnist Banksie Eaten by Jaws.

But, if they're around, the sharks are far too intimidated and the self-acclaimed Banks of England swims back to the beach and is relieved to see he's still got arms and legs intact.

He returns to the hotel, takes a second shower and dresses for lunch. He goes down to the station. A train pulls in and he climbs aboard and watches the city centre skyline drawing nearer. Under his arm, he is carrying a copy of his old paper, the *Australian,* for everyone to see. He's still very proud of it.

Tunbridge Wells: After her long day, Sharon Marris makes dinner, watches TV and chats to friends on Facebook.

West End: *Marie Claire's* Helen Russell arrives in the Soho *quartier* and steps into a swish restaurant looking forward to dinner. She's meeting a former colleague who has set up a contract publishing company. It's recently been bought out for an eye-watering sum. Her friend has become very rich.

They sit down and start with some wine.

'It's New York Fashion Week next week,' says Russell. 'I'm going.'

'Sounds exciting.'

'Yes, but hard work.'

Cambridge: Bob Satchwell heads for home with his work day far from over. He has yet more to catch up on, the personal price he has to pay for the Leveson Inquiry.

He's not complaining. He's got ink in his veins. He's just mainlining on his habit of choice.

Basildon: Having feasted on chilli con carne and tea, Greg Figeon starts copy tasting – selecting stories – for the *Chingford Times*. Then he sees the breaking news appear on screen.

Capello resigns.

No way.

He checks BBC Sport, Twitter and Facebook. It really is true.

He resumes copy tasting, this time listening to heavy metal music. The only other person present is the cleaner, manoeuvring between desks with her duster. She empties bins around him while giving him a look which says: 'Haven't you got a home to go to?'

Guardian: Chief sports writer Richard Williams, formerly deputy editor of *Melody Maker,* starts filing his comment for page one. He says the only thing Capello and Redknapp have in common is that they are both aged 65.

'Whereas Capello never seemed to respect the essential qualities of English football, Redknapp . . . is steeped in them.'

Wembley: There is a crowd massing outside the Football Association's headquarters. A few of them are curious fans. The majority are photographers, all gazing in the same direction, aware they're running up against a constant stream of deadlines.

Here he comes . . .!

They see a limousine approaching. It's the same one that delivered Fabio Capello a couple of hours ago. They raise cameras, point and shoot, generating that familiar background muzak to modern celebrity.

Whirr-whirr.

The car passes slowly, almost gracefully, offering unspoken cooperation, giving them precious seconds.

The flashlights only half bounce off the glass windscreen. Enough light penetrates to illuminate a face set rock hard in a show of . . . well, whatever an imaginative caption writer wants to read into it.

Grim determination. Passive resignation. Suppressed anger. Blandness. Concealed triumphalism. Relief. Sorrow. Joy.

The car sweeps away, whisking Fabio Capello back towards the heart of London.

Manchester: Sports reporters are seeking reactions. They get onto England's star striker Wayne Rooney. He gives everyone a quote: 'Gutted Capello has quit. Good guy and top coach. Got to be English to replace him.'

Then Rooney shows solidarity with the newspapers and the public: 'Harry Redknapp for me.'

CHAPTER 15

8pm-9pm
The First Draft of History

The Capello resignation strikes the newsrooms with the impact of a fragmentation grenade, shattering their carefully composed headlines. Now front pages which looked so fresh a few minutes ago are being ripped up and trampled upon and then put back together again. It's fun if you have the temperament of a wrecking crew. Destroy to create. This is what the old hands love, and where the young hands learn.

It needs cool heads, daredevil wit, a gift for word play and the insight that comes from an intuitive understanding of mass psychology. As these gifts are rarely embodied in one human form, it also requires teamwork.

At moments like this you can smell victory – or fear – in a newsroom just as you can in a football team's dressing room. It's now or never. The crowd awaits. Play to win, boys and girls. Give it all you've got. Death or glory. All the world's a stage.

Newsrooms exude a kind of sweat. In the old days it used to be real sweat making wet patches on nylon shirts overlaying string vests. Back then, the favoured olefactory barriers were tiny Manikin cigars or foul-smelling pipes or untipped Capstan cigarettes as dizzying as dope.

Now, in these more groomed and moisturised times, it's not the smell that creeps up on you so much as an unidentified metrosexual pheromone. It scatters on thermal columns above overheated computer screens, binding men and women together in an embrace which dare not speak to HR.

This is how the first draft of history is really written. You could almost vomit with the excitement.

And now, working against the clock, the rival newsrooms are each united in their urgency, mortally pitted against one another like warring Aboriginal tribes.

The Sun: '*Who's got a splash headline, for God's sake? We need a splash headline. Now!*'

Voices pipe up with suggestions.

194

Stale. They lack wit and originality. There must be something better linking the key words. *Harry – Fabio – Redknapp – Capello – a mutual good riddance.* How can they be joined, visually and intellectually.

Think, think.

Then some bright spark makes up a word and blurts it out.

Hey, I like that. Say it again.

'Arryvederci.

Pause.

Everyone still thinking. They chuckle. Then . . .

Brilliant!

Will it fit, will it fit? Scribble-scribble, tap-tap.

It fits . . .

They look. They have lift-off. It is a great headline. Almost up there with *Zip me up* etc.

Below it, they feed in copy under the byline of football reporter Dan Sales . . .

'Fabio Capello sensationally quit as England soccer boss last night – finally paving the way for the people's choice Harry Redknapp to take over.'

Then, on the back page, they don't mince words.

WE WANT HARRY.

The *Mirror* front-page splash is: *FAB BONUS FOR 'ARRY.* But the back page proves that great minds think alike (on a generous interpretation): *'ARRY VEDERCI.*

The *Daily Star* goes with: *HARRY FREE AS FABIO FLEES.*

Not everyone is carried away by this story, good as it is. At the *Daily Express*, wily Whittow remains cautious. He's thinking of his older readers, people more worried about the realities of daily life, getting to work, taking kids to school, doing the shopping. He only has to glance out the window to see now how cold it is. His faith in the editorial value of weather is being tested. And so, after some hard thought, he keeps his splash unchanged: *8 INCHES OF SNOW IN NEXT 24 HOURS.*

They may be bitter rivals – the *Express's* '5p cheaper than the *Daily Mail* and ten times better!' is designed to provoke – but *Mail* editor Dacre also has his doubts about Redknapp/Capello.

He doesn't want his paper to be just one of the pack. He likes his front page to look different. And, like Whittow, he's aware of his demographics.

He's conscious of every minute on the clock. This is approaching what he calls 'The Lonely Hour' when an editor will take other opinions and retreat to his office and sit alone, resting chin on hand, swivelling in his chair, staring out of the window, making up his mind for himself.

It's Dacre's call.

Newspapers are a monarchy, not a committee, and uneasy lies the head that wears the crown.

Dacre has worn that crown for 20 years, with impressive success. Now he interrogates his own decision-making process.

Will the football story appeal to the *Mail's* large female following?

Answer: No, it will not.

So he too decides to stick with his original choice: *BBC BOSS: I GOT IT WRONG ON OLDER WOMEN.*

He will run the football story across the top, above the splash: *Capello quits (as forecast by the Mail) . . . and now Harry's waiting in the wings after £10m tax trial victory.*

Interestingly, the broadsheet editors show greater solidarity with their red-top brethren than their mid-market siblings. They all go huge on Redknapp/Capello – half of page one for the *Guardian*, and most of page one for both *The Times* ('*ENGLAND EXPECTS*') and the *Independent* ('*A DAY OF TWO HALVES*').

Only the *Telegraph* breaks ranks, sticking with the Harry the Helicopter Pilot rather than 'Arry the Acquitted.

Everywhere, Death in Homs is steamrollered out of the way to make space.

Now, in vast sound-proofed warehouses across Britain the mighty printing presses tremble and roll . . .

The *Mail* emerges out of unlovely Surrey Quays, on the other side of London (in every sense) from their fashionable Kensington High Street offices. The *Express* and the *Star* come out from plants in Luton.

As for the *Sun,* it is printed at Broxbourne, Hertfordshire; Knowsley, Liverpool; and Motherwell, North Lanarkshire – on presses which also turn out *The Times*, the *Sunday Times*, the *Daily Telegraph*, the *Sunday Telegraph*, the *Financial Times* and many regional titles.

Such giant colour presses produce 80,000 copies an hour, or a pallet of newspapers every 2.5 minutes. They are loaded into trucks which now head for the motorways.

London: The train from Sheffield pulls into St Pancras station and disgorges its passengers, among them Professor Peter Cole, of Sheffield University's journalism department. He travels into Covent Garden and to the Garrick Club, founded 1831, where he has booked a room. He prepares for dinner with his eldest son.

Congleton: It is 15 hours since Jeremy Condliffe got out of bed and started work in his pyjamas. Apart from getting changed, he's hardly stopped since. Now he arrives back home ready to relax. But first, there are a couple of emails to check . . .

City: Alan Burkitt-Gray is on schedule for going to press in two days' time, although his designer says a couple of ads are still not in. He prints out six pages of proofs and puts them into his bag. He will check them at home.

He looks at the time and has seven minutes to catch the City Thameslink train. He sets off in hurry. Then, at London Bridge station, he has a 10-minute wait on a chilly platform and phones one of his two daughters, both now studying science at university. On the rest of the journey, he reads the inside gossip in the indispensible *Private Eye*.

Shepherd's Bush: Robin Lustig's *World Tonight* team record an interview about Republican candidate Rick Santorum. They'll probably not use it but it's reassuring backup.

Glasgow: Copy filed, and Twitter updated, Samantha Booth dares to wonder if it's time for a glass of wine yet. Can she relax, or will there be more emails? She stares at her screen and waits. Nothing. Finally she decides all must be well and makes the biggest decision of the evening.

She leaves her computer.

A little wine awaits.

Esher: Freelance Robin Corry sits in front of the TV and watches Michael Portillo's *Great Railway Journeys*. He says to himself: 'Not everyone loved Portillo as a politician, but he's a brilliant reporter.'

Sussex: Trainer Caroline Sutton's railway journey would not warrant Michael Portillo's praise, packed as it is with people staring with glazed eyes at their laptops. She is on the last leg from Bristol, and now nearing Brighton. She's tired and hungry, and can't help glaring at a man sitting across from her with an annoying tinny noise coming from his earphones. If he detects her disapproval, he doesn't show it.

Middlesex: Working away from home – his journalist wife Viki Wilson and their two children remain in Cornwall – Adam Carpenter uses his spare evenings to chase stories.

Tonight he phones a woman who's lost her 23-year-old daughter to cervical cancer and is now campaigning for lower age limits for smear tests. She's circulating a petition for people to print out and collect signatures so that she can deliver them to 10 Downing Street. She wants it all on sheaves of paper, the old-fashioned way.

He asks her: 'Why not do it online? You could start an e-petition?'

She says: 'It's too slow. E-petitions have to be online for a year and in that time another 60 young women will have died after being diagnosed too late. So I want to get 100,000 physical signatures – in ink, on paper – to present to the Prime Minister.'

Carpenter is impressed by her determination and courage but the trouble is, she is refusing to speak out about her daughter's 'personal and pre-diagnosis' story – the usual draw for true-life magazines.

He tries to think up a different approach.

Co. Donegal: Paddy Clancy gets a call from a local politician who says: 'Paddy, I want to talk to you about people driving on drugs. It's worth a story.'

Clancy's had enough for today. He reckons it's time for a glass of vino and a spot of telly with the missus.

He says: 'I'd like to do something. Can we talk tomorrow?'

Manchester: It has been a noisy ending to a excellent day for Damian Wild even if the banter in the champagne bar drowned his oratorical skills. Now he has left that behind for Piccadilly Station where he boards the train for his return journey. Soon he is speeding back south, his mind still ticking, going over all the ideas, topics and business they have been dealing with.

He is with a colleague and they decide to continue where they left off and order some wine. Well, they deserve it.

Then they start on an ambitious project: mapping out a five-year plan for *Estates Gazette*.

Enfield: Fourteen hours after leaving home, Arif Durrani arrives back to a wife who's spent her day dealing with two poorly children. He is just in time to kiss his eldest son goodnight. He knows it's not enough, of course – and the frazzled expression on his wife's face tells him who's had the hardest time.

Leeds: As an aspiring sports reporter, student David Spereall is riveted by the Capello/Redknapp story. In his head, he starts to plan a blogpost on TV journalism, based on the BBC's mistaken Redknapp announcement.

Walthamstow: Still without broadband, Nick McGrath is on the phone complaining. He's being dealt with by a woman in Delhi, who seems to be reading from a script.

It is making him even more annoyed. She shunts him off to someone else equally remote from what is really happening in his East London home.

McGrath tells her: 'It's hardly worked all day. I need my broadband. I'm a journalist.'

In a fairly robotic manner, the woman keeps saying: 'There is a broadband fault . . . We apologise . . . There is a broadband fault . . . '

He tries to control his anger. She is as much a victim of the technology as he is. It's not easy for either of them.

He slugs back some red wine.

Cambridge: Bob Satchwell is back at home and just about to try to relax. He has parked himself in front of the TV and a cookery programme is starting. But despite the chirpy music and rapid cutting, he's losing interest already. Then his phone rings and he seizes the chance to answer it.

The caller says: 'Mr Satchwell?'

'Yes.'

'I am a university law student researching privacy. I'd like to ask you a few questions.'

'Go ahead.'

The caller says he totally supports a free press. Satchwell thinks that's unusual for a lawyer and is happy to talk to him. The conversation lasts for 45 minutes. Is it a chore? No. He reckons it is lot more entertaining than TV chefs.

South London: Back at his computer, freelance Chris Wheal tries to do some more work but he can't concentrate properly. He realises he is too tired. Also, he's thinking about tomorrow.

He has to cover part of an event being run by the *Post* magazine. He needs to look professional. Could he take his suit and overcoat in his bicycle pannier? No, it's just a silly idea. He'll have to go by train.

At 8.45pm, Wheal turns off his computer and decides to have an early night. He goes to bed with his Kindle e-reader. He sets his alarm for 6.15 in the morning.

Tunbridge Wells: Ian Read finishes the last of his last tasks. Now he's hungry, having survived on two scotch eggs and a Kit Kat this afternoon. It is time to leave the office and go home, get some proper food and wind down.

He has worked 14 hours with hardly a break. He wouldn't have it any other way.

Stedham Village: In the shed behind his cottage, veteran columnist Colin Dunne has almost finished his latest humorous article. He cannot decide where it falls on the scale he uses, between 'incredibly bloody marvellous' and 'the same old crap'.

Let others decide.

Either way, he's savouring this moment. After half-a-century of writing, he hates starting, loves finishing and believes the finest sentence in English is 'I have written.'

He says to himself: 'And I have. Written that is. I'm a free man. Hooray!'

He traipses back to the house. Merlot time. One glass before eating. But his mind is still churning over.

Damn! Thought of a better intro. It will wait until tomorrow. Will it hell!

Dunne shuffles back to the shed and sits down again.

He starts tapping away.

He writes an intro comparing himself and his fictional character, Ross Thomas. Both read Raymond Chandler at an impressionable young age. Both resolved to write like him.

'Ross did. I didn't . . . I was obliged to park my Chandler dreams along with those of playing scrum-half for England, opening the batting for Yorkshire, and wooing Brigitte Bardot.'

Yes, much better.

He presses *send* before he can be tempted to fiddle with it again. It's writers' OCD (Obsessive Compulsive Disorder) and he has to fight it.

CHAPTER 16
9pm–10pm
Paps and Dinner

Basildon: It is 13 hours since the heroic Greg Figeon left home for work this morning. Now he starts laying out his last paper, the *Chingford Times*. He begins by looking at a front-page exclusive. A family have been waiting for an inquest for more than two years.

The *Times* asks: 'What's causing the delay – and why is a family's grief being drawn out?'

The hours have not diminished Figeon's enthusiasm one jot and he thinks: *That's a great story.*

London/Hertfordshire: Lindsay Nicholson and Kathryn Blundell have reached their respective homes, having brought pages of copy with them to read for their respective magazines, *Good Housekeeping* and *Mother & Baby*. Even at this late hour, they have admirable intentions . . .

Rwanda: Reuters' Graham Holliday makes a last check of Twitter. Nothing of interest. Bed.

Hertfordshire: Instead of being in the *Newsnight* studio, Susan Watts catches up with the third episode of the TV documentary *Putin, Russia and the West.*

KwaZulu-Natal: After finishing her pasta, travel writer Meera Dattani reckons everyone's bushed in the bush which is why early nights are the norm. She heads to her room, slips into bed and reads for all of 15 minutes before her eyelids feel heavy.

Bush babies are playing noisily on the roof but that's not enough to keep her awake. The day's heat and fresh air ensure a healthy sense of tiredness. She's out like a light.

Walthamstow: In his internet-free zone, Nick McGrath has had enough of foreign call centres and notices he has finished off his bottle of red.

Blackheath: Alan Burkitt-Gray emerges from the train station and buys a loaf of bread. He gets home and says hello to his son, who's working on a 3D printing project for a US client. He turns on the oven and puts in the remains of the sausage, carrot and tomato pasta he made on Monday. He is warming it up for supper ready for when his wife returns from her art class.

Mayfair: The paparazzi – fresh from snapping Duchess Kate in Trafalgar Square – are milling around outside the celebrity haunt, Aura. Then they see a target: *Desperate Scousewives* star Layla Flaherty. She is celebrating the birthday of her glamour model friend Louise Glover. Lots of spray-tanned flesh is being flaunted in defiance of the cold.

Flaherty, 27, poses in a white *Celeb Boutique* dress with a cut-out panel exposing her flat stomach.

They are good images and are quickly dispatched to picture desks.

Glasgow: Samantha Booth thought she'd finished for the evening but decides to have one last check of her emails. Eek! Now more messages start to come through about her stories.

9.25pm query number one;

9.35pm query number two;

9.40pm query number three.

Is that the lot? A further wait. Her email remains silent and she tells herself: 'Done – I think!'

Shepherd's Bush: There's only minutes to go before he's live on air and Robin Lustig is watching the clock. They've still got no one to talk about Capello on *The World Tonight*. He's anxious. It's a big story even if it is sport.

Then, a breakthrough. They get hold of BBC football supremo Mike Ingham.

'So, Mike, will they offer the England job to Harry?'

Ingham gives his thoughts and the interview is in the bag.

Lustig tells the team: 'That was superb. Crisis over.'

He does a live trailer for Radio 4, then pre-records the NHS discussion. Now the final headlines can be written and the scripts given a last polish.

As usual, it is a dash to the ten o'clock pips.

Stratford-upon-Avon: At the district council, Matt Wilson watches as the local politicians finally stop talking and start voting. Someone does the count. He tweets the result – *'Battle of Stratford: Cinema given go-ahead by 6 votes to 4'.*

He's not finished yet.

He leaves his little desk in the corner and hurries back to an otherwise silent office, puts an article up on the website, then flags it on Facebook and Twitter.

He sits in front of the screen and has the satisfaction of seeing the responses flood in. He has an audience out there, faceless yet in a way familiar. He drops in at the pub next door and gets to the bar. He orders one pint and drinks it quickly. Then he orders a second and downs that just as fast.

At that, Wilson goes home and to bed.

Basildon: Greg Figeon decides to have one last cup of tea. He gets up and goes into the office kitchen. He only has to make it for himself now. He carries the mug back to his desk and continues with his relentless subbing. The guy deserves a medal.

CHAPTER 17

10pm–11pm
World of Wine

London: After drinks and dinner, a woozy Marcus Harris arrives home and feels inspired, either despite alcohol, or because of it. He didn't wake up till 10am so this is not late for him.

He decides to start writing some *Mint* articles for tomorrow, chase up a few contributors and scatter a number of emails.

He begins bashing away at his keyboard, pleased see his fingers striking the right keys, most of the time.

Tunbridge Wells: Breakthrough in Edenbridge! Mystery woman found! Signature deciphered!

Although it's late, Sharon Marris has broken away from TV to check her emails. She sees one from the chairman of the Chamber of Commerce. He's been knocking on doors all evening.

He wants to tell her what happened.

Eventually he knocked on a door, showed a woman the illegible signature – and she exclaimed: 'That's me!'

He told her: 'Congratulations – you are the winner of our loyalty card draw.'

The woman was very excited.

It's a good story but there's nothing Marris can do about it right now. So she forwards it to the news editor for first thing tomorrow. There is still time to get it in this week's paper, before the final pages roll off the press.

She's feeling sleepy.

For two weeks she has been running on adrenalin and, now she's back from Afghanistan, her body is finally realising how long and tiring those days were.

That's a good thing. She is beginning to re-adjust, to being back in Kent, to the relative peace and quiet, to local stories about ordinary people, not soldiers and human bombs.

She goes to bed. She hopes she's going to sleep well and wake up fine.

Twitter: From his sickbed, Channel 4 News anchor Jon Snow informs his 34,000 followers worried about his unexplained absence from this evening's show – *'Grounded by flu today'*.

Unemployed Ex-Murdoch Reporter: Having self-medicated with Vimto and whisky, he climbs into bed early to save on the heating. He hopes tomorrow brings something better, but he knows he'll be awake in the early hours worrying about what he's going to do with his life.

While some people – like Steve Coogan in the High Court today – are leading a popular uprising now nicknamed 'the Murdoch Spring', there are many others facing personal disaster.

The 'Ex-Murdoch Reporter' is not alone in his despair at the collapse not just of his career but his life.

Some have contemplated suicide.

Sydney: Ex-*Mirror* editor David Banks steps off the commuter train and decides he's got time to fit in some more healthy exercise before lunch. There's no excuse for laziness. He'll walk to the restaurant. What with the swimming, he'll be a new man by the time he gets back to Northumberland.

He sets off hopefully.

Plod-plod.

A merciless sun beats down on him. He'd forgotten what a mountainous climb it is up to the Surrey Hills neighbourhood. But it's all coming back to him now and he starts to stream sweat.

Plod-plod, plod-plod.

It's a struggle but he pushes on, up and up the slopes in the midday heat, like someone illustrating the proverbial *Mad dogs and Englishmen...*

Plod-plod-plod.

He finds the restaurant, tries to compose himself and staggers through the door looking like a man who forgot to disrobe before stepping into the shower.

He is seated, gathers his breath and starts to recover.

Then Chris Mitchell arrives coiffed and cool, as you'd expect of the editor-in-chief of the *Australian*. He takes one look at his old mucker Banksie and says: 'Why didn't you come to the office? You could have shared my cab.'

Now he tells him.

London: Robin Lustig is on air with *The World Tonight,* his voice exuding a natural wisdom and authority. The programme moves seamlessly from one item to the next. Syria. NHS. Capello and Redknapp. There is no hint of the juggling and pressure that's been going on behind the scenes. It's like a duck in a storm, calm on the surface but paddling like hell underneath.

He reckons it's as smooth as ever.

As it draws to a close, Lustig looks at the clock and sees they are tight for time. The 'lovely Diana' in Radio 4 continuity agrees they can have extra at the end – all of 20 seconds. It doesn't sound much but as Lustig says: 'Every little bit helps.'

He finishes with his characteristic sign-off phrase: *'For now, from me, good night.'*

Another show floats away into the ether.

Lustig's work has ended.

Computer off, studio lights off, back to the production office for a debrief from a senior editor who was listening at home. She says she thought they did okay.

Okay's fine.

West End: Helen Russell has enjoyed her dinner and wine. They settle the restaurant bill. Her former employee is now wealthy enough to call a black cab to take her home. But not Russell.

She braves the cold slap of the February night and dashes along Soho's dark pavements towards the tube station.

Basildon: After a 15-hour day, Greg Figeon decides that enough is enough and switches off his screen. He's done for now. He will return early in the morning to finish the *Chingford Times* ahead of the midday deadline.

He leaves the office and sets off home. He's not gone far when he turns round and comes rushing back. He gets into the office. He's forgotten his notebooks. He leaves again. Definitely, he's going home this time.

Somewhere in the Midlands: Aboard an express train hurtling south, great thoughts are being born from a day charged with the energy and seriousness of big business, and nourished by some light champagne.

Estates Gazette's Damian Wild and his travelling companion are enjoying a wine and have discovered how to save the print industry in its hour of direst need. They, and only they, have come up with a new strategy for the transition to online.

It's brilliant, they both agree, and they raise a glass to their shared genius.

The train sways towards London through the black, wintry night . . .

Hertfordshire: At home, Susan Watts watches the BBC *Ten O'clock News* and then her own *Newsnight*. Later, as the credits roll, she goes to bed with the latest novel from Kate Atkinson (her first of hers) *Started Early, Took my Dog.*

Cambridge: Bob Satchwell is back in front of his computer, exchanging emails and updating the awards website which is being plagued by technical problems. In the end, he decides that announcing the awards will have to wait until the morning.

He watches a bit of *Newsnight* and enjoys Paxman scoffing at the FA management over the Capello resignation.

Hollywood: At Universal Studios, the BBC's Peter Bowes has finished his interviews and filming. Now he grabs a quick lunch of chicken breast and salad, and declines the sticky deserts. When he's not reporting, he's a triathlete. He's got his fitness to preserve.

He climbs back into his Landrover and sets off through the traffic of the City of Dreams, heading north.

Stedham: In the kitchen of his cottage, veteran columnist Colin Dunne is offered lamb chops by Mrs Dunne, who has prepared them while he's been in the shed. He tucks in and formally gives them, and her, his stamp of approval, announcing: 'These are delicious.'

He decides to tell her how his day's been. Some success, he explains, but a lot of frustration caused by editors and publishers.

He clears his plate and says with an air of finality: 'No more writing. Over, done with. I will retire tomorrow.'

When Mrs Dunne yawns and reaches for the Merlot, he thinks (but does not say): 'Heartless woman. It's as if she hears it every day.'

He decides to start a special love-match agency, 'Sympathetic Wives for Anguished Writers'.

CHAPTER 18
11pm-12 midnight
Midnight Massive

Euston Station, London: The train from Manchester eases alongside the platform and *Estates Gazette's* Damian Wild disembarks. As he and his travelling companion carry their bags up the platform, they are delighted at solving some of the world's greatest problems.

But even as they wonder onto the concourse, Wild is regretting they neglected to put pen to paper or finger to iPad.

'Now what was that brilliant idea again?'

'Well, I know it was earth-shattering, Damian.'

'But what exactly was it?'

Only minutes have passed since they were defining and refining the global transition to online print after some wine. Yet somehow it has become, well, a little vague.

Now, how to get home? For the moment, that must take priority . . .

London: Despite the late hour, and the alcohol, *Mint* mag's Marcus Harris surprises himself with his efforts at the keyboard. He manages to thrash out a thousand words – first, on which are the most terrifying deities, then on the perils of a Fatwa.

There is a theme there.

London: Greg Figeon arrives home. He has his last cup of tea, watches the Capello–Redknapp story on *Sky Sports News*, then gets to bed. He needs sleep. He's got to be up early to drive back to Basildon to finish the *Chingford Times*.

London: Robin Lustig arrives home. He pours himself a glass of wine, finds a snack and finally gets the chance to sit down and have a proper read of the *Financial Times*. He is already looking for ideas for tomorrow's *World Tonight*. He notes the Greece debt crisis is bubbling on . . . and on . . . and on. Perhaps that will make something more.

Glasgow: Samantha Booth goes to bed. Her final thought as her head hits the pillow: *Hopefully a decent night's sleep before doing it all again.*

Blackheath: Having finished his pasta supper, Alan Burkitt-Gray watches one of Michael Portillo's TV train journeys, which he has recorded on Sky Plus. After a high-pressured day, he finds it perfect undemanding late-night viewing – as does freelance Robin Corry on the other side of London.

When he starts to fall asleep in front of the set, he gets up and goes to bed.

Westminster: *Stylist*'s Anita Bhagwandas is finishing off at the Nivea dinner for beauty journalists at the Corinthia Hotel. For her, it's been a brilliant evening. She tells others that she's been on the go for 16 hours and adds: 'I can't function without at least 8 hours' sleep.'

They tell her this is excessive. Now, as she leaves, she wonders if she has a sleep disorder.

'No,' she concludes, 'I just like my bed. And that's where I'm heading.'

West London: One notable absentee from the Nivea dinner has been beauty editor Liz Wilde. She's seen it all before and leaves it to the younger eager-beavers. Instead, she has spent the evening drinking red wine in her local West London pub, not as super-trendy as the Corinthia but good fun.

She says: 'Regrettably, I'm the hardest-drinking beauty editor I know, but at least I have the products to reverse some of the damage. Externally anyway . . . '

London: *Marie Claire*'s Helen Russell arrives home. By her measure, it has not been a 'terribly exciting day'. Other people might disagree. Now she goes to bed, looking forward to New York, Wintour *et al*. She must remember to collect her dry cleaning.

Cambridge: Bob Satchwell looks at the time and resists the compulsion to watch more Leveson recordings. He goes to bed. Even there, before his eyes close, he wonders if media addiction is a sad life. Well, not to him, he thinks. He's very happy with it.

Santa Carlita, California: The drive back to the ranch was easy and now the BBC's Peter Bowes sits in his home office, catching up with emails and planning the *Grammys* coverage on Sunday. He doesn't know that his plans will be overtaken by a dramatic tragedy.

Hollywood: The paparazzi reckon Whitney Houston must be up and about by now. They are getting on her trail, hanging about outside her Wilshire Boulevard hotel.

They sense something will happen shortly.

Brazil: The bodies of a man and a woman are found. The police arrive on the scene. Both victims have been murdered. They have been shot in the head.

After inquiries, the man is identified as Mario Randolfo, a c ampaigning journalist. The woman with him is his girlfriend, Maria Aparecide Guimarães.

Randolfo, 50, the editor-in-chief of the news website *Vassouras na Net*, was abducted from his home 12 hours ago, along with Guimarães.

His most recent article attacked corrupt judges in Barra do Piraí, Rio de Janeiro state.

A brave voice has been silenced but the gangsters should know that another will take his place.

Sydney: David Banks has cooled and calmed down and is drinking unusually sparingly, recognising that is the pattern in the new Australia these days – as he fears it is in London. Thank God he lives in the North-east, where the culture of sobriety remains a minority cause.

He and Chris Mitchell talk freely as they eat lunch – old times, Rupert Murdoch, journalism's digital future and, most importantly, phone hacking and where it leaves the Aussie media.

On the record and off is never mentioned. They both know what's on and what's not, and that Banks won't let him down (unless he reveals he's sired a Murdoch lovechild, in which case all bets are off).

Stedham: In his cottage, Colin Dunne has one last glass of Merlot – or last-ish. Then, despite the dark, he makes a late dash down the garden to the shed to check his emails. He can't help it.

He looks at the screen.

Incredible! The golf mag loves his column.

The golf editor says: 'Best yet, Colin, hysterical.'

The books mag editor says: 'Perfect – what else can I say, Colin? Wouldn't change a word.'

Dunne returns to his wife in a happier mood and tells her: 'Fine fellow, Pete. Marvellous editor. Heather is even better. What a w oman. What astonishing judgement. Genius, if you ask me.

'One last Merlot. Day of triumph. Double triumph. Admiration of peers. Small but grateful cheque in post. Greatest feeling in world. Better even than . . . Wonder if Viagra actually works.'

New York: On Wall Street, Murdoch-watchers are desperate to know more about the impact of the British phone-hacking scandal. The media analysts want answers they can give to shareholders and investors. What can they tell their clients? Do they mark *News Corp* shares as a *buy, hold* or *sell*?

They need facts, information and the latest data. They have a stack of questions.

How much is it damaging News Corp?
What is it costing?
What are the legal fees?
Will there be a change at the top?
Is this the death-knell of the Murdoch dynasty?

They are desperate to hear the company's views and now they are about to get the chance. News Corp's chief financial officer David Devoe is preparing to hold a teleconference call with them.

Okay, they'd rather it were Rupert, or even James, and face-to-face so they can see the whites of their eyes.

But Devoe is fine.

CHAPTER 19

12 midnight–1am
Once Upon A Midnight

London: Finally, Anita Bhagwandas unlocks her door and steps into the home she left 18 hours ago. It has been such a long day.

Although tired she's not quite ready to sleep and she starts pecking away at her phone. She cannot resist sending a few tweets at this unlikely hour, reporting her wonderful dinner and safe return. Having done that, she goes to bed asking herself whether she must really annoy people by using Twitter so late. Before reaching a verdict, she falls fast asleep.

Leeds: Looking forward to another day at the *Evening Post*, student David Spereall goes to bed. Before he closes his eyes, he thinks that thought again: *journalism is the best job in the world.*

That's why he wants to do it.

Melbourne, Australia: It is mid-morning and the sun is shining on Cruden Farm again after the most important date in its calendar. The estate looks wonderful with its vineyards and gardens, horse paddocks and pools.

Dame Elisabeth Murdoch quite understands why her son Rupert and grandson James were unable to attend her 103rd birthday. They are busy running the planet's second largest media empire.

Some people say they're trying to run the world.

New York: Rupert and James Murdoch are leaving it to their chief financial officer David Devoe at the moment. As News Corp's quarterly figures are released, Devoe is holding a teleconference with analysts and financial journalists.

Overall, he sounds upbeat.

The Murdochs may be under pressure but this is the real source of their power: making billions. They are still brilliant at it.

That's why they retain the backing of the News Corp board.

As Devoe finishes the conference, Reuters sends out a report to desks around the globe.

'Rupert Murdoch's News Corp beat Wall Street profit forecasts on Wednesday . . . but warned the cost of the phone-hacking scandal remains an unpredictable issue . . .'

CHAPTER 20

1am–2am
Up All Night

London: *Mint* mag's Marcus Harris stops working. Aside from the project launch, he reckons it has been a slow day, which he hates. He thinks he might go to bed soon.

Sydney: As their relatively sober lunch draws to a close, David Banks accepts an invitation from Chris Mitchell to pop in and say hello to people at his old paper, the *Australian*. No more walking like a mad dog in the midday sun. He's had enough of that for the day. They grab a cab.

When they arrive, Banks is greeted by a few old-stagers who are keen to say hello.

There's a new face, too: Paul Whittaker, editor of the *Daily Telegraph*, which Banks once edited. He gives him a coffee in his old office and recalls his first week there when Banks introduced him to two big names: Col Allen, now editor of the *New York Post* but then his deputy, and Jack Daniel's, Banks's drink of choice at afternoon conference.

Those were the days.

Whittaker is very open and rightly proud of his newspaper and donates another stack of on/off-the-record quotes to his visitor's growing dissertation. Banks thinks: *it just gets better.*

Stedham: Colin Dunne is in bed but cannot sleep as he reflects on a day which saw his golf fail and his writing succeed. He decides the cheques will pay for golf lessons. But then, success at golf would leave less time for writing. More anguish. Stomach churns. Thank God for Rennies. If Shakespeare had Rennies, *Hamlet* would have had a happy ending.

Dunne's mind turns to his only current failure – the extremely daring *How I Made Sex the Popular Pastime It Is Today, with the Help of Maureen Ashton.*

It's probably just as well as the current Mrs Dunne is not too keen on hearing about Maureen Ashton.

Marblehead, Massachusetts: Rhod Sharp kicks off his talk show, *Up All Night*, on BBC Radio 5 Live.

Most of his British listeners think he broadcasts from London. Few realise he does it sitting in an attic studio at his home across the Atlantic, in an old port just north of Boston.

With modern technology, it makes not a jot difference.

Sharp says: 'It's Fabio Capello night . . . '

He gets Italian TV sports commentator Massimo Marianella on the line and adds: 'It's the next best thing to being inside Capello's head. What do you think, Massimo?'

Massimo replies: 'As soon as Capello heard that John Terry had been sacked behind his back, he was out that door.'

CHAPTER 21

2am–3am
War Goes On

Task Force Helmand HQ: Lt-Col Gordon Mackenzie wakes up at the crack of dawn and starts to prepare for another crammed day in Afghanistan.

Santa Carlita, California: Early evening and the BBC's Peter Bowes goes to the gym. It's February and the New Year Resolution crowd is still out in force. The gym is doing a New Year Fat Loss Challenge. The team which loses most fat wins $5,000. More than 200 people are taking part, including Bowes.

He does the Total Body class, intense rounds of strength training and cardio. He chats with a gym buddy who is the PR of a local police force. They discuss ideas for radio features.

What about the 20th anniversary of the LA riots?

Yes, sounds a great idea.

Helmand: Still out on ops, the BBC's Quentin Sommerville wakes up in his tent. It's been a cold night. He eases himself out of bed, gets ready and starts to collect his thoughts. He calls the producer in the Kabul bureau and talks through what's happening.

It is a risk-cost analysis of the type conducted by any business, except here they have to factor in life and death. They have to balance the ever-present dangers against the quality of material he's gathering.

He's not being given access to Afghani troops.

Sommerville consults his team – his cameraman and assistant producer Mahfouz Zubaide, and they reach a decision. They will continue. They will try to finish what they set out to do.

They are ready to resume the patrol with the convoy. But there is trouble with the transport and now they are delayed. More frustration.

Can covering war traumatise journalists?

An answer to this interesting question was given by Kim Sengupta, defence correspondent of the *Independent*, in the *British Journalism Review*, March 2012.

Sengupta wrote: 'It would be unrealistic to think that spending a working lifetime covering terrible happenings would not affect members of the media. Occasionally, journalists will talk about it.

'Last year in Kandahar, on an evening before we were to go out on a difficult operation with US forces, a group of us were speaking unusually openly about what troubled us.

'An eminent writer with *The New Yorker* reflected on his increasing explosions of rage when he returned home from Afghanistan. On one occasion he, a middle-aged man, found himself rolling on the street outside his home in a fight with a stranger over parking. Listening to him, another writer, from *The Times,* a veteran of many wars, quietly described his own bursts of anger often directed to those close to him, and then bouts of depression that followed. Were the mood swings caused by trauma? Who knows?'

[Sixteen days after 8 February, the *Sunday Times* reporter Marie Colvin, and her photographer, Remi Ochlik, are killed in Homs, along with an estimated 80 activists, in one day.]

Marblehead, Massachusetts: On his Radio 5 Live talkshow, Rhod Sharp switches from football to war. He gets through to a man in Babr Amr, in the Syrian city of Homs.

Sharp: 'What's happening there, Omar?'

Omar: 'My neighbour's house took a direct hit from a shell or rocket. His infant daughter was killed outright. He is in shock and cannot speak for crying.'

As an experienced journalist, the Scots-born Sharp realises he is taking Omar's interview on trust but thinks: 'He'd have to be the best actor in the world . . . '

Sharp tells him: 'It doesn't look like help is coming any time.'

Omar agrees. He says a sad goodbye and the call ends.

Stedham: At 2am, Colin Dunne is still wide awake, and suffering his own kind of personal trauma, a panic attack about retirement. He wakes up his long-suffering wife and asks her: 'I don't have to retire, do I?'

'No, Colin,' she says. 'You don't.'

Thus reassured, he finally falls asleep.

CHAPTER 22

3am–4am
More Fun

Delhi: In her flat/office, Helen Roberts is woken up by the arrival of her cleaner. She's not used to employing a domestic but in India people are so desperate for work that she felt obliged. She's a sweet lady with a couple of kids. As she rattles about with her broom, Roberts starts to plan another fun-filled day.

Sydney: David Banks leaves the Murdoch offices and heads back to his hotel at Cronulla. He checks emails and finds one from *Press Gazette* asking: 'Banksie, do you have a column yet?'

He's got the material. He's just got to write it . . .

He emails Miranda Devine, a top Aussie columnist, to invite her for drinks and more quotes. Within 30 minutes she's back with the quotes, explaining why she's being so efficient.

She says: 'So we can concentrate on our drinks tomorrow.'

Banks exclaims: 'That's my kind of woman.'

Santa Carlita: Peter Bowes checks his iPhone and sees he's got an email from a BBC producer in London.

'Hi Peter, are you able to send us a report on Russell Brand's divorce?' it says. 'It's just been made official today by an LA judge. We'd like something for radio?'

Bowes abandons his social plans for the evening. He leaves the gym and drives back through the canyons to his home and goes straight into his studio.

He resumes work.

CHAPTER 23

4am–5am
World News

Delhi: Helen Roberts starts her day with fruit, muesli and yoghurt and takes a look through the morning news. She sees a new movie, *The Best Exotic Marigold Hotel*, is just being released in Britain.

It gives her an idea.

It was filmed in India and stars two British Dames, Judy Dench and Maggie Smith. But of more interest to Roberts is the young actress from Mumbai who played alongside them. She is called Teena Desae.

Roberts abandons her breakfast and locates her agent.

She asks: 'Is Teena available for interview?'

'Yes.'

'Excellent.'

'When do you want to talk to her?'

'Now.'

'Oh, I'll see what I can do.'

Santa Carlita: Peter Bowes puts together his piece on Russell Brand and files it for BBC Radio 2 and BBC 5 Live. Most pre-recorded reports are sent electronically these day, as .wav or .mp3 files. He can do that from any computer, even his iPhone.

Task Force Helmand HQ: Press chief Mackenzie attends a morning meeting of heads of department. Afterwards, he reviews notices with press officer Tom Bennett and authorises their release.

Marblehead, Massachusetts: On his Radio 5 talkshow, Rhod Sharp switches to Lauren, a friend from New York who is working for Sudanese returnees in Juba.

He asks: 'What's happening in Sudan right now?'

She says: 'All we ever hear about is the cattle raids up north but Sudanese entrepreneurs are coming back to try to build prosperity in the new country.

Right now in Britain, bundles of newspapers are being loaded into vans for delivery to the front-line newspaper shops and supermarkets.

CHAPTER 24
5am–6am
Once Upon A Morning

We have been following journalists at work, practising the reality of their trade in all its many varieties, from checking lipstick shades to risking death by bullet or bomb. Now that 24-hour period is drawing to a close . . .

Santa Carlita: At his ranch, the BBC's Peter Bowes calls it a night and goes to bed.

Delhi: The agent has come back to Helen Roberts and now she is interviewing Teena Desae, the up-and-coming Bollywood star starring in her first western film.
'What's it like to kiss Dev Patel?'
'I was very nervous.'
When she's finished she starts to write it up for magazines in the UK and Dubai. It's a good start to the day.

Task Force Helmand HQ: After seeing heads of department, Mackenzie holds a morning update with his team.
'Any thoughts?'
A voice pipes up: 'Valentine's Day is next week. We can do something for that.'
Someone else says: 'Yes, perhaps we can link up husbands and wives and other couples on the day . . . '
Good idea. They start to organise it.

Kingston: Freelance Natalie Dye opens her eyes to the sound of her husband, Gino, preparing for his early-morning swim. She's been having a nightmare, something about the space–time continuum. Oh no . . .

London: Showbiz writer Nick McGrath wakes up with a bad head and a dry mouth. He's got a hangover. *Damn that red wine.* He has two big interviews

220

lined up for today. As the clock approaches six o'clock, his two-year-old son wants to play and starts poking him with a plastic dinosaur and he gives muted scream.

Hollywood: The paparazzi are out in force for *Essence* magazine's 'Black Women in Music'. It is a pre-Grammy star-studded event with one notable absentee: Whitney Houston.

Later today Houston will leave her hotel and the photographers will get the kind of images they want of her. They will snap her bloated and dishevelled, in mismatched clothes and with hair dripping with either sweat or water.

In 48 hours, those last pictures will rocket in value for one reason: Houston is found dead in her hotel bath.

Ker-ching-ker-ching!

Any Town, UK: A newsagent slams up his shutters and sees a van screech to a halt alongside the pavement. A man jumps out, grunts 'Morning', and drops a fat bundle of newspapers on his shop step. As the vehicle speeds away, the newsagent cuts it open, removes the cardboard packing and is greeted by a one-word headline . . .

'Arryvederci.

The first draft of history is ready for its audience. Let a new day dawn . . .

THE END (for now . . .)

AUTHOR's NOTE:
Project 2013 – you can join in next time

Monday, 11 March, 2013.

All I know for sure is that it is the date of Rupert Murdoch's 82nd birthday, and you are free to praise or pan him. Otherwise, anything could be happening: World War III, Obama joins the Moonies, maybe an extraterrestial invasion - shock is the USP of news.

As I finished this first book, I had other journalists saying they wished they'd taken part. Well, this will be their chance.

Because of the interest, I intend to produce a new version for 2013 – I stress it will be new, with many different characters and different individual stories (although current contributors will be welcome as well).

I hope it will be even more global, enlightening and compelling.

If you are a journalist, or affected by journalists, or involved in journalism in any way, then please email me a written snapshot of your day – 24 hours from 6am (GMT) Monday, 11 March to 6am (GMT) Tuesday, 12 March, 2013.

Add colour and dialogue, friendship and conflict. I am also interested in quiet, routine days. I want local journalists, as well as big shots.

221

Like this one, Project 2013 will be turned into a nar rative ranging from Europe to India, from America to China, and all stops in-between.
Please adjust your times to GMT.
Email: 24hours2013@hotmail.co.uk
Website: 24hoursinjournalism2013.com
I look forward to hearing from you.